NON NOBIS

Published by Logos Press
P.O. Box 8729, Moscow, Idaho 83843
800.488.2034 | www.logospressonline.com

Tom Garfield, *Non Nobis: The Story of the First Generation of Logos School*

Cover design by James Engerbretson
Front cover photograph (top) by Mark LaMoreaux
Front cover photograph (bottom) and back cover photographs by Tom Garfield
Interior photographs used by permission of copyright holders
Interior design by Valerie Anne Bost

Printed in the United States of America.

17 18 19 20 21 22 23 24 10 9 8 7 6 5 4 3 2 1

NON NOBIS

The Story of the First Generation of Logos School

TOM GARFIELD

CONTENTS

Preface 1

Prologue 3

CHAPTER I *The Basement* 11

CHAPTER II *Growth* 40

CHAPTER III *Challenges* 75

CHAPTER IV *The Roller Rink* 103

CHAPTER V *Doug Wrote A Book* 133

CHAPTER VI *A Bigger Menu* 159

CHAPTER VII *Further Up and Further In* 188

CHAPTER VIII *The New Millennium* 221

APPENDIX A *Lost Tools Illustrated Chart* 248

APPENDIX B *Logos School Timeline* 251

APPENDIX C *The Particular Prospects of the Pre-Polly Stage* 257

APPENDIX D *An Apologetic for Logos Grammar School's Approach to Teaching History* 266

APPENDIX E *The Arts and the Christian Worldview* 270

APPENDIX F *Holiday Guidelines* 276

APPENDIX G *A Few Alum Stories* 278

APPENDIX H *Photos* 283

DEDICATION

To Julie and Carolyn, Seth, Kajsa, and Kathryn – because of you and for you, by the grace of the Lord Jesus Christ

PREFACE

"Not to us, O Lord, not to us,
but to Thy Name give glory!" Psalm 115:1

It's almost become cliché that Christian schools start in church basements. Well, then I guess Logos School didn't break the pattern. It did, however, go on to have a rather profound effect on thousands of folks who never saw the basement—or the roller rink, for that matter. By God's own design and grace, Logos School grew from a small beginning in a town tucked away in north Idaho, to influence dear people as far away as the Marshall Islands, China, northern Iraq, as well as other far-flung countries. I could also mention Nigeria and South Korea, and most of the states of the Union.

Doug Wilson, Logos School's founder, wrote a book published in 1991 entitled *Recovering the Lost Tools of Learning*. If you haven't read that book, you really should. He does a brilliant job of laying out exactly what was unique about the educational philosophy that Logos School embraced and promulgated.

My purpose in this book is not to offer additional philosophical underpinnings for a classical, Christian school. I am an administrator, not a visionary. My job for thirty-five years was to build a school to follow that unique philosophy, grounded in and saturated by the Word of God. Along the way, I worked under more board members than I can recall. But regardless of the specific individuals, my board consistently and fervently adhered to our original mission: to offer a classical and Christ-centered education to as many families as the Lord brought to us.

So, I simply present to you, the reader, a look back at the founding and development of what became the greatest part of my life's work and, more importantly, the means God used to bless thousands of families in Moscow and across the world. This is the story, from my viewpoint, of Logos School's first 35 years, presented in mostly anecdotal pieces. It is far from a complete history, someone else would have to write that. I wrote this primarily to have a brief record of this amazing work of God. And, selfishly, to have something to read that would remind me in years to come just how much and why I loved this place.

If you are a Logos alum, you may recognize some of these stories. You graced our halls and classrooms and meant a great deal to me. You made all the labor a joy! If you worked at Logos, I thank you and highly value the time we shared in this ministry. If you are a Logos parent, you will certainly recognize some of these stories, depending on when and how long you were with us. Thank you for your commitment in giving your family this education! It was an honor and delight to serve you. If you work in or attend another classical school, you will likely relate to much of what we went through. That said, this is the first book of its kind as far as I'm aware, coming from the founders of classical Christian education in this country, and that distinction alone may make it worth reading.

Whatever the reason you find yourself picking this book up, I hope you will be blessed by discovering yet another story and another reason to give all glory and praise to the Father.

Non Nobis!
TOM GARFIELD
April 2016

PROLOGUE

Logos School opened its doors (actually a church's doors) on September 8, 1981. That's when it opened, yes, but when did it really begin? Since it's my joy and privilege to tell this story, I can say that Logos School began with a very unique family, the Jim Wilson family. And the story begins long before 1981. By God's grace and for His own purposes, He has given me a front-row seat for over forty years seeing the Wilsons prepared and used to accomplish great things for Christ's kingdom. So to understand where Logos School came from and why it is the kind of school it is today (and, I pray, will be for generations to come), you need to know some of the history of the Jim Wilsons.

I cannot begin to do justice or even accuracy to the breadth of Jim Wilson's life here, nor will I try. For a book that contains a somewhat short, but still magnificent biographical account, I highly recommend his grandson's outstanding book, *Death By Living*, by N.D. Wilson (or Nathan, as I knew him originally, but I'm getting ahead of myself). For my purposes, I will simply start with my first association with the Wilson family and what came of it.

For reasons known at the time only to God, a few years after being converted to Christ, Jim Wilson was miraculously spared from certain death while on sea duty during the Korean War. That incident was just one of the many amazing stories of God s direction and provision for this man and his family (for instance, at one point Jim was called away from his duty station just before it was hit by an enemy shell). After the Korean War, Jim continued to serve as an officer in the United States Navy, and he and his family moved to Annapolis, Maryland.

In 1969, after ten years there, they moved again, this time to Ann Arbor, Michigan. He had begun a Christian bookstore ministry in Annapolis, one that inaugurated his lifelong, strategic delivery system for the Gospel. I say "strategic" because that's how Jim put it himself: he believed in applying warfare tactics in the spiritual warfare to which all Christians are called. So he sought to evangelize, biblically counsel, and distribute Christian literature to a captive, unique audience: college students. At no other time in these young people's lives would they be so ripe for hearing the Truth, and so vulnerable to the rampant lies manifest on college campuses. After graduation, these grads would go out to further the Kingdom's work all their lives, or be lost in the world's landfill. So after pioneering this work in Annapolis, and in nearby College Park at the University of Maryland, Jim's next tactical invasion was to the University of Michigan in Ann Arbor.

As it turned out, Ann Arbor was not only a tactical target for Jim's ministry, it was also my hometown. My parents, Bob and Lois Garfield, had moved to Ann Arbor shortly after being married in 1947. My father was pursuing a medical career and attended the med school at the University of Michigan. God changed that path and Dad became a college administrator instead. Our home was filled with Christ's love and instruction. My parents also made sure that their four children were given a love for books (particularly the Narnia series and anything else by C.S. Lewis) and frequent lessons in hospitality to visiting friends and missionaries. We attended a Baptist church (more precisely Swedish Baptist and, no, I never figured that flavor out) called Huron Hills Baptist.

Not long after my family began attending Huron Hills, the Wilsons arrived not only in Ann Arbor, but also in our church. It was 1968 and, if you know anything about that unique period of time, you know we baby boomers were a tad caught up with ourselves. Or, to put it more accurately, we believed the universe now revolved around our post-WWII, spoiled generation. Sadly, that attitude and culture affected Christian young people as well. That's not really any excuse for the dumb and weird things we did, but it is somewhat of a reason. All this is to frame what follows. As Doug Wilson has often said, we all see the world through our own two eyes, and what you're getting here is from my ocular vantage.

Jim and Bessie (Elizabeth) Wilson came to town with their four children: Doug (then 15), Evan (14), Heather (12), and Gordon (7). Evan, being my age, appeared in my Sunday School class and Youth Group. My first impressions of him were not positive, to put it mildly. He never took off his coat with its Nehru collar, regardless of the weather, and made the most sarcastic comments. It was almost like he thought that a lot of what we were doing was ridiculous. (Of course he was right, but I didn't see it at the time.) Doug was making quite an impression in the older high school group, as well. While not as sarcastic as Evan, he was nevertheless taking the Youth Group leader and some peers to task fairly regularly. (I heard this from my older sisters who saw him in action—they, too, wondered who this guy was and why he couldn't go along to get along.)

What I didn't discover until many years later was that Jim Wilson was causing a somewhat similar bestirring of feelings amongst the adults. Again, not because he thought he was the greatest and newest thing since sliced bread, but because he felt compelled to state his understanding of Scripture, graciously and clearly. Some congregants were drawn to his wise and clear insights; others saw him as a threat to the norm. Either way, no one found Jim Wilson boring or easy to dismiss, and some saw him as a challenge to the church leadership. (This response would concern him to such a degree that, years later when he moved to Idaho, he chose to start a new church, rather than potentially divide an established congregation.)

Not long after the Wilsons began worshiping with us, my dear folks asked them over for dinner. The Wilsons reciprocated, and after dinner in their home, I found myself in Evan's room while our parents chatted downstairs. Then Evan put on a Bill Cosby record and we laughed ourselves into friendship. In the three years that followed, Evan and I worked at being Christian hippies (whatever that meant), while Doug was being, well, Doug. It was Doug's idea, for instance, to write a Christian student newsletter, *ZEI,* which is Greek for "He lives." The three of us and a few friends wrote articles and even poems for it, then ran off and distributed hundreds of copies to our 2,500 student body high school (apparently the ACLU wasn't paying attention).

Tempting as it is to relate many other tales from our teen years, suffice it to say, I'd never seen a family like the Wilsons before. My folks were very strong Christians, and they became good friends with Jim and Bessie. The Wilson home, located near downtown Ann Arbor, was Spartan in decor, but rock solid on the Gospel, and it became my second home. I was witness to Jim in action many times, in Bible studies, dinners, and just informal chats, with every sort of person who frequents a college campus. From professors to street people, all were welcome and all showed up in the Wilsons' living room.

By his senior year, Doug had become more of a force to be reckoned with, following closely in his father's spiritual footsteps. Then, in 1971, Jim received a request from some Christian businessmen in faraway Moscow, Idaho, to come and start a Christian bookstore on not one, but two college campuses (University of Idaho and Washington State University). This was right in line with Jim's strategy. So, after Doug graduated from Pioneer High School in the spring of 1971, the Wilsons left Michigan to head West, or more precisely, the Pacific Northwest. Shortly thereafter, Doug enlisted and went off to start a four-year tour of duty in the United States Naval sub service.

Evan and I stayed in touch, and I visited him in Moscow after Christmas, 1971. I found the Northwest and Moscow to be delightful! Coming from a university town I already felt at home in the culture, but Moscow's small size and lovely setting attracted me very much, too. During that first visit I saw Jim and Doug (home on leave from the Navy) work together to bring the gospel to some pretty tough teens. Jim used his garage (soon called God's Garage by the kids) to make a hang-out near the local high school—another great tactic.

After graduating from our respective high schools in the spring of 1972, Evan and I decided to follow our fathers' examples and join the

U.S. Navy. Through the Navy's buddy program, we were able to go to boot-camp together in San Diego; he coming from Idaho, I from Michigan. The nine weeks there were not just an intense training in the ways of a sailor; more importantly Evan challenged and encouraged me to grow in my faith. We prayed, read the Psalms and other Scriptures together many times, particularly when illness and discouragement hit me hard. I can honestly say the Lord used Evan to help prepare me spiritually for the subsequent years of military life. Evan got orders to a shore duty station in southern California (i.e., the desert) and I ended up aboard a very large, very smelly ship called a fleet oiler, for three and half years. The *U.S.S. Neosho* (AO-143) had her home port in Norfolk, Virginia, but she was sent to sea quite frequently. My job as a storekeeper kept me busy organizing storerooms (not a store, just to be clear). While I put in my time living and working on the ship, I was convinced that there was absolutely no way this work would ever be useful to me in real life.

Evan may have been literally on the other side of the United States, but Doug, who had entered the service a year before his brother and I did, was stationed on a nuclear sub in the Atlantic. None of us had worked very hard at staying in touch. One warm afternoon when my ship was in port in Norfolk, I returned from an errand ashore and was told a visitor was waiting for me in the Supply Office. Upon entering, it took me a moment (and gave me a bit of a shock) to behold Doug Wilson, now fully bearded, sitting in my desk chair. It turned out his sub was in port for a few months. In that brief time, not only did he introduce me to a great church, Tabernacle Church of Norfolk, he helped me clean house spiritually, not the first or last time. Interestingly, our church was located immediately next to a Christian school. Neither of us gave it much thought at the time.

I won't take this opportunity to recount salty sea stories, as former sailors are apt to do. Suffice it to say, the Lord showed me His faithfulness and sanctifying work in a multitude of ways during those four years. By His design I saw some fascinating sites in countries around the Mediterranean Sea, particularly Greece and Italy, the birthplace of the classical world. Given the education I received, I had virtually no idea of the value or history of what I was seeing. And I blithely assumed that I would never have anything more to do with these places and that history.

When I had about 18 months left to serve and after much prayer (and some clear answers to those prayers), I became convinced that after I was discharged, I should move to Moscow, Idaho, and attend the U of I there.

Doug was discharged in 1975 and shortly thereafter married Nancy Greensides. In September of 1976, their first child, Rebekah, was born. Doug was attending the U of I, majoring in philosophy. He was also serving as the song leader in the non-denominational church Jim had been involved with starting in Moscow.

Shortly before my discharge, my parents moved out to Portland, Oregon, leaving their home of 30 years in Ann Arbor, to be nearer to their children (and grandchildren). My father was in his early fifties at the time and, though he had no specific job yet, he and my mother believed their faithful Lord would provide as needed. He did. I made my own westward migration in my trusty Toyota Celica upon being processed out of the service in December, 1976. There was much to celebrate that Christmas!

It was a very snowy winter in the Northwest that year. So when my folks helped me move to Moscow to register for the second semester at the U of I in January, 1977, we had a bit of a dicey drive coming up from Portland. But the thick snow mounded up all over the town made it all the more charming to me. Once I was settled in my dorm, we paid a visit to Jim and Bessie Wilson's home. They were delighted to see my folks for the first time since leaving Ann Arbor six years earlier. After a pleasant visit, the Wilsons told us we should also stop by to see Doug and Nancy, who lived just a block away. As a single guy I was a bit disconcerted when Nancy placed Bekah, now four months old, in my arms.

It was that same little girl, Bekah Wilson, who became the human catalyst for what would become Logos School. While her father became conversant in classical and philosophical studies at the U of I, she grew into a Toddler and was soon joined by a brother, then a sister.

Doug also became the default preacher in our church (through our losing the previous pastor). Faith Fellowship (later "Community Evangelical Fellowship," then finally "Christ Church") was comprised of a slowly growing congregation of about 50–70 folks on a given Sunday. We met most often in Green's Body and Paint Shop, but also used the city park and other various places for worship. By the time Bekah was getting to school-age, Nancy let Doug know that they couldn't send their daughter to the local public schools, to be taught that Christ was irrelevant by teachers who didn't love Him. Doug not only concurred, he promised Nancy that he would somehow make a school for Bekah that was grounded in God's Word.

Doug got to work immediately. In short order he was meeting with a small group of like-minded parents, mostly young dads. Often these guys would have their own meeting after we concluded our regular Brothers Meetings for the church. I noted their activity, but sought no part in it. Even though I had married my dear Julie (a fourth generation Moscow gal) in September of 1977, and we had a little girl by 1979, a Christian school held no interest for me. My initial reaction to hearing what Doug was up to was skepticism, to put it mildly. I even remarked to Julie at least once: *Our church meets in an auto body shop. We sing hymns while facing a wall of car bumpers. Our church nursery is in an apartment where a massive husky lives and sheds constantly. I mean, can't we just be normal about where we send our kids to school?*

Plans for the theoretical school went on, nevertheless. A first school board was put together comprised of three committed individuals: Mrs. Shirley Quist (the wife of a local farmer, Don, and mother of Jim, a fourteen-year old young man), Mr. Larry Lucas (a young father of four children and an accountant just starting out in business in Moscow), and of course Doug.

Which brings us to the autumn of 1980. It was an election year and Ronald Reagan was challenging the incumbent president, Jimmy Carter. The Iranians were still holding about 50 Americans hostage in Tehran. Mount St. Helen's had exploded not far from us (near Portland) in May, inflation was running at over 13%, gas had recently climbed to over a dollar a gallon (shocking!), and all the Beatles were still living.

Micro-computers were just coming on the market. Even though they cost a good bit, they were being snatched up by individuals wanting a computer in their home. Pac-Man and the Rubik's Cube were popular games. The United States was only seven years out from the end of the Vietnam War, and only five years from the last helicopter out of Saigon. Disco was largely over (amen!) and the *Empire Strikes Back* had blown out the box offices earlier that summer.

In the fall of 1980, Moscow, Idaho, the split pea and lentil capital of the world, had about 13,000 residents, of which about 5,000 were students at the University of Idaho. The thousands of acres of rolling wheat fields surrounding Moscow were recently harvested. The basement of the Paradise Hills Church of God, a large facility on the south side, sat unfinished, housing only the occasional mouse family or two. On the west side of town, a new roller skating rink was being completed.

Such was the time, such was the place, and these were the people when Logos School began. God was writing a very unique story.

CHAPTER I

THE BASEMENT

DOUG AND HIS IDEAS

It wasn't the first time Doug Wilson had thrown me a curve ball. I've already mentioned his Christian newspaper, for which we all were enlisted to hand out in high school. And in Norfolk, VA, I'd been church-hopping for two years; Doug helped me find a church home within weeks of his arrival. Then not long after moving to Moscow, I was delighted to be asked to join Doug's band, "Mountain Angel" (formerly "Morning Star"). This time, however, he had the most outrageous, life-altering idea. "I'd like you to consider heading up the Christian school we're starting next fall. You know, be its administrator or principal or whatever. What do you think? Of course you'd need to be interviewed by the board we have."

Doug stood there, looking at me with his you-see-this-is-a-really-great-idea-don't-you look. We were conversing in Crossroads Bookstore, a Christian bookstore begun by his father, Jim, back in 1971. It was now late autumn of 1980. I was in the middle of my student teaching stint at the local public high school, as the final requirement for finishing my undergraduate education degree at the University of Idaho, in Moscow. I was student teaching in secondary art, to be precise. To date, my classroom experience had consisted of about four weeks of watching the high school art teacher conduct—what else?—art classes. True, I had assisted some of the students in their clay and painting projects, so I was not utterly devoid of hands-on, meaningful, student-teacher interaction.

Nevertheless, as I stood there on that fall day, watching Doug's sincere face and hearing his sincere tone, I had to pause. I should not dismiss his proposal out of hand. This was not an offer to take lightly. Some serious possibilities had to be faced: perhaps this was a vital ministry to which God was calling me, perhaps it would help change the lives of many children, perhaps it would lead to a life-long career, perhaps I could use my interest in art at the fledgling school to teach finger-painting! But I didn't think of any of the aforementioned possibilities, with perhaps the exception of the last one.

"You've got to be kidding!," I blurted out, "I am graduating in December with a B.F.A., Doug! That's a Bachelor of Fine Arts degree, and it's in *secondary art*, for goodness sake. In spite of the ed courses I have taken, I couldn't write a lesson plan to save my life. My most profound and recent educational experience with young children was successfully changing my daughter's diaper. And you want me to consider being a principal of a Christian school?" I laughed in a rather derisive tone. Actually, it was a very derisive tone. Anyone else being laughed at like that, after a sincere offer, either would have been just plain hurt and offended, or would possibly have shoved a nearby Christian book on *Loving Unconditionally* into my laughing mouth. Not Doug.

"Well, why don't you and Julie think and pray about it, just the same. If you have any questions about what we're doing, you could ask me, or give Larry Lucas or Shirley Quist a call. They're on the board, too. See ya!" And with that, if my memory serves, he smiled and exited the scene.

Upon returning home to my wife, Julie, I recounted Doug's proposition, with a fresh burst of chortling. Julie, while not seeing it in exactly the same hilarious light I had, did express some profound amazement. I would like to think that she was amazed by the many unknowns of such an offer, and not by the possibility of Doug having a temporary loss of sanity.

In any case, by that time in our lives, both Julie and I had known Doug long enough to normally hold his judgment in high esteem. Julie had been born and raised in Moscow, where agriculture and the university employ the vast majority of Moscow's residents. In the summer following her graduation from high school, Julie had also met the Jim Wilson family, who by then had opened a bookstore in Pullman, Washington, (Moscow's neighbor city eight miles to the west) and would open another near the University of Idaho campus shortly afterward.

By that time in 1980, Doug had been meeting regularly with Larry Lucas and Shirley Quist, as I mentioned. Larry and Shirley were of a mind with Doug, in terms of the necessity of a establishing a non-denominational Christian school (at the time there were only two other private schools in Moscow, a Catholic school and a Seventh Day Adventist school). These three individuals, with the advice and support of a number of other area Christians, had spent the majority of 1980 putting plans together. By fall they had completed a survey of a number of churches to determine the interest in a potential school. The results convinced them that there was indeed enough interest to move ahead. Although no other church actually wanted to be officially connected or financially supportive of a Christian school, a number of individual families had stated their strong desire to see such a project become reality. The planners had continued their work. Curriculum materials were to be obtained from a popular Christian textbook publisher. Based on the interest indicated in the surveys, the fledgling school board decided to "limit" enrollment to sixty students. Then, using a 15:1 student-teacher ratio, they planned to hire four teachers, including the principal.

The board had begun the search for these staff members; they would look for a facility later. Now was the time to seek those capable, loving, far-seeing individuals who would form the first staff of this little school. And like any solid, spiritually worthwhile missions effort, these staff members, like many missionaries before, would need very little in terms of money to sustain them. In fact, salaries, as such, were not part of the board's budget planning. Tuitions would only cover overhead costs. Teachers' pay? Well, that would come from the many gifts that would no doubt be poured out on such a project. In spite of such sketchy visions, the board had rather quickly found two young ladies willing to work under these conditions: Debbie Quist, the daughter of Don and Shirley Quist, would carry the largest load of teaching for any older students; Meredith Gillespie, also a single gal, would teach Kindergarten and science for older students. The Lord had already blessed Logos with two very capable, loving, and intelligent teachers.

Thus it came to the point where Doug confronted me in Crossroads Bookstore with his wild proposition. After easily brushing aside such a harebrained idea, I completed my student teaching at the local government high school. At the same time I sent out the requisite resumes, with the intention of teaching art somewhere locally, if possible. I received at least two art teaching job offers and did a lot of thinking and praying during the months of November and December of 1980. Prior to the idea, or more accurately, the *seed* of the idea of working at a Christian school had been planted in my mind, I probably would have jumped at either job offer. After all, I had loved art all my life, it was what I had been trained for, or at least, it would keep food on the table for my young family. Our first child, Carolyn, had been born in January of 1979, so there were three of us to think about.

Now, with the public school job offers to consider, I paused and gave serious ruminations to that pesky idea of Doug's; it somehow wouldn't just fade away. Julie was no help at all in my wavering about my future vocation ... she just "trusted me to make the right decision." *Great.* I would like to say that I found a number of Scripture passages that guided me to make an inspired choice, but that's not the truth. It finally came down to just not having peace in my mind until I chased this idea down and stared it in the eye. So, after a fair bit of prayer, in January, 1981, I met with Doug and asked to be interviewed by the school board. My uncertainty must have been evident to them, but they were gracious and kind anyway. I basically told them that I knew they were mature Christians, so I would consider their decision, either way, as God's direction for me.

As would be the requirement for all staff hirings in years to come, the board voted unanimously in its decision. Doug called to let me know they would like to offer me the job. If I accepted it, I would serve as principal and the fourth board member. God's timing is so good. By this point, I had been substitute teaching for the district for several weeks after obtaining my degree and certificate. I didn't know much yet, but after working in a variety of public school classes, I knew that this was not what I wanted to do as a career. There had to be a better way to teach children and even enjoy doing it than what I was seeing in these schools. Julie and I prayed again, and, gulping down the remainders of my foolish, pricked pride at being the only one to apply, I accepted the job offer. The first step into the immense gulf of the unknown future began with a short "OK."

HOME LIFE

Carolyn had turned two years old by the time I accepted the job at Logos. Being a quick learner, she was also working on driving her mother and me nuts by singing the alphabet song repeatedly. She needed some steadying influence. How about another sibling in the home? Along about February we discovered that a small bundle of steadying influence would be arriving in October. So, while I continued subbing in the Moscow public schools and planning for the new Christian school, Julie worked on preparing our apartment for another small tenant.

As the spring of 1981 progressed, the board and staff met quite a few times to discuss plans and look at curriculum ideas. We decided that a public informational meeting, both to disseminate information about the school and possibly garner interest, would take place in March. We held it in a local restaurant's banquet room and about thirty people showed up. Our board chairman, Larry Lucas, did an admirable job of outlining the mission and purpose of the proposed non-denominational Christian school. However, opening ourselves up for questions may have been a mistake. We were handling them pretty well until someone asked where the school would call home.

"Well, we're still looking for a place. We are sure open to suggestions," Larry answered hopefully. The attendees exchanged concerned looks. But, overall, the evening was a modest success, with a couple of families expressing interest in enrolling their little ones.

Where *would* we have the school? It couldn't be avoided any longer. We hadn't exactly been avoiding the need, but with summer coming on, the issue moved to front burner status. Knocking on several church's doors produced no offers of hospitality, not even the suggestion of a stable out back. Creative ideas were thrown on the table. A helpful realtor even showed us a couple of houses "that might work for you, at least to get started." However, even with only sixteen students, we would need a pretty good-sized house. "Cheaper by the dozen" was certainly not the story for us.

Other work went on in between searches for a facility. We decided to go with the most popular Christian school materials' publisher to supply our curriculum needs. By June, some of the ordered materials had arrived and we scrutinized them with all the excitement and keen insight of a teenager buying his first used car. Gee, they were colorful, and there were posters and everything!

Finally, thank God, in late June a wonderful group of Christian folks at the Paradise Hills Church of God came through for us. We met with their church council, among whom were Larry and Betty Lacey, and Jay and Marva McCoy—folks who would become long-term friends and supporters. Larry was a local contractor and Jay was one of three brothers (Oba and Len being the other two) who owned McCoy Plumbing and Heating. The council offered to let us finish their basement with funds they would borrow from their church district. We would repay their loan through our rent payments. The small congregation had huge hearts and a large building they had built themselves. The unfinished basement area was big enough to house several classrooms. For our first year we planned to construct three classrooms, one each for kindergarten, lower elementary, and upper elementary. In addition, two bathrooms and a small school office would be constructed. All those spaces only took up about half of the unfinished basement area. The church would allow us to use their main floor sanctuary for assemblies and their downstairs fellowship hall for indoor PE, lunch, and other fun events. What a real blessing! Much better than that split-level house (or the large barn we had considered briefly). Plans and construction moved into high gear.

However, while the school home problem was being solved, a very serious problem was developing in my home. Julie was only about five-and-a-half months pregnant but she began to have contractions. Her doctor sent her to get bed rest in the Pullman hospital. In March I had begun a part-time, temporary job at Skipper's restaurant. Now, without Julie at home, I had to care for Carolyn alone. Christian friends watched her when I went to work, but leaving her weeping day after day at other homes burned itself on my heart.

Time in the hospital didn't seem to be stabilizing things for Julie. Even so, when the crisis came on July 14, it was a real surprise. On that warm, sunny morning I had left Carolyn with our next-door neighbor. Before going to work, I showed the new school facility to our final teacher to be hired for the year, Debbie Wilson (no relation). She would have the first and second graders in a mixed level class. After comparing notes with her for preparations for her class, I left the church and arrived at Skipper's only to be told that I was needed at home, pronto. But by the time I got home, my baby-sitting neighbor informed me that the Pullman hospital had sent Julie to Deaconess Hospital in Spokane by ambulance.

Taking time only to kiss Carolyn good-bye, I cruised as fast as I lawfully could (or a little more) to Spokane, eighty miles to the north. After an anxious trip, I arrived at the wrong hospital. I was given directions and made it to the correct facility, where I was informed Julie was on the third floor, Obstetrics and Maternity. A nurse there let me know Julie was just about to go into surgery to deliver the baby. She also couldn't resist saying, "It's about time someone got here for that poor gal!"

For a while things were on fast-forward, as it seemed to me. I remember putting on the pale green paper clothes that doctors wear and being told to "stand there," near Julie's head. Intense lights, mumbling, and softly shifting people in green, rustling outfits. Low hums, clinks. More mumbling, higher pitched. Prayer came easily: "Father, please just get us through this. Help Julie!"

"Mr. Garfield?" a green person said over the hum and mumbles. I looked up to see a doctor holding a gangly, red little body about a foot long. "You have a son, Mr. Garfield." I had honestly momentarily forgotten about the fact that a baby was also involved in this whole operation. After allowing me a brief glance at our very tiny boy, they whisked him into a wheeled isolette (a special incubator) and told me I could check on him later in the NICU (Neonatal Intensive Care Unit), a place Julie and I would learn to love and loathe in months to come. The rest of the day was spent tending Julie, calling our moms, listening to them cry, and, finally being able to see Seth Thomas. After weaving among several other aquarium-like isolettes, I found Seth. On the card under his name was written, "2 lbs., 3 oz." He lay, red as a sausage, under more lights, wires sprouting from him like the back of a stereo. I measured the size of his hand from finger-tip to wrist by comparing it to my fingers. His whole hand was the size of the last knuckle on my thumb. My son…born three months early. What a guy!

Then came the days and weeks of being separated as Julie stayed in Spokane with dear friends of Shirley Quist. Days and weeks of three steps forward and two back, as we prayed and willed Seth to grow stronger. Though never requiring a respirator, he was given oxygen, with the goal of reducing the amount to that found in normal air. Two and a half months would go by before, handling him like a Delft plate, we were able take him home.

One day, as we knew it would, the hospital's business office asked to meet with us to discuss our somewhat sizable tab. The woman we met with was extremely nice and understanding, even when we let the cat out of the bag and told her that not only did we not have insurance, but that I would not actually be paid a salary in my new school job.

"You d-don't know what you will make each month?"

"Nope. See, it's sort of like missions work. You know, where we'll receive gifts, as they come in."

Nodding as though this was the most reasonable idea she'd ever heard, she asked us what we could commit to as a regular monthly payment. Seeing as how we were in the process of racking up a hospital bill equivalent to the sticker price of a modest new house, I threw out a figure I hoped wouldn't sound too ridiculous, considering everything. She accepted it right off and drew up the forms. Julie and

I looked at each other, both with one thought, "How in the world will we pay what we've just committed to?"

A special note of profound thanks to our parents needs to be inserted here. Both sets would have been perfectly justified in telling us that, in light of our current situation, going ahead with the new school job would be like investing in eight-track players. That's putting it very mildly—they would have been justified in telling me to get a "real" job! And they would have been echoing my own thoughts and fears. But they didn't say anything like that; instead they just poured loads of love and support into us as we waited and prayed day after day.

Was this whole episode with Seth a test of our faith, or our vision for the ministry we were entering? I honestly don't know, and would not presume to know my Father's mind. We were set on a course and to veer from it never seemed to be a viable option. Seth did grow and much more happened to him and us during that tense time than I can relate here. Suffice it to say that I do know that the timing of Seth's homecoming—just days before the school opened—was a tangible blessing to me. Knowing he was home made both Julie's and my burden lighter. Seeing what it can take to get a little baby safely into the world also taught me how precious each child is; I would have a hard time taking a child for granted after this.

A final note about that trying period of our lives: our dear Father truly put a hedge of protection from fear around our hearts. I always expected Seth to live; I honestly never doubted that he would. Only later, much later, did I find out he had had a one-in-three "chance" of living. Such is the Holy One's sovereignty and kindness.

During the time Seth was in Spokane, a school family and staff barbecue was held in August. We cooked the obligatory burgers and dogs, watching our charges-to-be charging around the backyard of Jim and Bessie Wilson's home. The fledgling teachers and administration were wondering how all this was going to work, but the kids had no problem figuring it out. They quickly discovered who was in whose class and expressed the joy and excitement of meeting new friends. After the meal, I called all the families together, and we had the kids group up by grades, with the appropriate teacher. They looked more like teams for kick-the-can than classes of school children, but the kids thought it was neat. I still marvel at the faith and trust of the parents gathered there. Competence and professionalism did not exactly describe the teachers and administration present. Especially the administration, dressed in the ever-present jeans. Yet, to my knowledge, none of the parents backed out that night. Rather, they made all the staff feel appreciated and supported.

As the summer of '81 ended, my new son and the new school were both off to a somewhat shaky start. And, also with both, only God could bring growth and stability.

THE GRAND OPENING

Oh, mercy! It would have to be on the third floor! Sigh. Oh, well. It was the only piano we had seen, so I bid on it. The other auction attendees, being smarter than I was, allowed me to gain the top bid rather easily. In fact, no one else bid. ("Check out the idiot bidding on a piano on the third floor!" Snort, guffaw!) "Sold!...to the guy about to get a hernia!" Eruption of laughter among the auction attendees, with the exclusion of one.

The piano wasn't the only thing we bought that day, but it was the most memorable. Shirley Quist, Larry Lucas, and I had driven to Spokane in early August, 1981, to get some used school furniture at the public school auction. Over many years to come, I would be able to obtain the vast majority of our school's furniture by taking advantage of the Spokane District's use-it-or-lose-it budgeting policy. We saved literally tens of thousands of dollars buying used furniture with years of life left.

This particular auction was an all-day affair due to the tremendous amount of stock to sell off. We had all been astounded at the huge warehouse rooms stacked with desks, chairs, bookshelves, kitchen equipment, lab supplies, and shop tools, just to mention a few specifics. Table tops were covered with odd bits and pieces of electronic equipment, maps, art supplies, P.E. items, and other identifiable and unidentifiable gewgaws. We had brought a shopping list and tried very hard to stick to it. But we couldn't get through any room without at least one of us saying, "Hey! Check this out! Won't we need one of these, sometime?" And, depending on how convincing the person's reasons were, we would either bid on it, or just say, "Well, let's see how much it goes for..."

We were able to purchase enough chairs, desks, blackboards, and one piano, among other miscellaneous neat stuff to outfit our little school. We loaded the Quists' grain truck, drove back to Moscow, unloaded the furniture, and surveyed the overall readiness of the school. In just a few weeks the school doors would open for the first time. The newly sheetrocked walls for the three classrooms were ready for paint. The bathrooms still needed the fixtures installed, but the plumbing contractors (the McCoys, of course) were great guys and we knew we could count on them. (In fact, they would be of incalculable blessing to the school for years to come.) The carpeting would be laid after the painting was done. I looked into "my" office: a ten-by-twelve foot room that would house the secretary's desk, my desk, and some teacher-work items, e.g., the duplicating machine. (A photocopier was a far-off dream.) It all looked wonderful!

The lower level of the church was a daylight basement with windows facing east and a door to the outside play area. The school would be located in the half of the basement closest to the stairs and fellowship hall. The unfinished, back half of the same wing would provide future expansion possibilities. For now, it contained church storage and a sizable population of mice.

After the others left, I went outside to cool off from the long, hot day of work. The grassy yard that would be the playground for the kids was a relatively narrow piece of ground that quickly dropped off to a fairly steep, weed-covered slope of about a hundred yards. At the bottom of this hill was a farmer's field of fifteen acres.

From the top of the hill behind the church, you could see much of the north and east views of Moscow. It really was a beautiful view. From my office window the Moscow mountains, a long, undulating ridge of hills about a thousand feet high, could be easily seen. While in the Navy, I came to love the ocean's ability to shift and change its colors and texture daily. The mountains were like that too, their colors and shadows never looked the same two days running. The green and blue hues would shift constantly, according to the each day's light and the season. The highest tree tops would get the first frosty dusting of snow around late October, letting us know winter was coming. In the spring, the hillsides would be a rich aquamarine, the forest of firs looking bushier somehow than they had in the winter.

But that day I wasn't thinking about how the mountains would look year after year. I was thinking about how small the "playground" was, and the fact that there wasn't one thing for the kids to play with or climb on. We had spent many hours preparing the inside of the school, but the outside would have to wait until after school began, there just wasn't time to do it all. The weedy, wide slope of the hill on which the church sat would provide some diversion, as it turned out. The boys especially would find it of great interest. Again, though, I was spared any foreboding; ignorance can be bliss, for a while.

The last few weeks of preparation were a strange mix of time perceptions for me: the days weren't long enough in readying the school, and yet they weren't short enough as I monitored, long-distance, Seth's progress in the hospital. The school work was definitely therapeutic, though. It displaced, for a while, my anxiety about Seth still struggling in the hospital eighty miles away. Along with the teachers, I immersed myself in moving furniture around the rooms, watching the carpet being laid, carrying in far more books than I could imagine seventeen students needing, and painting, painting, and more painting.

As August's last days ticked off, the teachers feverishly put lesson plans together (based on absolutely no guidance from me or any other clear directives) and decorated their walls with those colorful posters. I worked on the office—adjusting my desk-top items, determining which side was best for my phone, trying out my chair, and generally trying to figure what in the world I was going to do once the kids got there. Oh yes, I also obtained a nice, tall bookshelf from a generous family. Of course, then I had to find some intellectual-looking books to put on it. Nothing is so naked as an empty bookshelf. Perhaps some well-placed models would suffice? Ah, yes. Work, work, work.

We had set the Tuesday after Labor Day (the 8th) in early September as the grand opening date. As with many such incidental decisions, this too would become a tradition for years to come. None of the staff spent much time away from the school that holiday weekend. Quite a few school families also spent their Labor Day helping to clean, organize, and generally make the school look more like a school than a done-over basement. And, by George, it really did look a lot like a school! From the carpeted hallways, to the neat rows of desks in the three classrooms, each with an orderly pile of books on top, the place just might pass for a school. A very small one, but a school nonetheless. I counted the desks in each room for the zillionth time; six in the kindergarten, eight in the combined first and second grade room, and three (one each for our token fifth, sixth, and ninth graders) in the corner room.

Monday, Labor Day, came to a close. It was rather late in the evening when the last teacher finally heaved a sigh and shut her door. We had done all we could to be ready in such a short time. Still no playground equipment, but that wouldn't be a problem, I assured myself.

I didn't sleep well that night. I lay in bed and considered what we were embarking upon. I recalled one significant, recent conversation we had as a staff and board. We had been discussing a variety of business items, including the school's name. Debbie Quist had been doing some thinking along those lines already.

"Let's call it *Logos*.* That's Greek for *word*, and I think that would be far more appropriate than 'Moscow Christian School'" (our initial idea). We had already decided on the motto of "A Classical and Christian School," based on our agreement with Dorothy Sayer's points on the Trivium in her article, *The Lost Tools of Learning*. "Logos has the double meaning of a reference to classical roots, as well as Jesus being referred to as the Word of God in John," Debbie went on.

Doug added, "If we're going to use 'Logos,' let's just call it 'Logos School,' versus 'Logos Christian School.' That doesn't sound very good, and seems rather redundant to boot."

Thus the school was christened. No fanfare, no great announcement. Just a name that sounded appropriate to the small group that would see the school out of the starting blocks. Logos School. Short, easy...I liked it, too.

* Incidentally, we determined to make the pronunciation of this word "Loh-goss," as opposed to "Loh-gohs" or "Law-goss." No one is absolutely certain how Greek vowels were pronounced back then anyway. So we used both long and short. It just sounded better.

Tuesday morning. The first day. I unlocked the glass front doors of the church (the school wouldn't have its own entrance until next year). The teachers arrived early and so we gathered for a brief time in the kindergarten room for prayer and final notes. Where to eat lunch? Who's got the first recess? Shall we all get together for an assembly first? What's an "assembly?" After a brief explanation by the teachers..."Um, yes, let's meet in the fellowship hall at about 9:00 for a short, first assembly."

I'm not sure what we each expected the first day to be like. I thought it would be something like slowly but gradually idling back a revved up engine, until you heard just the quiet, smooth hum of a happy motor. It was almost anti-climatic in a way. The parents were excited, the kids were dubious, and then we started the classes. The day began and then, well, just went on. Quietly, with no need to idle the noise back or anything. I wandered professionally about the only hall, ever-ready to leap into action should a teacher holler for help with a nasty pencil sharpener. But no such cries issued forth, so I returned to my office to see what my secretary was doing.

When the first recess came, all seventeen kids trickled out to the grassy area behind the church. All five staff members came out, too, to enjoy the sight of happy children frolicking and laughing in the warm September sun. However, for the first few minutes, the inaugural recess took on all the jovial appearance of a doctor's waiting room. Every child's face silently was asking the same question: What do we do now? No play equipment, no balls, just grass lawn and a steep, weed-covered slope down to a field. What was there to do? Restlessness and confusion hung heavily in the air.

Finally, someone, somewhere obtained a real ball, and it could have been an ice cream truck for the enthusiastic response it received from the children! The ball's presence energized all the kids, even those unable to get their hands on it. Once the first ball broke the ice, the boys found that the weeds were an Aladdin's cave of treasures. In weeks to come they found it to be rich and full of wildlife. They could echo Lewis and Clark's sentiments, "We have come into a great and good country!" (It was too bad the girls would come to feel quite differently about the same area—even when the boys enthusiastically shared their significant findings with the ladies, such as healthy garter snakes.)

The first lunch was eaten in the respective classrooms. In days to come we would set up a couple of tables in the fellowship hall and eat all together. After lunch, I had the opportunity to introduce our three older students, one each in fifth, sixth, and ninth grade, to the history and art I would be teaching them. It felt more like a committee than a class, but we got off to a good start anyway. Among the four of us teachers, we covered all the older students' various subjects. The fact that Jim, our ninth grader, would be taught by his older sister was a concern before school began, but once the work actually started there was never any awkwardness.

Three o'clock came and so did the parents to retrieve their offspring. Each parent came equipped with the same two questions: First, to their child, "Did you have a good time?," and second, to the teacher and/or me, "How did it go?" To the first question, the answers were varied, but the ones I overheard were rather benign: "It was OK. But Mom, there isn't much to play with." To the second question, the answers from the teachers were very similar: "It went really well!" accompanied by sighs of relief. We had begun. The first day was finished, learning had actually occurred, the parents hadn't been disappointed, and only one student had thrown up. Not bad.

Logos School was underway!

MORE FIRSTS

One pleasant aspect of having no idea of what you're doing is that you aren't easily discouraged. Almost any idea sounds not only good, but even plausible. So, at Logos, we went from day to day, making it up as we went. Thankfully, the teachers took planning their lessons very seriously, so the bulk of time was well spent in the classrooms. So, I guess when I say we were making it up as we went, I largely mean I was.

I sincerely had no idea what administrating a school entailed. I mean zip, nada, zero, no clue. All my interest in education up to that time was built around art and the teaching thereof. I needed lots of practical help! To my rescue came the Association of Christian Schools,

International (ACSI). This organization already had thousands of member schools (we quickly joined) and a good amount of helpful resources. One such resource was a binder entitled, *Beginning A Christian School,* and it came with a plastic case full of cassette tapes about various topics in administering such a school. Yay! Just what I needed. I literally spent hours and hours that first year, sitting at my desk and listening to the tapes, reading in the binder and writing notes.

"So we need report cards?" I would say to myself after listening, then I wrote on my yellow legal pad of notes: MAKE REPORT CARDS. In the binder, ACSI had thoughtfully even included sample forms and documents (like a Report Card) that might come in handy.

My office also served as the only office of the school. My secretary's desk was close to the hall door, my desk was by the window. A low table held our mimeograph machine, so the teachers and/or mom volunteers had to come in there to run off any worksheets, notes, etc., for their classes. It was a very busy place! It was also where I held our daily before-school staff meetings—all four of us, and my secretary, would meet briefly to pray and discuss anything that might need to be...discussed.

A word about Logos School's first secretary: Heather Wilson. If you were paying attention to the Prologue of this volume, you may have noted that Heather was mentioned as being the only daughter of Jim and Bessie Wilson. When Logos opened, she kindly offered to be our part-time school secretary. Considering that we received few phone calls and I was still trying to figure out my own job, much less knowing how to make good use of a secretary, Heather didn't have loads to occupy her time. But she certainly didn't mind seeing a bit of her first little niece, Bekah, who was in the kindergarten class.

The school's phone number caused some interesting calls that first year. It turned out the phone company had issued us the number of a former auto salvage yard that had closed some years back. Apparently, quite a few backyard mechanics either never got new phone books or had just memorized the number, since we frequently got calls like:

Ring!

"Good morning, Logos School."

"Yeah, I'm looking for a front bumper for a '59 Chevy Bel Air...ya think ya got one of those?"

"I'm sorry, this is Logos School, we aren't a—"

"What d'ya mean a school? You ain't the salvage yard? Did I get the wrong number?"

"No, you got the right number, but we're a Christian school."

"Oh...so you ain't got any front bumpers...?"

We quickly slipped into the daily routine of starting the school day: unlocking the doors, turning on lights, checking to see if our volunteer janitors (parents) had come the night before (if they hadn't, which happened from time to time, we did a quick cleaning of the bathrooms), welcoming our little band of students as they arrived at the church, and beginning the day's schedule of classes. It didn't take long before we all relaxed and enjoyed being together. Being in close proximity (one hallway), and essentially feeling more like a large family than a school, any special occasion was shared by everyone. Kittens brought into kindergarten show-and-tell? How fun! We all gathered around the basket of mewing fur-balls. A guest speaker in second grade? Yup, we all went in to hear about Lewis and Clark.

Our first 'official' guest speaker, by the way, was Mr. Tom Trail. He happened to be the landlord of the apartments where my family lived. But more to the point, he was a world traveler and a university professor (later to become an Idaho State Representative). He brought us all an interesting presentation on the Holy Land, which the kids listened to very politely.

Not long after we were up and running, someone suggested we get school photos taken. The selection of the photographer was easy: Mark LaMoreaux. He and his wife Chris had their oldest child, John, in our kindergarten. Mark was an artist with the camera and agreed to come and take a lot of pictures. I let the parents know the date and cost, and the kids dressed up for school picture day. (Golly, it felt almost like a real school!) Mark took individual photos of all the children, then for good measure took a photo of the entire school, like a family portrait. He also took some of the four faculty members. What we would ever do with those, I had no idea, but it seemed like a good idea at the time (and now, you can see it in Appendix H). The local paper (at that time called the *Daily Idahonian*) got wind of our new educational enterprise and did a fairly decent-sized spread of a story on page one. They really enjoyed the angle of our not paying our teachers and "living on faith." The story got the attention of some of the local public educators and shortly thereafter I received a very kind invitation from one of the elementary principals. You should understand that at this time, the early '80s, the local district had a good many long-term teachers and administrators. Most of the principals of the four elementary schools, for instance, were women who had served in the schools for well over 30 years. They referred to themselves as "dinosaurs." How do I know that? Well, the invitation I received was from one of these ladies, and it was to take a trip to Lewiston to hear a presentation on state accreditation standards.

I thought, "Why not?" (Remember how desperate I was for any training and information I could get?) On the day appointed, four very matronly ladies in a smallish sedan arrived at the door of the Church of God to pick me up. I was placed in the middle of the back seat and thus got to hear all their quips and conversations, as well as get a bit overwhelmed by the heavy lavender aroma, on our forty-five minute drive south to Lewiston. That's when I heard them refer to each other as dinosaurs, and laugh uproariously about it. I had the distinctly strange impression of being taken under their (pterodactyl?) wings. But they were sincerely wanting to help me and my little school get the lay of the land.

We arrived at the Lewiston high school auditorium where we heard an Idaho State Board of Education member speak about how to get accredited by the State of Idaho that year. There were forms handed out and the ladies made sure I got a copy of each form. In glancing through the numerous important standards schools would have to meet to be state accredited, I noticed one I wouldn't have thought would make the list: the height and number of drinking fountains. Apparently, I deduced, if students have to either stretch to get a drink or bend over too far, this would negatively affect their learning. Man, there was a lot I didn't know.

Afterward, the ladies decided that it was time for lunch and knew just the place to go eat. They insisted on paying for my lunch, too. Again, I felt like I was out with four aunts I never knew I had. At the restaurant, we all sat around the table and, after ordering, one of the ladies noticed the placard in the center of the table.

"Oh, look! They're putting on a lingerie modeling show during lunch today!"

I may not have known much about administration, but I knew I was in the wrong place at the wrong time. Sadly, our orders hadn't come before the models started making the rounds of the tables. So I found myself studying the fascinating aspects of my water glass and dearly wishing there was a trapdoor in the floor under our table. Then suddenly an already awkward situation went into hyper-drive...

"Well, hello, Tom!"

One of the 'models' (most of whom, I couldn't help noticing, were on the far side of 35 years old) had come by our table and recognized me. I didn't want to be rude, so I looked up, way up, and said hi. I vaguely recalled that she was one of the many ladies who knew my mother-in-law, possibly even a relation. All I could think of, though, was how long the odds had to be that someone I had met briefly in Moscow would be modeling lingerie in this particular Lewiston restaurant in which I was cringing.

As with many of life's dark moments, time blurred and I recall being dropped off back at Logos by the bevy of lady principals that afternoon. I staggered back to the comfort and relative seclusion of my office, still holding on to the state accreditation forms. "What had *that* been all about?" I asked the Father silently. "What was I supposed to glean from that bizarre trip?"

In the following days, I actually read through the forms carefully and came to the conclusion that there should never be a time when Logos should seek to be accredited by the state. The actual scriptural principles against such a compromise would be clearer to me in years to come. For now I just knew it would be wrong, regardless of the delightful trip with the dinosaurs.

FIRST LOGOS NEWSLETTER – SEPTEMBER 16, 1981

Dear Parents and Friends,

Just think, our first whole week has already gone by for Logos School! I believe all of us, students and teachers, have learned a lot about each other and the school in this short time. We are still revising our daily schedule to make sure all the classes run smoothly and our volunteer teachers can make the most of their time. Daily we discover things to be done and ways to do things better. Overall, though, we are having a very enjoyable education.

As you probably know, we had our first field trip for the school on Friday, the 11th. The Palouse Fair was not only fun to see, but I think we all learned something about farming and animals. All the kids were very well behaved and we as teachers were very proud of them. I had some jitters about taking nineteen children to a fair, having observed similar endeavors that did not meet with very much success. Now, however, I am anxious to take the kids to a lot of other places. A hearty thank you to Greg Pole and Irma Davis for helping out.

A few items that should be noted:

1. The staff's upcoming ACSI (Association of Christian Schools, Intl.) convention in Seattle is on the first and second of October. The school will be closed during those days while we learn from other school staffs, administrators, and pastors. There will also be Christian text book publishers displaying their wares at the convention.
2. We are planning an "open house" for the school on the evening of October 8 from 6:30 – 9:00 pm. This will be a time for anyone interested in the school to drop by to meet the teachers, have some refreshments, and see the facilities. We will be there to answer questions and show you around. The kids will very likely want you to see their work also, so please plan on coming and enjoying yourself.
3. The school board is hoping to establish a Parent-Teacher Fellowship basically to keep communication lines open between the school and the parents. It is in the formative stages now and if you are at all interested in taking part in the leadership of such an organization, please contact me at home or at the school. I think this could become a very important part of our

school's impact on the community, as well as improving the functioning of the school.

4. Finally, about the lists attached, the first is a list of things that we need volunteers to do. I greatly encourage you to see if you could spare an hour or two a week to work at the school or at home to help us get these things done. The second list is of items that the school could use if you have them on hand and want to donate those items. We are not asking you to go out and buy them, only to donate those items that you are not using.

As always, if you have any suggestions, questions, or problems concerning the school, please let me know. Thank you. Keep us in your prayers, our Lord is listening and answering.

In Him,
Thomas Garfield
Principal

FALL CARNIVAL

The summer weather waned and suddenly it was October. Our first holiday of sorts was looming and we had to decide what, if anything, we would do about it (the idea of a Reformation Day wouldn't even occur to us for many years). Halloween. It didn't seem right to just ignore it. Yet we somehow knew instinctively that it wouldn't be good to decorate the rooms with construction paper witches and ghosts. I don't know who had the idea, but we agreed this would be a good time to have a Fall Carnival. We would try to steal a little thunder from the pagan holiday.

We told the students they could wear costumes on Friday, the 30th, little knowing what we were unleashing. Of course, we all wore fun outfits, too. I didn't have to look too far for a costume; my Navy uniform actually still fit me (for the last time) after four years as a civilian. Those with a better understanding of children and education than we had would've been able to predict what would happen when you combine costumes and children—not much school would happen, that's what. But that was ok.

With whoops and hollers and general laughter we greeted each arriving costumed student. The hilarity rose exponentially with each new arrival. Cowboys, fairies, and even Raggedy Ann came through the door. There were games, with parental help, like bobbing for apples and decorating cookies. In years to come, we moved this event to the evening (thereby getting a school day back) and eventually had all sorts of booths of fun filling the entire fellowship hall of the church basement.

SUCTION

Considering the wear and tear we put on the church building, I must emphasize how tremendously gracious the congregation of the Church of God was to us. With lots of sweat equity they had built a lovely two-story facility that we had invaded with lots of young, energized, little people. We were even allowed to use their sanctuary for our weekly assemblies. I had only one significant disagreement with the planning that had gone into this structure: the central vacuum system.

I can understand the thinking behind such a device: there would be no need of lugging a vacuum up and down hallways or stairs. All you needed to have was a hose and wand, then just open one of the many small, round suction vents located throughout the building and stick in the hose. The vacuum would automatically start and there you'd go. The dust and dirt would be sucked eventually into a large R2–D2 look-alike mounted in a basement closet. And therein, as Shakespeare would say, was the rub.

In our newly finished half of the basement wing, we used the same vacuum system, which meant that we would, from time to time, have to empty R2–D2. Or, to be more precise, I would have to empty and change the vacuum bag; there was no way I'd ask the ladies to do it and parental help was usually not around when it needed to be done. How did we know when? Well, it was usually after school, when the teachers were vacuuming their rooms, or attempting to do so. I'd hear the vacuum start up, an unearthly whine, then pretty quickly it shut off and a humble, needy face would appear at my office door:

"Tom...the vacuum isn't sucking again."

"Did you check to see if any ports are open?" (Note: If *any* of the multitude of little ports were open anywhere in the entire building, the suction would be diminished. Considering how just one small piece of gravel could jam one port open, this was a frequent event.)

"Uhmm...I haven't looked..." (Said with a sorrowful, I've-had-a-long-day-teaching, pleading tone.)

Sigh. "Right. OK, let me take a look."And thus would begin my odyssey throughout the entire facility, visually checking to see if every port was tightly closed. Once I determined that, indeed, every little plastic cover was as it should be, I knew there was only one other option: I must empty R2–D2. Steeling myself for the chore included mentally composing excuses to Julie for when I got home. That's because I knew, no matter how carefully and slowly I handled the change, I was in for a dust bath. And since I rarely wore old clothes to school, Julie would have to deal with the state of my shirt and slacks (not to mention my tie).

Yet, every time was a challenge—could I unlatch all the connections between R2–D2's head (as I thought of it) and his 'body' without jostling the vacuum bag? Then, like handling an unexploded nuke, I would slowly extract the large, amorphous, dust-coated bag, packed to the rim with...gray stuff. Could I make it past the edge and get it into the garbage can without...(bump!) WHOOMPFFF! The bag would hit the floor and the whole world would immediately turn gray. I did learn to hold my breath just before the dust cloud enveloped me.

THE LONG WINTER

The winter of 1981–82 in Moscow was amazing! It was like the Lord felt sorry for us and gave the kids tons of snow to play in during recess. Remember our tiny playground? In a very short time, well over a foot of snow accumulated everywhere, including our hill, and thus our Winter Olympics began. It wasn't very organized, but there were many events each recess time: fort-building, snowman-making, snow angels, but very quickly the favorites became sledding and the luge. Luge? Yes. Well, sort of. The snow kept falling and with several feet of depth on the hill's slope, it became possible to build tunnels all the way down the hillside. After a few brave boys in slick snowsuits worked at smoothing out the tunnel walls, we had, ta-da!, a luge run! A student (usually a boy) would thrust himself into the entry point at the top of the hill and disappear. A few moments later, as we watched from the hilltop...POP!...out he'd come from the other end far below and skid into the field. The only down-side was that with recess only being fifteen minutes, there was only enough time to make one luge run per kid, what with the time it took to make the trek back uphill.

Sledding or tobogganing was a delight for the non-luge types. Here, too, the trails became thick but packed (i.e., slicker and faster). This is when the ominous music should start. You know what they say—it's all good fun until someone gets hurt. Though I had taken a fair number of turns going down the hill with various children, I was inside when it happened. A frantic teacher burst into my office and shouted, "Mr. Garfield, there's been a sledding accident! I think some kids are really hurt!" In shirt sleeves I dashed out the door and into the snow.

When I got to the top of the hill, the teacher explained that five children had gone down on one toboggan. They apparently found a ditch no one else had and crashed into it rather spectacularly. Three of the children were crying, but otherwise ok and back up on top. Two sisters, Beth and Becky, made up the balance of the five on the fateful ride. Becky, a second-grader, was being helped up the hill by other students and a teacher. She was bleeding badly from her mouth. But she was more concerned about her sister, still lying in the snow at the base of the hill.

"I think Beth is hurt real bad, Mr. Garfield! Please help her!"

I assured her that I would and, without much idea of what I could actually do for Beth, I took giant steps down the slope. Upon arriving by the prone body of our only sixth grader, I asked her how she was.

"I can't find my glasses!" was her first concern. I looked around and actually found them and placed them on her face. That calmed her a bit, and she told me her leg hurt a lot. Even without knowing much first aid, I knew that trying to walk up a hill on a possibly broken leg was a bad idea. I also remember thinking that any EMTs would take quite a while to get there and would have to come down the hill, too. So, I carefully picked Beth up in my arms (she was a very small, thin sixth grader) and made my way up the hill, avoiding the slick sled paths.

Meanwhile back in at the school office, Becky was being ministered to by one of the teachers. Heather, our secretary, phoned Becky's parents to tell them about the accident. When their mom asked how the girls were, Heather was succinct, if not a bit tactless: "Well, we think Beth's leg is broken, and Becky's bleeding like a stuck pig."

Thankfully the girls' mom, Mary Lou Busby, was made of pretty sturdy stuff and took this news in stride. She asked that we get the girls to the hospital and she'd meet us there. One of the school moms happened to be volunteering that day and she had a pick-up truck. The girls were loaded gently: Beth in the covered truck-bed with one of our teachers to ride with her and Becky up front in the cab. Later we learned that Beth had indeed broken her leg and would need a cast. Becky got some stitches in her upper lip (in years to come she would point to the barely visible scar whenever she wanted me to do something special for her).

What had we learned from our first serious accident? Well, one policy we put in place right away: no more than three people on a toboggan. We also altered the sledding paths away from the ditch. And next time I would let the EMTs go down the hill.

The days, weeks, and months of that first year sped by, as school years always would. We presented our first Christmas program (written by our three oldest students) in the church sanctuary and attended by a small, but appreciative group of families. Beth had directed the play, even while on crutches. We also had our first broken window—a baseball went through a window in that same sanctuary.

We had our first awkward school vs. parent situation: two new children were enrolled part-way through the year by their recently divorced mother. Several weeks later, the children's father and his parents showed up mid-day at Logos and told me they were taking the children out for the day. Being fairly new to these situations and having a high degree of respect for parental authority, I saw no objection. That afternoon, the children's mom showed up expecting to collect her offspring. She knew nothing of her ex taking the children. As I said—awkward situation, to say the least. Again, by God's kind grace, the mom didn't bring her lawyer into play. Instead, she told us she knew where they were headed (Colorado, I believe) and would sic the law on them there. Right. We never saw any of them again, not surprisingly. I added another to-do item to our enrollment process: in any divorce situation, find out who has legal custody of the child(ren), ideally with proof on paper. Oh yes, and if a stranger shows up to claim any kids, check with the known parent first!

Valentine's Day came and cards, candy, and cookies magically appeared in every room. Then, a few weeks later, the snow melted away, the grass grew in our little yard, the snakes returned to the slope, and we knew the year was winding down. We celebrated Easter with an assembly, hymns, and a half-day on Good Friday. The kids were all obviously taller and older than they looked way back on School Picture Day. The weather was warm, the teachers took their little classes outside as often as possible to soak up the sun, sing, and learn things. It suddenly dawned on me one day—we were actually completing our first year!

SPRING ARRIVES

During that same springtime, I couldn't resist being out at recess as much as possible. I loved playing with the kids and it seemed to be mutual. One very warm day we were playing a fore-shortened version of baseball. I was the catcher, with my back to one wall of the church. The ball was hit, caught, and thrown home to tag out the runner. I lunged and caught the ball. At that same moment, I heard an unmistakable ripping sound and felt an immediate, personal draft where there hadn't been one, if you follow me.

Thankfully recess time was over and I stayed right where I was and sent the children in. Once they were safely inside the building, I backed carefully over to the sliding doors of the fellowship hall and slipped in. The hallway was clear, so I walked briskly to my office with the intention of calling Julie to bring a spare pair of pants STAT. My secretary only worked in the morning and, glory be, it was the afternoon, so I was alone in my office. I sank gratefully into the chair behind my desk and was just about to call Julie when, lo and behold, two of the Church of God council members appeared at my door. I suddenly remembered, with horror, that we had an appointment to walk through the church and discuss Logos' needs for next year.

So, doing the only thing I could think of, I grabbed the large, black wool, long-sleeved sweater I happened to have hanging by my desk and slipped it on. It covered the indiscreet portion at the back of my pants, but, on that warm day, certainly got some odd looks from the council members. Neither they nor I actually said anything and we proceeded with our tour.

How to end this unique, shake-down cruise of a year? I didn't have any amazing insights; everything about the year had been rather informal. Back in September I had started a photo album/scrapbook. It seemed like the right thing to do since we were just starting out. In it I put the first newspaper article about Logos School, copies of our various programs (Back to School, Christmas, etc.), and photos of the kids and staff. One photo showed me trying to look administrative at my desk. Under it I wrote, "Tom Garfield, Logos School's First Principal, 1981–...." I recall thinking that some day, perhaps in a few years, someone else would fill in the second date. Then whoever it was, would put the new principal's photo on a fresh page in that same book. Being 27 years old when we opened, I naturally assumed that, like all the jobs I'd had before this one, I would move on to...some other job. This had been a delightful year, but there was no real sense of permanence, yet.

So, the last morning arrived, like the first one had so many months ago—quietly but definitively. Like the first day, this one felt very important and sort of weird. After cleaning out desks, cleaning the rooms, and playing some games outside, everyone assembled in our largest classroom (the one at the bend in the hallway). We were all dressed in jeans or shorts and T-shirts. We may have passed out some certificates, but I don't recall what they said. I asked the kids what we should sing for our last song of the year. They wanted to sing "I Am a Promise." It was a short chorus that had found its way into Logos from the Nazarene Church Sunday School:

> I am a promise,
> I am a possibility!

I am promise, with a capital P,
I am a great big bundle of [beat] po-tential-ity!"

That was the chorus—I'm pretty sure there were verses, but they escape me now.

Then...we were done. It didn't take long for the parents to pick up their progeny and soon the teachers and I were left alone in the now empty school in the church basement.

What had we accomplished in our first year? Well, considering how everything we did was new to us, one of Indiana Jones' lines would fit pretty nicely: "I don't know! I'm making this up as I go!"

That's not entirely accurate; we had made a rather important discovery (with very long-range effects) regarding our curriculum and the materials we had purchased. We had discovered that what we wanted to *do* (a classical approach to teaching) didn't match the *means* (the Christian publishers' materials) with which we were trying to do it. It was sort of like we had been trying to saw some wood with a hammer: slow going, at best. It had taken a while to figure out, but the teachers and I finally came to the conclusion that the kinds of activities and pacing the materials wanted us to use weren't consistent with the kinds of teaching methods Dorothy Sayers had described.

We resolved, in the year to come, that we would just go ahead and write our own curriculum for Logos and then find materials to match it. How hard could that be? (Insert maniacal laughter here.)

As I reflected on the school year just finished, I came to some other conclusions:

1. We needed some actual playground equipment. Snakes and snow slides are good as far as they go, but we needed more consistent (and safe) activities for the kids to do at recess.
2. We needed a new secretary. Heather had given notice. Fun as it had been, she had other fish to fry (such as getting a real job).
3. We had had only one family from Pullman, Washington. Could we attract more families from there if we had a bus route? (Future self to 1982 self: "Stop, you fool! That is the devil's voice you're hearing!" More on this later.)

4. Amazingly, we were getting even more applications for enrollment for our second year! We needed a bigger school—or at least a few more classrooms, and more teachers.
5. It was summer time. That meant I had time to do some more planning. But first, since I didn't have any salary, I should probably find some summer employment...

CHAPTER II

GROWTH

There would never again be another year quite like the first one for Logos. I've often thought of it like the first year of a marriage. There are a lot of similarities:

- The teachers and students were all new to this relationship.
- We were living together in one "home" for many hours each day—that meant we had to learn how to get along and seek each others' good in daily living. (Kind of along the lines of remembering to put the toilet seat down.)
- We were establishing new traditions and how to celebrate holidays together.
- We had to learn how to biblically deal with mistakes, "bumps," and even sin between us. And then we had to learn how to express love for one another after dealing with those awkward moments.
- We did almost everything together, and there wasn't much that went on in the school that everyone didn't know about.

But change is inevitable in marriage and in schools and, in God's plans, it's always a good thing. Unbeknownst to me, a fair number of local families had been watching our first year with great interest. In seeking to recruit more students and spread the word about Logos School, I began asking churches if I could come and make a presentation about the school. Sometimes I was even allowed to take a few minutes of the morning service to give a short slide show (not a power point, but real cardboard-framed slides). Afterward, families would often ask me some questions. In many cases, small as our enrollment had been, these folks knew a family at Logos.

Growth in enrollment came then as a result of our first families spreading good reviews to other families; I quickly learned that this was *the* means of all growth thereafter. At best my presentations were informative and/or a reminder about Logos School being a viable ministry. But it was the parent-to-parent interaction that would convince families to make the decision for enrollment. Logos more than doubled, with over forty students enrolled for the second year!

REMODELING

So, change necessarily came in the summer of 1982. The Logos board asked the Paradise Hills Church of God council if we could finish out the rest of the basement, which would give us four more classrooms. They were cheerfully hospitable and accommodating, as they would be for all six years we would spend under their roof. Work began early in the summer. In addition to the new rooms, we would now have our very own entrance on the south end of the basement. Therefore, an outdoor cement stairway was built from the parking lot down to the school entrance.

Other campus improvements were made: one of our dads who was a logger had a great idea for building playground equipment. Rather than trying to buy fancy metal swing sets and slides, which we couldn't afford, he offered to build several such items out of logs! How could I say no? Why would I say no? (Of course *now* I know why I would say no…) He went out to Moscow Mountain and in short order we had a half-dozen or more, ten to twelve inch thick logs laying in our little playground. The logs were then pealed of bark and cut up in various lengths. Slowly but surely wooden structures began rising from the ground, as he dug post holes, put in the logs and poured concrete bases. A tall, two-seat swing set was connected to some monkey bars. This dad really liked ropes, too, so a large rope net rose up to one side of the monkey bars. But the *piece d'resistance* was the huge rope-climbing unit. It soared at least fifteen feet into the air with a cross bar and two ropes dangling down. We had the most rustic-looking playground in all of Moscow!

As summer ended, we had an all-school picnic in the fellowship hall, as the kids played out on the new equipment. They loved it! They particularly liked the swinging ropes, or that was how the 'climbing' ropes would be used for the rest of our time there. The children found that you could get up on the top of the monkey bars, have someone else hand you one of the hanging ropes, then leap into space. The goal, of course, was to see how far and high you could swing. They also learned by trial and error that you had to either jump off or drag your feet to a stop on the back stroke, or you would bean yourself royally against the monkey bars. Great fun!

Oh, yes, and I'm pretty sure that over our six years at the church, we removed enough splinters to supply a family with a winter's worth of firewood.

At that same back-to-school picnic, as one of the board members was giving a talk to the all the parents, I vividly recall thinking, "This little school could go on without me." I wasn't being morose; it just seemed so much more 'real' than it had the first year. We were getting so...organized, I thought. There was also a much more serious sense of purpose. Where we had all been pretty comfortable as essentially one multi-grade class before, now we were going to be a bit more school-like. We were even starting a small library in one fairly large storage closet. In addition, several eight foot tables had been purchased so all the kids could eat lunch together in the fellowship hall.

SPORTS?

With the addition of several more 'older' (above fifth grade) boys by our second year, it didn't take long for someone to suggest that we needed sports. Considering that all we had for any physical activity was the basement fellowship hall (which had two metal support poles in the middle of the room—bonk!) or the small patch of grass outside, it wasn't an unexpected suggestion. What could we do, though, with just a handful of (young) guys and no money for equipment or facility for practices? Not to mention the lack of a coach, uniforms, etc.

Again, I don't recall who should get the credit, but the idea of flag football came up. It had a lot to recommend it: very cheap equipment (Velcro flags on belts and a football), little training/practice needed, no uniforms (though we did get matching jerseys) and even a willing, volunteer coach, Mr. Chris Owsley. Hey, let's play ball!

But wait! We needed a school mascot and colors first. We conducted a school-wide (!) survey and the results were quite hilarious: Penguins, Dragons, Ponies (can you tell what age the majority of students were?). The winning mascot was picked because it was the least bizarre—Leopards. It had alliteration going for it ("Logos Leopards"), as well making our color choices obvious: black and orange. (As you may already know, we didn't stick with that mascot or colors, by the grace of God. Besides the horrific choice of colors, "Leopards" announced over a PA system can sound a lot like "Lepers," which would be rather creepy.)

So the Logos Leopards practiced perhaps a half-dozen times and then we arranged an actual game against a local power house: Elk River. This was during a time when Elk River, a very small town about fifty miles east of Moscow in what we refer to as the 'wilderness,' had about two dozen kids in its entire school system. Really. The local junior high football field was reserved and the teams, fans and 'refs' turned up on a brisk, but sunny November morning in 1982 for the big game! After four short quarters, the Leopards emerged...defeated 0–24.

But we had a team! And, to tell the rest of this story, the next fall we faced Elk River again...this time we crushed them 19–0!

BOARD GROWTH

It only took a couple years to figure out that the Logos School Board needed more wisdom in the form of additional members. So, in 1984, two other school fathers were asked to join the four original members (or 'founding members' as we called ourselves then): Bill Twigg, a wheelwright, and John Sawyer, a U of I veteran affairs director, agreed to come 'on board.' Both men had little ones in Logos and were happy to offer whatever counsel they could to help Logos succeed.

A long-overdue task the larger board took on that year was the creation of the school's official goals. We already had adopted the motto of "a classical and Christ-centered education," but we needed to flesh that out a bit for our staff, parents, and marketing purposes. After a good bit of discussion, based on our motto, the following six basic goals became our marching orders for the future:

Christ-Centered

A. Teach all subjects as parts of an integrated whole with the Scriptures at the center. [II Timothy 3:16–17; Colossians 1:15–20]

B. Provide a clear model of the biblical Christian life through our staff and board. [Matthew 22:37–40, Matthew 5:13–16]

C. Encourage every child to begin and develop his relationship with God the Father through Jesus Christ. [Matthew 28:18–20; 19:13–15]

Classical

A. Emphasize grammar, logic, and rhetoric in all subjects.

B. Encourage every student to develop a love for learning and live up to his academic potential.

C. Provide an orderly atmosphere conducive to the attainment of the above goals.

Unlike many, if not most, of our early policies, these goals not only stood the test of time without any tweaking, but after the Association of Classical Christian Schools (ACCS) began in 1993, many sister schools used ours as a template for their own.

The board continued to meet weekly, often at Logos, but also at Larry Lucas' accounting office. The agendas were largely full of administrative issues; we hadn't learned about the dangers of 'micro-managing' yet, so we just went ahead and did it. Looking back, the board acted very much like a multi-headed administrator, which actually made my job easier. Though it is a practice I discourage (for good reasons) in counseling other schools, I believe God knew I needed lots of additional wisdom to make even the smallest decisions at that point in our history. We did not and could not know how precedent setting those early calls would be in the shaping of our future school programs and culture. So, in spite of the board having to put out many 'fires,' by and large, there was much wisdom in many counselors.

That doesn't mean the board's work was all just long, tedious meetings…

A MEMORABLE MEETING

Some vague sense, nibbling at the edge of my awareness, told me this was going to be a slightly different board meeting than the usual fare. Perhaps it was the way Larry Lucas, our board chairman, firmly called the meeting to order; or maybe it was the extremely crowded conditions; or just maybe it was the fact that we were gathered for our meeting in a two-seated, open carriage being pulled by a very large black horse. Otherwise it was pretty much business as usual.

We had initially gathered, as we did many times, in Larry's downtown, downstairs office. This week, among other items, the board would be discussing the acceptance of a deaf boy, what to do about low income and high bills (a standard agenda item for numerous years), and the hiring of several new staff members. Bill Twigg had arrived in his carriage on this beautiful late-summer afternoon.

"Say," Larry blurted, just as we were sitting down to grind through the work ahead, "Why don't we have the meeting in Bill's buggy and get a ride at the same time?"

That was Larry, all business, from top to bottom. And since Bill, in his usual jean overalls, would be the last person to insist on decorum, it was pretty quickly a done deal. To be fair, I don't believe any of us strongly objected to a buggy ride, versus staying and working in a stuffy office.

Bill took the reins in his leathery hands, gave a small chirrup, and we were off at a nice walking pace through and out of downtown Moscow. In spite of being stared at and feeling like something in a Macy's Day parade, we actually got some work completed.

As we clopped along the main road on the east side of Moscow, near Les Schwab Tires, we were in the thick of discussing acceptance of the deaf boy. Suddenly the carriage jolted as Charlie (the horse) shied at some unseen object in the ditch. Fearing for his life, I suppose, he then broke into a rather awkward canter. At the same time, one of the braces attaching the carriage to Charlie fell off, rendering the reins virtually useless to Bill. America's Funniest Home Videos hadn't been thought up yet, so we were the only ones to enjoy every moment of a real-life, run-away horse and carriage, in the mid-1980s, for goodness sake. "Enjoy" may be the wrong word there, since, speaking for myself, scared spit-less more or less described my feelings.

My life didn't pass before my eyes, but every western movie scene of runaway carriages did:

LONG DISTANCE SHOT: Foam-flecked horses drag rickety carriage, filled with screaming minor actors, along dangerous, rock-filled road.

CUT TO CLOSE SHOT: Terror-filled faces of expendable pioneers.

CUT TO CLOSE SHOT: Riders behind carriage racing to stop horses.

CUT TO CLOSE-UP: Back wheel of carriage starts fiercely wobbling.

CUT TO GROUND SHOT, ANGLE UP: Carriage approaches nasty bend in road at about 150 mph.

CUT TO MEDIUM DISTANCE SHOT, GROUND LEVEL: Horses reach bend, execute neat slice to right; carriage reaches bend, fails to execute neat slice; separates from horses (NO ANIMALS WERE HARMED IN THE MAKING OF THIS MOVIE); carriage hits rock, back wheel flies off; carriage and settlers flip skyward over nearby high cliff...scream volume UP.

Nevertheless, Bill stayed calm, and called firmly to Charlie to take it easy. Charlie dragged us across an unoccupied (providentially) intersection and up into the Les Schwab lot, where the slight incline, along with our considerable weight, slowed him to a halt. For once, the "Fast Action Team" at Les Schwab didn't dash out to help us; actually they seemed a bit nonplussed at finding a carriage-full of very pale people at their doorstep.

Bill fixed up the carriage in no time, Charlie got his attitude straight, and we had a rather pleasant, uneventful ride out to the country. We even finished our business in record time. And we all really enjoyed Larry's stuffy office the next week.

COME ONE, COME ALL

During the early '80s, several older students, closer to Jim Quist's age, joined the school. Some stayed for a year or two, but none of them went the distance to graduation. As things would turn out, Jim would be the only and the oldest student for four years (1981–85), through his senior year. This was partly due to our enrollment philosophy at the time. Put in a nutshell, it was this: "If you want to come to Logos and behave yourself during the interview, you will probably get in." A bit more stringent than being a warm body, but not that far off, either:

RING! "Good afternoon, Logos School..."

"Hello. I'm wondering who I could talk to about getting our son enrolled in your high school. You see, he's really a good boy, but he's been hanging around a bad group of friends and, well, he has done some things that, well...he's been expelled from his school. What do I need to do to get him into Logos? There doesn't seem to be any other option for us at this time. Can you help us out?"

That introduction, virtually verbatim, I heard far too many times over the first years of Logos. I say too many times for a couple of reasons. One is that sadly far too many students "hit the wall," having done something bad enough for even the government schools to notice and boot the student out. Another reason is that many people in our community initially thought of, and treated, a Christian school as a reform school for students who can't "make it" in the public schools.

I think the reasoning for that last assumption goes something along the lines of the following:

Historically churches have accepted anyone, especially the downtrodden and the outcasts, and we are a "Christian" institution, so we should accept and help these troubled students. Also, the reasoning continues, not only should we accept them, but being a "religious" school and since we have tougher discipline and academic standards, somehow just being *there* will straighten these students out. However, very often, as I suspect with a reform school, the time at Logos was practically considered a 'sentence' to be filled before the student earned the privilege to return to his rightful place in society (i.e., back to the public school).

So, within a short time after we opened, we were faced with this dilemma: Do we accept these problem students and count on our Christian love and program to turn them around, or do we cold-heartedly reject them and be labeled as a school for only the "best and the brightest?" In our educational infancy and naiveté, we chose the former, since it was "obvious" that these students *needed* the kind of education and atmosphere we could offer. I remember assuming there was no way one, or even two, such students could out-gun the Christian influence practiced among our adult staff members.

Imagine our naive shock when, time and time again, we saw that not only were we *not* seeing these students repent and achieve; they were actually having the effect of dragging other students down with them! We did not, at least in practice, believe the scriptures that teach "bad company corrupts good morals." The reason it took us literally years to realize this ageless truth is due, I believe, to our thinking that when Scripture says that good should and will triumph over evil, we acted as though Logos School was *the* agent for that "good," instead of the Lord and the students' parents. As much as we loved and prayed for the students, only God alone, through Jesus Christ can truly make men new.

So…how then were we to live, as a Christian school? Were we failing at our mission?

FRIENDS IN TIME OF NEED

Thankfully, by God's grace we did have some specific people turn up from time to time who helped us along the path of maturing as a school. A very wise, grandfatherly man, who had known our Lord and worked in the ministry for many years, visited our school several years after we began operating. Not surprisingly, in some ways, he was brought to Logos one morning by Jim Wilson. Jim and his guest arrived just in time for one of our staff meetings. In the space of five minutes, Dr. Bob Smith (yes, his real name and quite an evangelist) encapsulated our mission dilemma, which I thought was unique to us and unsolvable. He had had a good exposure to many Christian schools, he said, and he wanted us to be clear on one thing in our work:

"You will have to decide," he said quietly, but firmly, "whether you will be a school that primarily assists Christian parents in training up their children in the Lord, or if you will be a school that primarily reaches out to unsaved, and troubled kids. You have to decide which because you cannot successfully do both."

The structure of every aspect of the school would be different, based on the choice we made. Though the ramifications were not comfortable to contemplate, the decision was not difficult to make. We had started with the purpose of being a Christian school. The board had set our six primary, mission-defining goals in 1984. Though we still would accept non-Christian families into Logos, our focus would be to train all our students from a Biblical perspective. If a family or student was unwilling or unable to accept this purpose, Logos would not be the school for them. This decision, based on our goals, clarified our acceptance policies, and that in turn, certainly set the tone for our student body for many years to come. There were times when my heart literally ached for parents who had come to our school since they "had no other place to go" for help with their rebellious student. But unless there was an obvious desire and commitment to change, that student would have to be turned away. We could not, and would not, do what the parents had been unable, or unwilling to do, for their own child.

MARKETING A SCHOOL

Another friend in time of need, to whom we are greatly indebted, was Mr. Allen Cumings. I had had the privilege of first hearing and meeting Allen at one of the annual A.C.S.I. in Seattle. He had done a couple of seminars on development and school financing. He made the mistake of offering to help any school that would be interested in having him come. I say "mistake" because I quickly obtained his number and address, and then, after receiving my board's permission, invited him to come to Logos to share his insights with us.

Allen was working in Portland, Oregon, with a ministry to police officers. He was also very much in demand as a development adviser for businesses and educational institutions. We were very fortunate to be able to get him so quickly and easily. Our board members took time off their work schedules and spent a whole day with Allen. He had already looked over our newsletters, budget, and other financial documents, and told us what he thought of them. He was polite, but candid. For instance, at one point, he held up a copy of our newsletter and said, "Now, would you really want to read this?"

Since I was the primary author of that epistle, I had to resist the temptation to say, "Well, yeah!" He made a good point though. It was boring. Actually he made quite a few good points, not only about how to improve our newsletters, but also about our payroll: "You need to pay your teachers much more than you are and there is no excuse for not seeking to do so!"

The day was extremely profitable for the board primarily and for the school in general, as the board began to implement Allen's wise counsel. In later years, we turned to him a number of times for practical assistance. Development became a critical element to establishing Logos School's support network, and we gained much insight into development work because of Allen's generous and practical guidance. (This was a wonderful example to us when, many years later, other schools and individuals looked to *us* for some guidance.)

ADOPT-A-GRANDPARENT

Just down the same street, Styner Avenue, from where the Paradise Hills Church of God stood, was a care facility for the elderly, Paradise Villa. The teachers and I determined that it would be a mutual blessing for the kids and the residents to get to know each other. It was just a short walk even for the littlest of our charges to get over and visit once a week. We set up an informal arrangement with the management of the Villa that we called Adopt-a-Grandparent and let the parents know our intentions, of course. Everyone agreed it would be worth pursuing.

A typical visit would be maybe twenty to thirty minutes, sometimes longer if the kids had a song or two to sing to some assembled folks.

The kids would frequently prepare hand-made cards to give to their 'grandparents.' On their side, the residents of the Villa and the staff often had homemade cookies for the students, so pretty much everyone looked forward to the visits. Admittedly there was, once in a while, someone like the 'pinching lady' who earned her nickname quickly among the kids, who also quickly learned how to stay just out of her reach. But overall it was one of the first and best outreach programs Logos began. When years later we knew we would be leaving and moving across town, the staff of Paradise Villa threw a big ice cream party for our whole school as a goodbye and thank-you.

BUSES: A LOVE-HATE RELATIONSHIP

I noted earlier that we didn't have many students from Pullman, only one in fact, when we began. There was a good, but rather odd, reason for that. For the reader's benefit, a bit of geography is necessary to insert here. Geography and, well, how to describe this? Uniquely local attitudes? That doesn't really nail it. Well, anyway, first the geography lesson. Moscow, Idaho, is located one mile from the Idaho-Washington border, at about 46 degrees north latitude. It is home to the University of Idaho (current student population about 10,000). Surrounding Moscow on all sides are lovely undulating hills, often covered in wheat, peas, or oats. The larger region in which Moscow is but one town, is referred to as the Palouse. The Palouse is known for those hills and their rich top soil.

Pullman, Washington, could be referred to as Moscow's sister city, since it also lies in the Palouse, but nobody who lives in either town would claim city sibling status. True, Pullman is only eight miles from Moscow, seven miles of which are in Washington. Further, Washington State University (current student population about 20,000) takes up a rather large portion of Pullman. The year-round citizenry of both towns is roughly the same number, about 12–13,000 people. The towns may seem on the surface to be quite similar.

Ah, but here is the weird local reality—folks living in Moscow just don't like to go to Pullman, unless there is a really good reason. It's not that Moscowites dislike Pullman folks; it's that it just takes too much time to make the trip. Even with our relatively new four-lane highway ("the corridor"), it still takes *at least* fifteen minutes to get from town to town.

Usually, therefore, a Moscow dweller will have to have a very good reason, perhaps the saving of a substantial amount of money at a store, or a life-saving medical procedure, to drive to Pullman.

One might logically assume that Pullman citizens felt the same way about making the trek over to Moscow. *Au contraire!* Here is an actual quote from a friend who lives in Pullman: "It's eight miles from Pullman to Moscow, but it's a hundred miles from Moscow to Pullman!" And he is quite right, or at least Pullman folks feel that way, based on the attitudes they pick up when hobnobbing with Moscow friends. One is tempted to feel bad about this and wish to make one's friends feel better about where they live. But that would probably require going to Pullman more often, and, well, it's just so dang far away!

Since I am writing this, I will take this opportunity to briefly present my theory on *why* this strange phenomenon exists. It's not that Moscow people really think eight miles is a long distance—it's more a matter of timing. When your entire day-to-day existence is made up of, at most, ten minutes of driving to get anywhere you ever need to be, well, then fifteen, twenty, or, Heavens!, forty-five minutes (say to get to Lewiston) is a big deal! Spokane, for example, is about eighty miles north of Moscow—the drive takes about an hour and a half. We are almost tempted to pack an over-night bag for such a journey.

All this is to help the reader understand why, in Logos' second year, I thought getting a school bus would be a good idea. What if we ran a bus route to faraway Pullman? Perhaps that would help families manage that significant distance. Also, I have to admit, I liked the idea of Logos School having its own school bus. It was sort of a rite of passage. "Real" schools had buses; it was time Logos put its name on the side of something that literally said 'school' to everyone who saw it.

I made the pitch to the board and they agreed it might be a good idea to get a bus. I believe we paid all of $500 for the first one (a bit of foreshadowing here) and thus began our love-hate relationship with school buses.

The Pullman route actually seemed to work; more Pullman families joined Logos and used the bus route for their children. We charged a separate bus fee, but, as with everything involving money, we kept the fees as low as possible.

Well, I thought, if one bus is good, two would be that much better! So, it wasn't long before our bus, now named "Issachar," was joined by "Reuben." What's with the names, one might ask? It's like this: the local district had for some time painted cartoon names on the front bumpers of their numerous buses—Mickey Mouse, Snoopy, Donald Duck, etc. This was no doubt to help the student riders to not only know which bus to hop aboard when there was a line-up after school, but also to possibly engender some friendly feelings toward the otherwise massive trucks. So, not to be outdone, and in keeping with our Abrahamic heritage, I thought we should paint names of the twelve tribes of Israel on our buses. (Yes, I did assume that we might actually end up with at least twelve.) I went so far as to ask a local pastor who was up on Hebrew to write out the tribal names in Hebrew for me, then I painted them in white on the bumpers. Thus, in my arrogance I managed to render both purposes the district had adopted useless to us; the children already knew which bus was theirs (the one that came), and they couldn't read Hebrew, thus no warm fuzzy feelings toward the buses.

In years to come, there would be even fewer reasons for most of us to feel friendly toward our buses. But first the good points:

- There is something awesome about the size and look of a school bus. After all, it is a *big* truck!
- Driving a bus loaded with young, first-time riders (such as Preschoolers on their way to the local county fair) is a shared, exhilarating experience. The gasps and small shrieks of joy (and some terror) as the bus makes its first lumbering, sharp turn. Very quickly these little people figure out that they are safe inside a very high, large vehicle. So then every small bump and jostle is a thrill which they soon want to repeat.

But it wasn't long before our investment in buses seemed more like experiencing the Dark Side of the Force:

- Firstly, buying a bus was deceptively easy and looked (in my naiveté) to be a sweet deal. I knew that a new bus (back in the '80s) could cost around $35–40,000. So when I heard that a local public school district would accept a bid of $1,500 for a twenty-year-old bus, I jumped on it. At one point I bought a bus, with my board's permission, while my family and I were visiting my folks in Portland. There was a large used bus site there so I figured we'd have a good chance of obtaining a great deal. I test drove one and that, combined with my vast mechanical knowledge, convinced me that I had found that "great deal." It also meant I had to drive our 'new' vehicle back to Moscow with a small caravan behind me: Julie in our car and my dear folks in theirs. (I'm pretty sure they expected the bus to blow up on the way and they wanted to be there to keep us from being stranded in the vast wastelands of eastern Washington.) The drive normally took us six hours; in the bus it took ten. The kids initially enjoyed being in the bus, changing seats to their delight every time we stopped. However, by the end of the long drive, I was alone in the cold bus, hunched over the wheel, vowing not to drive another bus for at least thirty years.
- Inevitably, as I sadly came to learn, the district bus mechanics somehow knew, almost to the mile and minute, when a bus was going to expire. Thus the 'great deal' on a used one.
- That didn't stop us from trying to nurse various yellow beasts back to life. Though, of course, the only time our mechanically gifted school dads (we rarely could afford going to a real shop) were able to come and try to fix something was in the evenings. The evenings, to my memory, were also frequently cold and either rainy or snowy. I knew my uselessness with all things mechanical, so my job was to hold the flashlight (steady—with freezing hands, right!), and pass various tools and parts to the poor dad underneath the engine/transmission/axle.

All this would be kind of fun, in a pathetic, Model-T antique sort of way, if we didn't actually need to rely on these beasts to rise each morning and pick up our children waiting in the cold. The Pullman bus route was just the beginning; eventually we had a grand total of *four* bus routes each day: two in Moscow city limits, the Pullman route, and a route coming from Princeton (famous name, small town), about seventeen miles north of Moscow. The Princeton route was driven by one of the bravest women I've ever known. She kept the smallest bus at her rural home and then each morning would pick up a handful of students on her way into Moscow, where she worked.

I knew it was vital that we stay in communication with our bus drivers (how else would we know when an engine caught fire?), so eventually we set up a CB radio base at Logos, with a radio in each bus. When it worked, it was quite helpful in giving us current news. I distinctly remember a driver (another school mom, Ann Casebolt) calling the school one morning and letting me know that my six-year-old Carolyn had thrown up on the bus.

I also easily recall the winter morning when our brave Princeton mom calmly radioed that she couldn't see the road. She was driving through what is commonly known as a "white-out," when the snow is so thick and swirling you can't see five feet ahead. By God's kind grace she didn't drive off the road, but actually made it to Logos.

Time and space won't allow me to recount the many stalls, inexperienced drivers, empty gas tanks, and other delightful events that made having buses and routes so memorable. More than once, while heading home after school, I was pulled over by a local policeman who informed me that the Idaho State Patrol had radioed in to report one of our school buses had died on the Lewiston grade (a steep, eight-mile hill). I would then race back to Logos, pray that one of our other buses would start, then drive as fast as legally and physically possible to rescue the stranded team of students.

The owner of the auto salvage yard in Lewiston and I became first-name friends. When even mechanically adept Logos dads could no longer nurse a bus back to health and we knew we had to put it down, so to speak, I would call Walter. If the bus could still sort of drive, I might get $500 for it. If he had to come and tow it, well, he would come and tow it.

Among our alums, especially the oldest ones, bus disaster stories are among their favorite recollections. Thankfully, even with those ancient buses, 'disasters' were relative. I firmly believe God often protects His children from their own folly. The only actual, significant accident with one of our buses occurred many years later when one of male teachers drove one into a light pole in parking lot. (A Mormon Church parking lot—it's a long story.) No one was hurt, but the light pole completely fell over, which was cool to watch from a distance (I was driving another bus and saw it all).

One of the favorite bus stories the alums often bring up happened near Coeur d'Alene, about eighty miles north of Moscow. Our volleyball team was on its way home after an evening game when, shortly after passing the large, reservation-run casino, the bus died. The girls were still in uniform and began to get chilled. Someone from the casino not only took notice, but took sympathy on our students. A limo was dispatched from the casino and our young ladies were driven in luxury to the warmth and comfort of... the casino. There they were treated to nourishing goodies and drinks (non-alcoholic), all for free. Our bus driver and volleyball coach made some phone calls and parents with vans drove the long distance from Moscow to rescue the girls (not that they felt they needed to be rescued—they had greatly enjoyed the evening's activities).

It often fell to my lot to drive not only for field trips and sporting events, but in the days of our bus routes, I filled in as needed. One morning I was returning through town with a good load of students on our way to Logos. As we passed the local high school, I became painfully aware that a police car was behind me and apparently, from his flashing lights, desiring me to pull over.

I pulled to the curb, directly opposite the high school with, seemingly, about a thousand or so students watching in delight at the Logos School bus. My passengers were in silent awe as the policeman made his way to the front of the bus. I opened the door and asked the requisite question:

"What seems to be the problem, officer?"

After examining the bus paperwork and my license, he said, "You were going twenty-five in a fifteen mile an hour school zone."

"Ah, yes. Sorry about that! You see, my speedometer is broken, so I wasn't aware of actually how fast I was going," I said with an apologetic smile.

His look of incredulity was only matched by his tone of voice. But he was polite:

"Well, I will just warn you for now, but get that speedometer fixed before you drive this bus again."

"Yes, sir."

With that, he went back to his patrol car. I sighed in relief. Not only was I relieved I hadn't gotten a ticket, I was relieved that he hadn't taken revenge on me. You see, I immediately recognized him as a dad whose daughter I had recently turned down for enrollment at Logos. I'm sure the recognition was mutual. Such is life in a small town.

My silent and fervent prayers on our way to Logos went unanswered; my riders all gleefully and repeatedly told everyone how I'd been pulled over by a cop! Sigh.

SAVING AND RAISING MONEY

I've heard of certain enterprises being started 'on a wing and a prayer.' If that means not having much of anything to begin with and relying heavily on God's kindnesses, that expression fits Logos to a T. I don't really know if we, the board, ever seriously entertained the idea of seeking any financial capital to get Logos going. I don't think we did because I'm pretty sure none of us knew anyone with a lot of money who we could approach to be an 'investor.'

The financial plan we adopted not surprisingly came from the way Jim and Bessie Wilson had lived when raising their children. That is, living on faith. What that meant was Jim did what he was called to—bookstore based evangelism—regardless of how much he would be paid (or not). He and Bessie were rock solid on their faith that the Lord would provide for their daily needs. And He did. Jim's stories of provision, 'on the mount of the Lord' (otherwise known as cliff-hanger situations), were always a fascination to me. He would often recount them in various contexts where I was present. During the three years the Wilsons lived in Ann Arbor, I was witness to the Lord's unique provision on a number of occasions. An envelope without a return address would arrive at just the right moment, containing a check for just the amount needed to pay a bill or buy groceries. Or bags of groceries would appear mysteriously on their front porch.

Thus the budgeting plan was simple for Logos: To make Logos affordable for almost any family, the parents would pay a minimal tuition amount that would just cover the overhead expenses (rent to the church, utilities, materials, etc.). The faculty would be paid through any gifts given to Logos. We four employees would live on faith. This plan was clearly laid out to each of us as we were offered our jobs. I can't speak for the three single gals, but as the only married person (with two children) on staff, I agreed but had a caveat. I let the board know that if there ever came a time when I fell behind in paying our home bills or in meeting my children's needs, I would resign and seek other employment. I would take that lack as a sign that the Lord wanted me to work somewhere else. The other board members heartily agreed with that principle, having families of their own.

The parents were informed of this rather unique budgeting approach. The board wanted to be careful, though, how staff needs were communicated. On one hand, the board rightly felt responsible for the staff members' needs being met and disclosing those needs to the parents. On the other hand, the board didn't want the parents to think we were subtly soliciting them for constant gifts. It made for a rather interesting balancing act at times.

However, the school parents were usually not in any financial position to pay for those needs, even if we'd been asking. Instead, many parents sought to help the teachers more directly in the form of dropping off groceries at the school. I don't recall who organized it, but pretty soon in our first year, the school had a 'Food Pantry': a set of metal shelves in one of the store rooms off the fellowship hall.

About every couple of weeks, a parent or two would arrive in the morning with arms full of grocery bags. The shelves would be filled with colorful cans, boxes and bags of various food items. The reaction among the four faculty members was always kind of fun to watch, in an objective sort of way. We all knew that, regardless of the time of day, making a mad dash for the food pantry would be rather tacky. So, once the school day ended, we would all amble out into the hall and chat amiably as we sauntered down to the fellowship hall. Upon arriving in the room, we would stand back and just kind of gaze at the wonderful site—not dissimilar to children gazing in awe at the stack of presents under the tree on Christmas morn.

Then, we would start verbally identifying the foodstuffs by name, as though the others were illiterate. But no offense was meant or taken; this was a necessary part of the ritual. We all knew, by the inflection in the person's voice, which items that person really wanted.

"Canned green beans."

"Quaker Oatmeal."

"Salt."

"Yeah, and, oh look, SUGAR! Five pounds of white SUGAR!"

"Oh, I've got some sugar at home, do you want to go ahead and take that?"

"Really? You guys OK if I do?" (She says as she hugs the bag like a long-lost sister.)

And, in most cases, we would take turns garnering the specific box, can, or bag most desired. I always found these times rather awkward for a couple of reasons: I was the only male, and my father raised me to be a gentleman, to allow ladies to go first. But I was also the only married person, and I had *two children*. I knew this was an ace card, but I don't believe I ever played it. At least not too often.

"Uhhnn…(I might mutter), look at that…a whole package of chocolate chips. Gosh. My little Carolyn just loves her mom's chocolate chip cookies. Of course, I cannot recall the last time we had them, but she sure likes them…What? Oh no, no, really, you girls must like…are you sure, because Carolyn doesn't really need any cookies this year…Well, OK, thanks!"

Even with this rather unique approach to payroll, not only were no staff members found dead in their apartments from starvation, we actually increased our staff numbers during the three years we all lived on faith. The Lord met my family's personal needs in many of the same amazing (but often nail-biting) ways. Yes, there were times when I was preparing to go job-hunting the next day, but it never came to that in reality.

The food pantry, like manna after the forty years in the desert, eventually ceased to be necessary. One lonely, small can of oysters remained for many months after we instituted salaries. Canned oysters? Really? But I'm sure it was well meant.

Another way we found to save money was to buy used school furniture from the Spokane School District. (Moscow and Pullman were obviously closer, but they didn't do auctions or have the used inventory we could find in Spokane.) I mentioned our first foray north earlier, when we bought our piano. For quite a few years, every July I could usually count on getting information about the district's annual auction and I would make plans to go see what I could find.

Typically it would require that I set aside a Saturday, call the Quists to see about borrowing one of their large grain trucks, then try to find at least one other person to help me. Once we had other males on staff, I would cajole one of them to go with me. But it so happened that more than once my intrepid secretary, Carol Smith, would be a sport and give me hand.

The auction would normally be held in large warehouses, with wooden student desks and teacher desks stacked two stories high. Other rooms would contain hundreds of student chairs of various heights. Then there were rooms stuffed with literally everything, including kitchen sinks. Several dozen people might show up, all seeking a deal. Here are a few true stories of auction adventures:

I would always have a shopping list of things Logos needed, but I would also need to be prepared for the unexpected item which wasn't on my list. Such was the case one Saturday morning as I came across a whole bin full of at least fifty school globes! They were in every size and condition, with several immense globes on stands. (This was before the U.S.S.R. collapsed, so the globes were still accurate, for the most part.) The auctioneer finally worked his way around to the bin. I don't think I was the only one who expected him to bid them out individually. Instead, being tired I suppose, he said, "I'm going to take bids for all the globes at once, the entire bin!"

That put a number of globe-hunters off, but I noticed how many folks looked disappointed. Charging in, I won the bid rather easily.

As soon as the auction was over, as I had hoped, folks swarmed to our truck as we loaded the dozens of globes. Most folks wanted just one or two. We priced the small ones at $5 and the large ones at $10, keeping the best ones for Logos.

We made enough from selling those globes to pay for all our purchases that day!

As Logos started making and collecting student records, I wanted to get a fireproof file cabinet to house them. But in pricing those cabinets in catalogs (pre-Amazon), I knew we couldn't afford a new one at $1200 each. Then, at one summer auction, I came across a four-drawer, legal sized, fireproof cabinet! It was on wheels, too, which was a blessing since it weighed well over two hundred pounds. I made sure I was on hand when the auctioneer got to it. Pretty quickly, though, I was up against another bidder, a rough-looking fellow who seemed determined to out-bid me.

"What's my bid? Do I hear 150?"

And we were off to the races. The bid climbed quickly past my mental limit.

"275! Do I hear 300?" Silence. I shook my head, indicating I was done.

"Sold to you, sir, for two hundred and seventy five dollars!" the auctioneer hollered, pointing to my opponent.

"$275?" he asked the auctioneer. (In his defense, it was the first time the auctioneer had said "dollars.") The winning guy shook his head, "I thought you meant $2.75. I can't afford $275!"

The auctioneer was livid, as everyone else laughed uproariously at the guy's lack of auction protocol.

"Do you have any idea what these things are WORTH!??" yelled the auctioneer. The other guy just shook his head again and moved to the back of the crowd.

Disgusted, the auctioneer turned to me. "Do YOU know what this is worth?"

"Yes, sir!"

"How much are you willing to pay for it?"

"$175?"

"SOLD!"

It wasn't easy to load it, but we still have it to this day.

Another impulse buy when Carol was helping me caused a major traffic jam. Among the many delightful items that day, I found two folding cafeteria tables, with benches. These contained two six-foot-long tables each. Again, I knew their value if we were to buy them new. I bid and got them for a steal. It wasn't until I won that it occurred to me that we would have to load those monsters into the back of the truck! Some Good Samaritans saw our plight and helped us heft them up, laying them down in the truck bed, one on top of the other, and hanging out a bit.

On our drive out of the warehouse area, I got my directions confused (a life-long gift), and we quickly found ourselves in downtown Spokane. The truck stalled as a light turned from red to green. Horns honked as I mashed down on the clutch and finally got the engine started. I jammed the truck into first gear; we lurched forward with a huge jolt. Simultaneously we heard a great crash behind us! Looking in my side mirror, I saw that both tables had slid off the back of the truck, landing in the middle of one of the busiest intersections in downtown Spokane.

This time there weren't any good or any other kind of Samaritans in the business district as Carol and I struggled and finally got the tables back into the truck. I pretended not to notice the lines of vehicles extending for blocks in every direction as we climbed back into the truck cab. As I slowly pulled away, I saw a Spokane police car, red and blue lights flashing, trying to move into the scene to determine the problem. I was able to turn a corner, which providentially led to the freeway. We made our escape!

A SAD DAY

One fall day I was at my desk when Meredith, our kindergarten teacher, dashed into the office.

"Tom, a lunch table fell on Trevor! I think he's really hurt!"

By that time, I had learned that very few "emergencies" turned out to be worth all the excitement, so I developed the habit of walking, not running when alerted. Panic is easy to instill in kids, and I felt by approaching crises calmly, the kids wouldn't be so upset. However, that day Meredith's face told me running would be very appropriate.

Remember those large, fold-up cafeteria tables we had purchased at the auction? Well, we now had a few more of that same type to accommodate the growing number of kids eating at the school. A wheel of one of the older tables had broken off, so it was not supposed to be used. This day, the broken table, for some reason, had not been chained against the wall, and some of the older elementary kids were attempting to set it up.

Trevor was a first grader. He had been in the lunchroom and had offered the kids his help with the table, Meredith gasped to me as we made our way to the fellowship hall. Another teacher was already with Trevor, who lay crying and screaming on the floor. The table had fallen across his lower leg, breaking both bones clear through. That was obvious to the casual observer, which I was anything but...casual, that is. Even I could see that Trevor's leg had a bend in it that hadn't been there before. We called an ambulance and a very competent team of EMTs arrived in what was actually a short time, but as Trevor was screaming the entire time, it seemed to take a few months.

Finally, after another few months, the team of professionals had him ready to move, and carefully carried him out to the ambulance on a stretcher board.

"Have you contacted his parents? It looks like he may need surgery so they'll need parental authorization," a blond-headed young man asked me. As a matter of fact we had been repeatedly trying to contact Trevor's folks, and had only just discovered that they were in Spokane for the day. Trevor was to have gone home with his pastor's family until evening.

It took a couple of hours, during which Trevor lay somewhat sedated (but not enough to completely remove the pain and moans), before a relative was found who could give the doctors permission to proceed with the surgery. (My, but we were learning all sorts of lessons as a school—Emergency Contact Forms on file from now on. Check.)

I went to the hospital later that afternoon to see Trevor, after spending most of the day mentally flagellating myself for

1. not making sure that stupid table had been better secured or thrown out;
2. not having a better system in place for obtaining emergency permission; and
3. allowing this to happen at all!

So, in that happy frame of mind I slunk into Trevor's room, where he lay with a huge cast over most of his poor little leg. The pastor's wife, Debbie, (who'd been a real trooper all day) was still there, reading to him. I came in the hospital room feeling like Admiral Yamamoto should have felt had he visited Pearl Harbor the evening of the December 7th, 1941. Debbie looked up and cheerily announced to the little patient:

"Oh look, Trevor, here's Mr. Garfield! Isn't this wonderful? It's sort of like Jesus Himself coming to visit you, isn't it!?

Right. *Sigh.* What a day.

DANGEROUS STAFF

As Logos grew, from sixteen students in 1981, to forty-five in 1982, and close to ninety by 1983, we hired more teachers. Among these were quite a number of intrepid and loving single ladies: Karen McFarland, Candace Bossart, Molly McRoberts, Carol Anderson, to name a few. We met every morning for a staff meeting in my office. At the time of this recollection, we had about ten teachers who would sit in a semi-circle facing my desk for our half-hour daily meeting. We typically sang a hymn, had some business items, and ended in prayer.

I wanted to foster a rather cheerful, somewhat informal atmosphere among the staff and school. So, one little practice I had was, if during a meeting a staff member asked or said something I deemed lame, I would lean down and pull out a dart gun from my desk drawer. Sometimes all I had to do was threaten to shoot the offender with the rubber-tipped dart. But other times I would just pull the trigger. It just depended on how I felt that day. All this without one leadership training class!

One morning it seemed like the teachers were trying to out-do each other in saying less-than astute things. That should've warned me.

Finally someone said something that I couldn't ignore. Sighing deeply, I leaned down, pulling my dart gun out of the desk drawer. As I raised my head and my gun, I froze. A complete semi-circle of various dart guns were all aimed straight at me! How they had pulled them out so silently was my second thought. My first thought was that I would be wise to promptly concede I was clearly out-gunned. I slowly put my own gun back. They hadn't said a word; kind of creepy, but in a very cool, ninja sort of way. I proceeded with the meeting and never drew on my teachers again.

FIRST FUNDRAISERS

It didn't take us long to figure out that just asking people for money was not going to bring all the necessary funds for bills or special equipment. We needed to be more assertive, to get out there and make money for Logos, in short, to sell hot dogs at the Renaissance Fair! The name alone says it all, but there are folks who may not have had the joy of seeing this sort of activity happen in a local park.

The Moscow Renaissance Fair actually had little to do with the historical revival of the arts and architecture in Italy and a lot to do with aging hippies reliving their "golden years." Colorful tents and booths were erected in our East City Park on the first weekend in May (calling for, of course, a May pole dance). Don't misunderstand; I harbor no ill will toward these gentle folk—after all, I lived through the original era of peace, dope, and love. That's also why it kind of grossed me out to see leather bandannas above graying ponytails, and the women were getting older, too.

But there were fun aspects, too: face-painting, balloon animals, and assorted games for the children, along with leather trinkets, tie-dyed shirts, and tables loaded down with lots of home-made ceramics. (An interesting element to the ceramics made locally was that in the early '80s many were made from Mt. St. Helen's ash. It had blown its top on May 20, 1980, and the immense cloud of dust and ash blew over us and fell to a depth of a couple inches over Moscow, as well as other points east of us. So enterprising pottery types collected tons of the stuff, apparently, and used it to make their pots, plates, cups and other dishes.)

Food booths abounded and unique smoky smells filled the air. There wasn't any electric power available to the vendors' booths, so most of the food was prepared over grills. However, they weren't cooking good old American hamburgers. No. The menus offered unique meats and vegetables not usually found in restaurants. Being a rather "selective" eater (derisively called "picky" by those with compromised palettes), I wasn't very interested in taste-testing what I can only say often looked like rat-on-a-stick.

Logos applied for and received a permit to have a food booth, too. We determined to offer something recognizable and tasty to anyone—chili dogs! The dogs and chili were cooked off site and then brought to our booth (a canopy with tables) within crock pots. Our decor and sign were blue and white (our newly adopted school colors), and our servers wore red gingham aprons. Not to put too fine a point on it, we sort of stood out like a Boy Scout troop at Woodstock. But we sold a lot of chili dogs!

Our first year at the fair, we made enough money (about $400) to buy our school's first computer: an Atari 400! But more on computers later. After just a few years of having our booth at the Fair, we were informed by the Fair people (irony there) that we would no longer be welcome there. Why? Because we didn't promote the "spirit" of the Fair. We were too, well, patriotic looking. It was our first, but hardly our last, encounter with liberal "tolerance."

Undeterred, we went on to try a plethora of fundraising activities in subsequent years:

We sold Christmas trees... once. I now have a great deal of respect for the work that goes into cutting, hauling, and selling these trees. Hours of standing in the bitter cold air, praying for someone to buy a tree, wasn't much fun.

We sold candy from a company that made very tasty candy! Eating the profits was actually a real danger. From that experience, though, we learned that going door-to-door, while probably not unbiblical, was still not how we wanted Logos School to be known. Nor did we want our kids (and their parents) to go through the experience of being unwanted salesmen.

So what *did* work for fundraising? Well, many years later we learned that just politely asking for help, say in a fun event like a dinner and an auction, or a concert, brought out the cheerful giving we desired. Sure, we still did car washes and bake sales, but those were for class purposes. At the end of the day, folks want to give to something they trust and want to see succeed. Our job was to convince folks that, by God's grace, we would be that kind of school.

THE FIRST SERIOUS THREAT

The word was spreading about our little school. Even a unique church in Pullman took interest in Logos. The pastor called me one day in the summer of 1983 and made an appointment to come and see me to find out more about Logos. When he arrived, I won't say I had a premonition or even bad vibes, but he did intimidate me from the get-go. He was stern and foreboding. I don't believe he smiled during the entire time he peppered me with questions. Considering my extreme lack of experience in all things related to starting a school, I didn't realize until later that he was examining Logos to see if it would meet not only his own family's needs, but those of the families in his small congregation.

Apparently I gave generally satisfactory answers, because it wasn't long after our meeting that Logos received a flurry of applications from this one church. In all about a dozen children were enrolled, quite a population boom for us!

However, it didn't take long before storm warnings appeared. We were only a month or two into the school year when I started hearing from my teachers (all female and single at the time). The common theme was that many of these new parents were challenging the teachers' methods and content of teaching the Bible particularly. As I could, I sought to field some of concerns and addressed the parents myself.

That didn't slow things down. I began to get phone calls from the pastor, urging me to encourage my teachers to be more dogmatic (not his word) in their Bible instruction and crack down on classroom discipline. The sky was definitely getting darker over Logos.

Then one day, as I was watching out my window as the children were out at recess, I saw the pastor's son clobber another boy. Oh great! I had the recess teacher send in both boys and I sat in Solomon's seat (wishing he were there instead) and tried to sort out what had happened. It wasn't all that difficult really; the smaller recipient of the punch had said the 'wrong' thing and the older boy nailed him. The older boy stated that his father said it was ok to hit others, if needed. The evidence was in and I had to put up or shut up. From our beginning we had informed all our families that corporal punishment, that is the ancient art of spanking, would be a disciplinary option at Logos. This situation certainly called for it.

So, with the sinking feeling that I was pulling the pin on a grenade, I spanked the pastor's son. I also asked the boys to seek reconciliation, which they did, somewhat begrudgingly on one side (guess which one).

Then, as my practice would become for many more years, I called the boys' fathers to let them know what had transpired between their progeny. The dad of the smaller boy was great, as I recall. The pastor? Well, I hadn't had the riot act read to me so thoroughly since my shipboard days in the USN. Among other things, he let me know that he taught his sons to defend themselves and it was up to the boys to determine when that "defending" was necessary.

I hoped things would calm down for a while after that. They didn't. Within a short time, not long before Thanksgiving I believe, one of my teachers who attended the local Nazarene Church came into my office one morning, weeping. She was not an emotional type, so my level of concern rose immediately. It turned out that one of "the families" (we all knew who we were talking about by this time) had invited her over for dinner. She accepted and soon found she was the main course. The parents obviously had an agenda which included calling her salvation into question because she went to a church that didn't teach "eternal security." They also questioned Logos' theological integrity in hiring a teacher who believed the way she did.

In my estimation the time had come for board action. We were still meeting weekly so it didn't take long for me to let the board know what was going on: the parents from this one church were hurting my teachers. The board agreed and wrote the pastor a respectful, but firm letter stating that this treatment of the teachers needed to stop or the families concerned would be asked to leave Logos.

The pastor mailed his response to Doug Wilson and me. It still stands as one of the most unique pieces of correspondence I have ever received (I think Doug would also rate it that way). The pastor had not written a reply; he had used a rubber stamp (with red ink) which contained the full text of "B---S---" and had thumped it down on our letter, then mailed it back to us. I wasn't sure which shocked me more—the fact that he had been so crude, or that he found it necessary to have such a stamp in his possession.

That, however, was just the opening volley. Shortly thereafter I received a letter from the pastor's attorney, notifying me, in legalese, that Logos was being sued for failure to provide the educational services we had promised. The letter also informed us that all the church's families would be leaving and demanding a full refund.

I would love to say that my first reaction was to pray for them and just trust that the Lord would see us through this crisis. But that's not what I did. I was stunned and discouraged. When I got home I told Julie that the experiment known as Logos School was over. In addition to the fear of going through a lawsuit, I knew that our budget couldn't take the hit of paying all those fees back, not to mention any actual court costs!

But my board was made of sterner and godlier stuff. They directed me to contact a friend of the school who was a Christian and an attorney (it is possible) and show him the letter from the opposing attorney. Our friend reviewed it, along with our school's application and policies. I'll never forget his phone call to me a few days later. He not only believed we had nothing to worry about, he was actually very anxious to get in the courtroom with the other attorney. He said something about how fun it would be to "eat his lunch," I believe. More professionally he let me know that these families had no legal leg to stand on; our application, which required their signature of agreement, and our other documents made it very clear that the families would abide by all the school's rules and policies. Among those policies was the statement that the fees were non-refundable.

In the meantime, one after another, some with tears of regret, all the church families pulled their children out of Logos. It was terribly sad in every way. Almost all the children were too young to understand, and I couldn't have helped them, even if I was asked to. I didn't understand that kind of blind and foolish adherence to a church's demands. A few of the families sent their own letters to me, threatening a lawsuit if we didn't return their money.

As our lawyer prepared a formal reply to the other attorney and his clients, stating that any suggestion that a lawsuit could hold water was ridiculous (he said it better), my board prepared its own letter. First, they determined to follow our Lord's injunction in Matthew 5:40: "And if anyone wants to sue you, and take your shirt, let him have your coat as well." Then our remaining families were informed of the basic situation and told that Logos would not only freely return the fees, but would double them. The response to this news was tremendous; even though it was getting close to Christmas, donations flowed in and we were able to do just what we said. The board wrote a concise, but pleasant letter to the departed families letting them know that, regardless of the unfounded demand, a check for twice the amount of their fees was enclosed, along with a basket of fruit and a wish for them to have a Merry Christmas.

Did we expect any of the families to be conscience-smitten and at least express thanks for the extra amount? No, I don't think so. And none of them did. But it certainly was a watershed moment for Logos. Yes, it put out the immediate fire, but more importantly it made it clear to all who were paying attention that the Logos School Board was putting Scripture and obedience to Christ ahead of budget worries and enrollment pressures.

I believe in the years that followed, one of the reasons that God blessed us so richly had to do with my board's faithfulness during our first serious threat.

TALENT NIGHT AND OTHER AWKWARD MOMENTS

This is as good a place as any to mention that in our early years, I not only was striving to become an administrator, I was also striving to help Logos look and act like a "real school." I knew we couldn't offer the bells and whistles the public schools offered, nor did I want to in most cases. But I did want to pursue opportunities and programs for our own students that might develop into traditions unique to Logos. My board felt the same way and supported my attempts.

Since we weren't able to offer a formal choral or instrumental program in our first years, I thought it might be fun to have an evening that featured the talents of the students. Thus Talent Night was born and debuted in April of 1983. It was never a competition—just a series of acts, sort of like the variety show that Ed Sullivan used to host on TV. OK, we probably wouldn't have the equivalent of presenting the Beatles, but it produced a lot of interest among the students and parents.

The idea of auditioning the acts or, at least as important, having a dress rehearsal, didn't enter my mind for the first few years. I do recall, though, when it struck me that knowing ahead of time what the kids would wear might be a good plan: it struck me during a program.

As they did with all their property, the folks of our host church were generous with their sanctuary and allowed us to use it for any evening programs. One Talent Night, I gathered the performers in the fellowship hall downstairs prior to going up to the sanctuary, where the audience of families and friends awaited. Some moms were still helping their children to get dressed for their acts. The rest of us trooped upstairs and I began the program (we had even printed up and handed out our first actual programs!).

One would rightly predict that piano pieces abounded; to this day, I can't really handle listening to one more rendition of Fur Elise after decades of Talent Nights. On this particular evening, I got up to announce the next act: a fifth grade young lady who would be baton twirling. Not having seen the act yet, I wasn't entirely sure what she was going to do, so I, along with the audience, was in for a surprise. She came out from the door and onto the stage at the front of the church. To fully appreciate the impact, one must recall the reverent, spiritual aura present in the architecture and symbols of most churches. It was thus here. And here came a sweet little thing in a brightly sequined, form-fitting, not to mention brief, costume. Then, to add to the visual dichotomy was her act—tossing and twirling a long silver baton. Now batons are all well and good in the hands of cheerleaders tossing them *outside* at a football game; inside a peaked, chandelier-filled sanctuary the shiny baton flipping into the air had the entire audience holding its collective breath! Amazingly, by God's kindness, our dancing, twirling little lady missed all of the lights.

I vowed then and there to audition and hold dress rehearsals in the future.

I should also include the act that I believe softened the impact of the circus act that evening. One of the last acts was a school father and his little daughter. They came up front, sat down side by side and, as he played his guitar they sang a precious hymn together. Amen!

One might recall that the church's fellowship hall served as our all-purpose room. It became our lunchroom, indoor recess area, assembly room, and our 'gym' for PE. However, any running was carefully coordinated to avoid collisions with the two steel columns in the center of the room.

PE was taught by volunteers, as we had no budget to pay such specialized teachers. Our full-time teachers were, well, full-time. We also hadn't really thoroughly considered how classical education affected physical education, yet. So, we tended to get whatever was offered by kind-hearted, usually athletic parents. One exception stands out, and I know he wouldn't take offense at not being considered "athletic." Bill Twigg, our wheelwright board member. He came by one day and offered to teach the boys wrestling. Somewhere, no doubt local school surplus, we came up with some wrestling mats. Or at least they were mats and we figured they would serve for wrestling. The guys loved it!

One might ask, "what about the girls?" Well, at about the same time, a school mom, Amber Thiemens, approached me with the idea (for which I got board approval) to offer the oldest girls a self-defense course. More specifically a course in Jukido, which is kind of a combination of karate and judo, from my observations. But before we would just begin such a personal defense program, I wanted the parents to see a demonstration of Jukido.

We set an evening date and, with the use of the wrestling mats, Amber put on a demo that few of the parents who were there would ever forget. She stood just about five-foot nothing. For her presentation that evening, she had brought along a martial arts student of hers, a well-built young man who towered over her. Though I knew she must have some idea of what she was doing, I still expected him to pick her up with one hand at some point.

Instead, wearing her black belt ninja outfit, Amber managed to get that guy on the mat (and potentially in an ambulance) time after time. He would even approach her from behind with a fake knife and... whip, twist, slam! He'd be looking up at her, trusting she wouldn't follow through with a threatening foot or fist thrust. Even seeing her go through her motions slowly was very impressive.

The parents were convinced—they were more than happy to have their adolescent daughters taught some basic self-defense techniques from this quiet, confident expert.

So, our PE program, albeit held in a carpeted fellowship hall, offered some rather cool options for our older kids.

FIRST GRADUATION

Certainly one of the proudest and happiest days we enjoyed was the day in late May, 1985. That was the day we held our first high school graduation! Jim Quist had been our oldest student to come to the school our first year. At that time he was in ninth grade, the youngest son of Shirley Quist, one of our founding board members. Jim was a very pleasant and bright young man who was top of his class for all four years of high school; in fact he was the only one in his class for all four years, but the point still stands. Jim didn't even have anyone near his age until he was a senior. That was the year another boy came as our only junior.

The younger students naturally looked up to and admired Jim. Thankfully, he always gave them good reason to do so. But it wasn't all a bed of roses, or perhaps it was, as long as you recall that thorns play a role in such a picture. Jim was a normal young man who at times longed for the company of other students his age, and opportunities we could not provide. For example, he and I both knew my offers to let him be quarterback on our high school football team didn't carry a lot of conviction. We had a number of long talks, and no doubt he and his folks did too, during those four years. But he stuck it out and his teachers enjoyed tutoring him immensely. Where possible, we taught him with some of the younger secondary students as they came along. But by and large he was on his own.

That's why that first graduation day meant a great deal to everyone in the school. Jim was graduating! He had made it, and Lord willing, there would be many more to follow him. His mom and the other older students, especially Beth (of the broken leg) who was three years his junior, had a great time decorating the church sanctuary for the evening ceremony. Beth also made sure she got to narrate a slide-show history of Jim's life, before and during Logos. The entire school board, and most of the student body (about one hundred and twenty by then), was there to recognize Jim's accomplishment. We sang "O The Deep, Deep Love of Jesus," the hymn chosen by the Class of 1985. Jim gave a valedictory address, which was fully earned in every way. He had done very well academically, in spite of the lack of any competition. (We didn't, however, have him do the salutatorian address.)

Don and Shirley Quist, and Jim's teaching sister, Debbie, sat in the front pew of the church sanctuary and glowed with pride. Jim humbly took in all the praise and attention, including a medallion as the first graduate of Logos School.

Afterward we held a reception for him in the fellowship hall downstairs. He commented on some of the many memories he would take with him to college. Where, by the way, he had received an honor's scholarship for being first in his class. Amen again!

CHAPTER III

CHALLENGES

KEEPING CLASSICAL

The meeting was taking on a noticeably unpleasant aspect. The parents were not very happy, and there wasn't much I was able to do about it; it was sort of like the feeling when one loses control of the steering wheel while sliding over a patch of black ice. In short, I wasn't sure where this was going, and it probably wouldn't end well.

The meeting had been called to address some concerns the school families had regarding the nature and amount of work being assigned to their children, particularly their older children. Logos was still a rather young school, only about four years old, and was still located in the basement of the Church of God.

Several parents were very vocal:

"The kids don't understand the stuff the teachers are having them read!"

"They're getting way too much homework assigned!"

"Perhaps Logos should just forget the idea of a secondary since so many kids are going to the public junior high and high schools anyway."

"We don't understand this 'classical' thing! Why don't you guys just drop that idea and be a *normal* Christian school?"

The really frustrating aspect to the whole thing was that, in many ways, the parents' criticisms were well-grounded. In all honesty, at that point in time, the teachers were sort of like the Israelites, that is, every man was doing what was right in his own eyes. They had received little actual instruction or guidance in what classical education was and how to apply it in their classes. So, one secondary teacher stressed reading only difficult, primary sources and was blowing our few seventh graders out of the water. Another teacher was indeed assigning way too much homework, as we discovered. In his defense, he thought this was a desirable hallmark of classical instruction. And it was true that we were constantly losing students to the public schools.

The next morning I was still stinging from some of the remarks and tone of the meeting. For not the first or last time, I felt our "grand experiment," as I often called Logos in private with Julie, was on the rocks. How would Logos School grow, how would it move ahead, if we didn't have the support of our families? Should we really toss out the idea of a classical education? Maybe it really was a pipe-dream. After all, even Dorothy Sayers never actually made a school based on her ideas, did she? Maybe she knew that in reality, with twentieth-century kids and culture, it would never fly, Orville. It was just too weird, archaic, and unrealistic.

Such were my despondent thoughts and feelings. Nevertheless, once again the Lord gave the board members more peace and wisdom than I had. After quite a few serious and vigorous meetings, the board determined to not only keep the idea of a full K-12 program, it reaffirmed its commitment to a classical education. The board also committed to provide more and clearer instruction on this philosophy to our teachers.

Shortly thereafter, we discovered the book entitled, *The Seven Laws of Teaching*, by John Milton Gregory. I was assigned to use it to help guide our teachers. Truly a Godsend, it would be the unequaled guide for instruction for us and thousands of other teachers in decades to come.

Though we couldn't know it then, the board's decision at this time was another watershed for the school. We never again pondered turning back from our original vision.

SEE DICK RUN. RUN, DICK, RUN. SEE DICK YAWN...

Everyone knows reading is without doubt the most important academic skill kids should be taught, and ideally as early as possible. Everything else they will learn manifestly relies on this ability. And besides, there are *so* many great books out there, the sooner one plunges into them, the more one may devour! Even with our very limited educational knowledge, the first Logos faculty members and I knew that truth. However, we were just learning that we had a lot to *unlearn*, when it came to making good choices for *teaching* those reading skills.

It was the children themselves who tipped us to the best way to encourage students to read. We had purchased a popular publisher's entire Reading Curriculum, complete with:

- Student Primers (that had stories in them)
- Teacher's Guide to the Primers
- Student Workbooks (to go with the Primers)
- Teacher's Answer Key to the Student Workbooks
- Supplemental Vocabulary and Activity Sheets (to run off on mimeograph machines)
- Teacher's Guide to the Supplemental Vocabulary and Activity Sheets
- Supplemental Android Reading Teacher, complete with AA batteries (ok, that one wasn't available, yet)

Our elementary teachers dutifully followed the directions in the Teacher's Guide and put the kids in reading groups, according to the students' apparent abilities. We also made a point, fairly early on, of scheduling weekly times to take the classes to the local public library to check out "free reading time" literature, i.e., real books. (We even used our one school bus to get them there!)

Then it started dawning on us: we noticed that the students who were in the lower reading groups would check out stacks of books that were, well, too *hard* for them. The books were written for a higher reading level in many cases. When a teacher would gently suggest another (easier) title, the typical reply was:

"But I like *this* one!"

So we let them check the books out, against our better judgment. Finally, we realized that our "better" judgment was, academically speaking, out to lunch. We actually looked at the books the kids liked, then compared their quality to that of the stories in the publisher's primers we were so carefully following. Frankly, there was no comparison. Artistically speaking, the real books were Norman Rockwell and the primers were Motel 6 wall decor. Worse, the stories were boring and insipid. Switching metaphors, we were feeding baby food to kids who had gotten a taste of hotdogs, ice cream, and crunchy Jonathan apples (to keep it healthy).

I don't know exactly when that epiphany hit us, but pretty soon I directed the teachers to put the primers in storage. And then began one of my favorite times ever at Logos School: we went shopping for children's literature! I asked the teachers to give me a list of as many titles as they could remember loving as children. I did the same thing. We also, providentially, found *Honey For a Child's Heart* by Gladys Hunt (she was a personal friend of my family). In that wonderful volume, Mrs. Hunt had compiled indexes crammed full of recommended titles for children of various ages, helping us to determine which approximate grade to assign our selections.

It was very much like Christmas present shopping for all our younger students! I found catalogs (no Internet yet) of book companies that carried the treasures we wanted: *Mike Mulligan and His Steam Shovel, Katie and the Big Snow, Frog and Toad Are Friends, The Cat in the Hat, Winnie the Pooh, The Chronicles of Narnia,* the *Little House* series, *Paddle to the Sea* (a personal childhood favorite since it's about the Great Lakes), *My Friend Flicka, Homer Price, Make Way for Ducklings, Blueberries for Sal, Bedtime for Francis, Good Night Moon, Johnny Tremain,* and dozens of other beloved titles.

When the boxes of books started arriving, the entire school came to see which friends (old or new) would come out. Yes, very much like many Christmas mornings!

Our very youngest students couldn't wait to master phonics so they could start reading "chapter books." No, we didn't have all the comprehension activities and vocab lists worked out yet, but those came in time. Now we had all the student motivation to read one could ask for.

Interestingly, not long after our major switch to real books, I was down at the Post Office one morning collecting our mail, quickly sorting and tossing the junk mail. One catalog caught my eye. Did I see that right? Yes! This company had actually written and published comprehension workbooks for many of our real books! My elementary teachers had been troopers and were already working on our own versions; even some parents were helping develop them.

I let out a loud "Yeehaw!" right there in the United States Post Office.

PCs COME TO MOSCOW

The dawn of a new age of technology crept up on Moscow and Logos School, slowly but surely. By the mid-1980s we were all hearing about "PCs," which we quickly came to understand was tech talk for "personal computers." I recall wondering what was so personal about them? They just looked like another small machine, not unlike the VCRs we were also just getting used to.

To be honest, I was more interested in the changing landscape on the home entertainment front than I was in giving much thought to the PCs. Growing up in a family that loved movies, going to the theater had been a frequent and delightful experience. So now being able to watch movies of your own choosing (without relying on the TV offerings) in the comfort of your own home, well, that was for me! OK, I didn't actually go out and buy one of the first video players. But thankfully one of our teachers, Chris Owsley, did.

Initially there was a marketing tug-of-war between something called a Beta machine and the VHS models. The Beta machine actually played large movie disks that looked like and were the size of record albums at the time. You slid the whole 'album' into the slot in the machine and pulled the cover back out. It worked quite well, even if the disks were rather large.

Chris bought a Beta video player and became quite a popular guy among the Logos staff, especially on weekends.

"Hey Chris, old buddy and pal of mine!" a fellow staff member would say, sidling up to him maybe on a Wednesday morning. "Any chance I could borrow your machine this Friday evening? I mean, if you weren't planning on using it yourself..." There might also be some kind of token gift, such as an offer to pick up some of Chris's favorite candy.

Thankfully, Chris was a kind and generous soul and managed to juggle the loans of his machine in such a way so as not to disappoint too many staff members too often. As I had with the food pantry, I was careful not to play the "having the only children among the staff" card in my own infrequent requests of Chris.

"Say, Chris, how're the classes going? Got all the textbooks you need? Desks working out ok for you?"

"Sure. Everything's going well in the math classes, Tom. Thanks for asking!"

"No problem. Just let me know if you need anything. I enjoyed observing your teaching the other day. You're really growing in your teaching skills."

"Thanks!"

"Oh, by the way, any chance your machine might be available this Saturday night? I was thinking of getting one of those Disney movies for the kids. Sometimes I wish we could afford to pay for cable, but the local PBS station isn't too bad. I mean, the kids probably gain a lot from only watching Masterpiece Theater and nature documentaries. Anyway, just wondering...?"

Good old Chris. He was very selfless. Too bad about his Beta machine, though. After a year or two, it became apparent that the VHS player won the market. The disks quickly disappeared from the rental stores and were replaced by the much smaller video cassettes. The new VCRs could not only play the cassettes, they could record shows off the TV, whoa!

Meanwhile the PCs continued making headlines. More specifically, headlines in the local newspaper. The Moscow School District got on the bandwagon and bought a couple dozen TRS-80s. Then they determined that the best place to try these babies out was in a refurbished former school bus (I am not making this up). That was to be their first computer lab. The article about this innovation went on to say that the district would also be looking to hire a teacher who might be able to figure out what to do with the computers!

So that actually made me feel pretty good about the Atari 400 we bought with money raised at our Renaissance Fair food booth. I had received the board's blessing to buy one computer and, as things turned out, that was all we could afford anyway. I easily recall how much the Atari was because it cost about the same amount as its model number—$400. What could it do for Logos School? Well, not much, to be honest. It came with a couple of cartridges (software) that were sort of "chunked" into a slot. It didn't come with a monitor; we were expected to provide that. Fortunately the Atari (and most other micro-computers) could be plugged into a standard color TV set. Ta-da! A monitor!

Over the next couple of years, the micro-computer market was flooded by companies seeking to be top dog in this booming industry: TRS-80s and Commodores became popular, along with the Ataris. Instead of just playing Pong or Pac-Man, each successive PC could do more and more sophisticated functions. Initially, educators (including Logos) thought that we should teach all students some basic programming called, well, BASIC. That lasted maybe a few months. Then the PC makers realized that most people just wanted the computer to do the thinking and so PCs became more "user friendly." That was a nice way of saying most of us were too dumb and lazy to figure out how the computers actually worked, so set-up instructions went from a manual the size of a New York City phone book to a Tri-fold, laminated card with color illustrations a two-year old could follow.

A new breed of super heroes started to emerge from the masses of normal people. They would initially be called derogatory names like "computer geeks" and "techno nerds." But, lo, it came to pass that at some point in our lives, the rest of us would be happy to lick their shoes if they would do their healing magic on our own computers!

Since Logos never really had a line item in the budget for computers, kind patrons would donate their cast-off, older computer models to us. I always said yes to any donations, so we accumulated enough ancient (more than six months old) computers to make a small "lab." We also garnered some used color TVs for monitors and we were set to join the latter part of the 20th century. Or at least let the kids play Pong and Pac-Man during breaks.

BREAKING AND ENTERING

It happened not long after Logos had purchased our first VCR, but I don't think there was any connection. Early one morning, a Monday, I think, one of the church members discovered a broken window downstairs. He went inside and turned on the hall lights; Logos School had had some nighttime visitors who were intent on vandalism and theft. They also apparently knew we were a Christian school, or perhaps because they were in a church they felt compelled to spray paint (in red) "Satan lives!" on a few walls. And our new VCR was gone.

I arrived shortly after the discovery of the criminal activity. The church member had already called the police. They got there about the same time as our staff and earliest students did. Yay. Another first—the Moscow PD coming to Logos. It wouldn't be the last time, that's for sure, but I was new at this whole crime scene thing and hadn't learned how to talk coolly and calmly with police officers. (Thirty plus years later it still wasn't enjoyable, but by then I knew some of the officers on a first name basis...because we all live in small town, that's why; not due to frequent infractions!)

Needless to say, not much learning went on that day, but it wasn't a boring day for the students, either. The walls were quickly repainted, the window repaired, but we never got our VCR back. However, a kind parent replaced it with a new one. Life went on.

Side note: Speaking of vandalism, the University of Idaho's team mascot is... the Vandals. Really. Ever since I visited in 1971, I have pondered that selection. Who picked that one? Did that person know any history at all? Why not the "Pillagers" or the "Goths." Michigan is the Wolverines, Ohio State is the Buckeyes (figures), even Washington State is the Cougars. Dolphins, Bears, Seahawks, Panthers, even Ducks (Oregon). "Vandals?" Just curious...

"ALL THE WORLD'S A STAGE" – FIRST DRAMA

Not long before Logos opened, it was my pleasure to discover that I loved doing drama! That was a real revelation, verily an epiphany, since in high school I would gladly have gone to the dentist, sans Novocaine, rather than go on stage. I won't elaborate here, but suffice it to say it had to do with a traumatic acting experience in front of about five hundred other eighth graders in junior high school.

Fine, I'll elaborate for you. It was during a condensed version of *Romeo and Juliet* that some misguided English teacher thought would be a good play for hormone-afflicted teens to present to other similarly afflicted teens. My role as Paris was even more condensed (line-wise) than most. I suppose that was due to my complete lack of acting abilities. So, as no doubt the reader will recall, Paris has a sword fight with Romeo, and Romeo ends up sticking it to Paris, so to speak. Well, the Bard gave Paris a lengthy farewell-to-the-world speech. My teacher trimmed my lines down to this: "Oh, I am hurt!" The imagination needs little help in picturing the scene as I performed that bit in live theater. At least it provided some comic relief to their otherwise drab junior high day. Thus my strong aversion to drama was born and would last for many years thereafter.

It was after my four years in the Navy and as I started at the University of Idaho that I gave drama another shot: I took a two-credit class in Beginning Acting. A Christian friend who was already an amazing actor at the UI saw one of my little acting assignments. He was slated to direct a Woody Allen comedy for the Moscow Community Theater. He asked me if I'd like a role as a wacky priest living in a U.S. Embassy who practiced magic acts. I said sure, for no really good reason. It was nothing less than a blast! I was hooked for life.

As our small secondary program began to grow at Logos in the latter part of the '80s, I thought it would be fun to introduce some drama to the kids. We were just getting into offering "electives" to the older students. These were two-day/week classes in various non-academic subjects, e.g., typing, band, and now drama. Not having much experience myself, I asked my friend who had directed me in my first real play if he'd like to teach the drama elective. He said sure, for possibly no good reason, but I was pleased.

That is, until one particular day, and it would of course be a day that the board was meeting in my office. We were discussing this and that when an elementary teacher poked her head into the office and said, in an off-hand-but-still-rather-concerned sort of way, "Did you know that the Drama Class is watching a James Bond video in the library?"

Well, as a matter of fact I didn't know that was happening. So, I calmly excused myself from the now very quiet board meeting and made my way to the library at the end of the hall. The upshot is fairly easy to summarize, in consecutive order:

1. I turned off the video and suggested to my friend the kids do something different, like, maybe acting.
2. I apologized to the board.
3. I wrote an apology to the parents of the kids in the drama elective. (One dad wrote back and said he actually liked James Bond movies, but that's not really the point.)
4. Shortly thereafter my friend became busy with other activities and I took over the drama elective.

I also added one more bit of knowledge to my growing understanding of the teaching vocation: Not everyone who can *do* something, can or should teach that thing.

In taking over the elective, it seemed to me that a significant direction and culmination of teaching students how to act should be to perform in a play. So, I found two one-act plays: *The Importance of Being Earnest* (one-act version), a long-time popular show, and *He Led Her To the Primrose Path (But Was Nipped In the Bud)* which was, for those not familiar with the genre, a melodrama. Both plays being comedies certainly helped in making our inaugural productions a success. The Church of God even let me use their small dais for the shows. All the older kids had a part in one of the plays—auditioning would have given them the mistaken idea that they had the option to not be in a show.

Those were the only plays we did at the Church of God; the next time we put together a production we were in our new home on Baker Street.

LOVING THE FATHERLESS

Sometime during our fourth or fifth year, I got a unique phone call from Mr. Jim Wilson, asking me if we would consider enrolling a pregnant young lady. Right away. Apparently there was a high school-aged young woman who lived not too far away and was facing a serious dilemma. Being pregnant during this Dark Age of abortion, she was trying to decide whether to quit school or kill her baby. She was leaning toward the latter since she wanted to finish school but didn't want to face the embarrassment of having her friends watch her "expand," so to speak.

How Jim knew the family of this girl I don't think I even bothered to ask; Santa Claus knows fewer people than Jim Wilson. He wanted to let this family know that there would be a way for this girl to have her schooling and keep her baby, too. She would need to move to Moscow and attend Logos until the baby was born, which was about six months away.

There was no other appropriate answer than "Yes." I didn't even have to consult the school board, I knew what they'd say, but I got their quick assurance just the same. However, inexperienced as I was, I knew that the tricky part was going to be informing the other students and their families. Particularly the little ones who were as yet a bit clueless about how these things happen, if you follow me. On one hand, I wanted all the students to accept this young lady lovingly and respectfully. On the other hand, I didn't want them to think that this situation was normal and fine.

So, before the young lady came, I let the parents know and asked them to support us by talking to their children about how to treat her. I then went to the classrooms and told the kids the essentials: a pregnant girl was coming to attend our school. I said she had sinned by not being married before she had a baby but God says that babies are *always* a gift from Him. We were all to love her and help her through this difficult time.

The kids and staff couldn't have done better by this girl than they did during the time she was with us. In fact, the older girls were so very supportive and kind I admit I was privately a bit worried. Especially when the baby finally came and they all visited their new friend in the hospital, showering her with gifts and attention. All their natural and good instincts to love babies came out, yet I didn't want them to think this was as joyful and right an occasion as it should have been, i.e., within a covenant blessed by God. Nevertheless, I was slowly learning that many times not saying everything I wanted to was the right thing. So I didn't say anything and was gratified that my concerns were groundless as time went by.

In fact, within the next few years, we took in two more young women in similar circumstances who came to us be educated and loved through their pregnancies. We were happy to accept them both (thankfully they came at different times).

We were all learning that a Christ-centered education must deal with *all* of life, not just the "academic" side, if there is such a thing. God presents life in all its complexities and nuances, from messy birth to hard-edged death and He sustains us throughout by His grace. He was helping us learn that in all the varied chapters of the story He was writing about Logos School.

TRUE-LIFE DRAMAS:
THE TURNING POINT FOR OUR SECONDARY...

By 1986–87, we knew we needed to resolve the matter of our hemorrhaging, so to speak, from the seventh and ninth grades. Putting it in less disgusting terms, we were losing kids to the "public" junior high and high schools each year. We theorized long and hard about this problem, and determined that it seemed to come down to two major reasons:

1. We didn't have all the bells and whistles (sports, dances, cool stuff) that the public secondary programs did, and...
2. Kids attract kids.

Since we were losing more than we were gaining at that level, getting more to attract others was rather problematic. It also wasn't hard to rank those reasons in terms of need for action: if we didn't retain the kids, starting any other extracurricular programs would be a bit difficult. A Catch-22 situation, if there ever was one.

Thus, in the spring of 1987, we were down to a Total of about fourteen seventh and eighth graders, with no high schoolers at all. The elementary was doing fine, numbers wise, but it looked like those parents who wanted us to stop at eighth grade were going to get their wish, de facto. The board made this issue a top priority of planning and discussion. We decided to hold a meeting with just the parents of our current eighth graders, five in all (down from twelve two years earlier). This would be an essentially do-or-die meeting. We were going to ask these parents to answer one, all-important question: "What would we have to do to, as a school, to persuade them to have their students graduate from Logos High School?" Considering that Logos High School was a theoretical program at the time, this was asking for a lot from these parents.

We met with the five sets of parents in Larry Lucas's home. After a bit of hemming and hawing we got down to The Question, and requested that they try not to let the others' answers influence their own. We needn't have worried. These families had already demonstrated their independent thinking just by having their students at Logos School for as long as they had. I will admit I was a bit on pins and needles. Very realistically, the future of Logos School's secondary program would be determined that night, by these parents. That was the thought that ran through my mind, causing me the same kind of sweaty anticipation political candidates must have on election night.

My fears dissipated and my stomach muscles relaxed in waves of relief, as each parent around the room gave essentially the same answer:

"Well, we aren't interested in sports or other programs that much. Otherwise we would have left sooner. We know Logos doesn't offer much in the way of nifty facilities, or fancy equipment. Basically, we put our kids in Logos to get the best, Christ-centered education we could find. Our bottom line for keeping our kids there is this: if you continue to hire and keep the kind of godly, loving teachers you have, we'll keep our kids in Logos until they graduate. That's the deal."

What a deal! It still implied a very serious responsibility on our part, but it was one we had embraced from the very beginning as an unchanging goal. We very happily accepted the terms of their deal. Later that spring, we made a big hoopla (promotion ceremony, cake, even letter jackets) celebrating these five students moving into our high school. Four years later, by God's sustaining grace, we had the joy of not only seeing those same five students receive their diplomas; we awarded six more to the students who had joined the class in the intervening years. This pioneering class and their parents blazed the path to graduation that many other secondary students would follow.

EARLY PROTOCOL

As it started to look like we might have older students sticking around, maybe even to graduation, we began to give more thought to what kind of students we were helping to raise. Was school just about classes, homework, and the occasional extra-curricular activity? Or was there more we could help the parents foster in the lives and characters of their children? We never wanted to be a para-church organization. That is, we were not another independent spiritual training center for these kids. We have always considered ourselves as essentially a 'tool' for parents to use in training up their children in the Lord. We aren't in any sense autonomous or even under a specific church; we serve families, plain and simple.

All to say that, as we considered how we should help shape our students' characters, we wanted to do all we did with the parents' clear blessing. So we decided to start addressing the students' interactions. Someone, possibly Nancy Wilson, suggested that we have an evening event for the older students, centered around etiquette and good food. I knew the food would be an attractive selling point, but I wasn't too sure about the idea of requiring proper manners. Not that I was against them; I just wondered how the students would react.

As we would discover with many issues, the adage about the speed of turning aircraft carriers is very true; it can't be done quickly. The adage certainly applied to our initial fits and starts with what would eventually be known as 'Protocol Night.'

Our first forays were, well, rough. Among the memories I have of those events are:

- Being at one of our very first such events, in a school family's home, where the boys found out how fun it was to flick water from their glasses at each other. This, predictably, lead to full glasses of water being spilled across the table, soaking several girls' dresses. Aircraft carriers.

- A first progressive dinner (each course at different homes) that began with a movie (!) and hors d'oeuvres at one family's home. Since I was tasked with picking the movie, I thought a "Christian" movie would be a good choice. The recent release of *The Hiding Place* made my choice easy. However, being Christian and well-produced weren't the only factors I should've taken into account. A very heart-rending, true story about the Holocaust was perhaps not the best kick-off to what was meant to be an enjoyable and pleasant evening for the students. By the end of the film, the entire living room was littered with balls of soggy Kleenexes, and even the boys were doing their best to hide the fact they had shed some tears, too.
- On another occasion we had a lovely evening dinner with students and some staff members at a board member's home. The unique factor of that event was that one of the girls was in her ninth month of pregnancy. (She had transferred to Logos from her previous school as an option to abortion. We had readily taken her in, of course.) That evening was punctuated with a few awkward moments of what we (adults) all thought were early contractions. As it turned out, the contractions were the real deal and she gave birth to twins the next day.

But the idea of a unique, protocol-enhancing evening was worth pursuing and refining, which we did. More on those later.

SNOW DAYS (OR NOT)

As I noted earlier, our first year, 1981–82, had a very snowy winter. That was God's gift for our students' recess times, especially considering we had no playground, much less playground equipment at that point.

Being from Michigan, where snowy days meant just allowing more time to get to work (or school), I was not all that familiar with calling "snow days" for school. Sure, we had them in my youth and I remember the eager, almost painful, anticipation I felt when Mom would turn on the radio to hear if our school was closed, as the snow mounded outside our windows. (Dad would've already headed into work, slowly.) Then, oh joy, the thrill of hearing my school's name listed among the casualties of the snow storm.

However, having lived in Moscow for four years before Logos opened, the amount of snowfall we typically received rarely impressed me. I believe we may have had one day that first winter when I thought it wise to close the school. But then it was pretty easy to get the word out; I just had to call a couple families and ask them to call a couple more and we were done. I personally called the other three teachers to let them know and, viola, all done.

As the school grew and, it seemed to me, the annual snowfall lessened, the need for calling a snow day not only lessened, as well, it became more problematic that all the families would get the word in time. The local radio stations were happy to assist us, as they did with all the local schools, if I called a special phone number to tell them we were caving.

At first I thought we should close whenever the local school district did, but it didn't take long to figure out that they closed more often than I felt necessary. I found out the reason: if they couldn't run their country bus routes safely, the administration shut down the whole district. Even though we had a few bus routes for a number of years, I didn't want to close the whole (!) school if the buses should not have been run.

The primary deciding factor, on whether to close or not, was obviously how much snow had fallen or was falling. I had no practical means of ascertaining that amount. Looking out my window in the dark morning and checking our thermometer were not very accurate measures. Hearing on the radio how many schools were closed was helpful, but took too much time in the morning since they usually only announced them on the half-hour. Parents, especially those coming from out of town, needed to know what Logos was going to do as soon as possible. Finally, I arrived at what seemed to be a pretty reliable indicator of just how bad it was out there: the local Catholic school had a daycare. Even when all other local schools were closed, that daycare rarely closed. I figured, usually rightly, that if parents could drop their poor little people off at the daycare on a snowy morning, the roads must not be all that bad.

So, it wasn't unusual on a very snowy morning to hear something like this on a popular local radio station, which had two DJs:

"...and locally both the Moscow and Pullman school districts are closed, as is St. Mary's Catholic school. However, St. Rose's Daycare will be open, and so will Logos School."

"Hey Darren, I don't think Logos has closed yet this winter! Have they?"

"I think you're right, Dan. Man, I feel sorry for those poor Logos kids...and teachers!"

"Yeah! Everyone else has a day off, but the administration at Logos makes those guys keep working!"

"Now, turning to sports..."

Believe it or not, that's pretty close to the actual comments made over the air. I didn't hear them myself very often, as I didn't listen to that station on my way to work. But the older students, coming in and taking off their snowshoes, were more than happy to let me know what they'd heard. All in all, though, the "poor Logos kids" were pretty good sports about coming in to school when their peers were home watching TV.

Predictably, every time we had a snowy day or two, a few older students would threaten to pile snow in my driveway because I had told them that if I could get to work, so could they. I had a four-wheel drive SUV and I parked on the street; I wasn't worried. One year a class came close to following through with the annual "threat." I was at home one snowy evening and the doorbell rang. When I opened the door, no one was there. But on our doorstep was a two-foot high snowman. He had an arrow through his head with a note on it. The note read: "If we don't get a snow day, this could happen to you!" I also noticed that someone (or several someones) had piled two mounds of snow, one of each side of my driveway. Julie and I both thought it was quite hilarious.

The next day at school (open for business), I had no trouble discovering who had been responsible for the evening visit. In fact, I didn't have to even ask: one of our sophomore boys came up to me and asked, "So, Mr. Garfield, did you find out who put the snow in your driveway?" I replied that, yes, I just did. His sudden realization of how dumb he'd been and the accompanying look on his face was all I could have desired. The other kids standing nearby let him know how clever they thought he was, too.

I must confess one time when my pride got the better of my discernment. It was not long after we had moved to the roller rink on Baker Street. We hadn't closed for a snow day in many years and this one morning didn't look that bad to me. So I went about getting my driveway cleared and headed off to Logos. Unbeknownst to me, even the daycare had closed; the canary in the tunnel had died and I didn't know it. Upon arriving at Logos, I quickly noticed that not only did we have at least three feet on the ground, neither Baker Street nor our parking lot had been plowed out. It was really bad and it was still snowing!

A few staff members and students had already arrived. I started recruiting adults to call school families and let them know not to come in: we were closing. By this point it was after 7:30 and a fair number of our outlying families were bravely making their way to Logos. (This was long before cell phones.) So, as each family arrived they had to be told that we were closed. Frowns and frustration grew exponentially!

To compound my humbling, during the following night a chinook wind (rapid warming) came in and all that snow began melting…too quickly. By morning the flooding was getting so bad in the city that even the University of Idaho closed, an almost unheard of event! The sky was blue, the temp in the high forties, but water was flowing over many streets. Logos closed for a "flood day."

Sigh.

THE MUSIC "MAN"

We hired our first red-head, Mrs. Patsy Huddleston, in 1985 and life at Logos suddenly took on a more musical bent. Not that her hair color had anything really to do with it, I suppose. But she was certainly a ball of energy and enthusiasm! Her cheerfulness was a constant and I know we all appreciated that each day.

Patsy taught our fifth grade. After some weeks, I noticed how much time she was devoting to music-related instruction per week; let's just say it was a bit excessive. In her defense, it should be noted that our curriculum guide was still very much in flux at this point. But I needed her to make some adjustments. Patsy loved music, and I didn't want to quench her spirit. We arrived at a mutually beneficial compromise: she would teach math, reading, history, etc., with adequate time for each. To give her an outlet for her musical passion, we organized our first band!

The "band" was initially, like all programs we began, small. But it grew along with the school's population. Where there were just a half-dozen, soon there were two dozen young musicians. I believe we reached our zenith when we got to actually march in the U of I Homecoming parade through downtown Moscow! We certainly didn't have anything close to marching band uniforms for our kids, but we wanted some way of identifying them as 'Logos School' students. I don't know who came up with the idea of sweatshirts, but I was called upon to design the logo to go on them. (A funny, sort of related note here: Our school name is a bit unique and many businesses over the years have gotten it wrong in addressing bills or solicitation to us. We have received mail to "Logas," "Lo-gas," "Logo," and my personal favorite, "Logo's" School: that's right, we're a school that designs graphics!)

So on that Saturday of Homecoming, our kids assembled with other parade participants in the large parking lot of a local grocery store in preparation for starting the parade. The sweatshirts were now an inspired element—it was a cold, wet, dreary morning. But by the time the first floats, tractors, horse riders, and new cars with important passengers waving started making their way down Main Street, the sun won out.

Our little band of elementary musicians hadn't had a lot of marching practice, but they only formed a few short lines anyway. Each time the parade would stop moving, our intrepid director, Mrs. Huddleston, would give the down-beat and the band played something akin to a Tune. It was the classic scene from the end of *The Music Man* as our proud school parents cheered their children throughout the entire parade route:

"Great job, Davey!"

"Hey Debbie! We're over here! Good work, honey!"

MATTHEW 18 APPLIES EVEN AT LOGOS

"And if your brother sins, go and reprove him in private; if he listens to you, you have won your brother. But if he does not listen to you, take one or two more with you, so that by the mouth of two or three witnesses every fact may be confirmed" (Matthew 18:15–16).

There. It had happened again. Though hopefully unnoticeable to the person on the other side of my desk, my knee had definitely jerked. Worse, my knuckles were whitening—surely I couldn't hide that. Breathe deeply, relax those muscles. Now, focus on what she is saying.

"...and after talking to all those other moms, I found that I'm really not the only parent in the class who feels this way about Mrs. Burkstock's science test last week. In fact, after I told them my concerns, several of them said they felt exactly the same way, but were not sure if they should say anything to her. I mean, nobody wants to hurt her feelings, you know what I mean?"

Yes, I knew what she meant. With the kindest of intentions, what she really meant was that gossiping is a whole lot easier and less awkward than individually confronting a teacher with her concerns. Gossip? Surely that is a bit harsh, isn't it? "He who goes about as a slanderer reveals secrets, therefore do not associate with a gossip" (Prov. 20:19). But surely there was no slander intended; she only wanted to see if others "felt the same way." And what "way" was that? Eliminating all the hyperbole, these parents believed the teacher had made a poor call, a significant lapse in judgment, in giving the test.

So, what's wrong with a few parents comparing "notes" about a teacher's (or administrator's or board's) actions, without consulting her? Don't they have the right to do that? After all, the teacher is teaching *their* children. A number of years ago I was asked to go to another Christian school to "trouble-shoot" and give them some advice. Oh boy. After arriving at the school, it took me all of half-a-day to ascertain two facts: 1) this school had the worst problems I had ever personally seen, and 2) that a great portion of those problems stemmed from parents, staff, and board members all "just talking" to each other; they just hadn't bothered to confront the *right* people (i.e., those that could do something) about the problems. It had been far easier and more gratifying to talk behind each other's backs. Among other suggestions, I urged their board to adopt the principle of Matthew 18 in their school.

Certainly in Matthew 18 our Lord is directly addressing a suspected sin versus bad judgment calls, but as with many portions of Scripture certain principles can be derived from the direct teaching. Gossip or slander is addressed frequently in the Bible, from Proverbs to James. (James devotes all of chapter three to just what damage the tongue can do!) If the purpose of our Lord's directives in Matthew 18 was *not* to avoid groundless rumors and slander, what is the point of going to the person privately? By going first to the person under suspicion, gossip (a real sin) is avoided. Besides, by going first to the correct person, both sides of an issue are then heard, and it often turns out that at least part of the concern was based on inaccurate information. (For example, kids don't always give all sides of a story.)

I have seen far more damage than good done, even when a specific "sin" was not the initial problem, by people discussing the concern with everyone except the person who could do something positive. As one of our own "prophets," Bob Dylan, has said, "If you're not part of the solution, you're part of the problem." Christian school staff members, like most folks, are susceptible to the hurt that comes from discovering others have been talking behind their backs. Almost always an immediate feeling of betrayal of trust and friendship results. (At the school mentioned above, peace was not restored before almost the entire staff had been fired or resigned.)

On the other hand, many parents feel they should apologize when they do bring a concern directly to me or a teacher. They feel that they may be regarded as "complaining" or being a nuisance. Nothing could be further from the truth; by coming directly to the "source," they have done the right thing and avoided complaining to others, which is a real nuisance. Confrontations are about as fun as a trip to the dentist, but usually they are just as necessary. They can also be even more productive for all involved.

When a common spirit of trust and application of the *principle* in Matthew 18 exists in a Christian school setting, rumors and gossip rarely get a toehold. When the opposite happens, that is parents and teachers slandering others in the name of "concern," even Christian schools can be destroyed. It has happened and happened too often. The enemy of our souls frequently works to poison a Christian institution from the inside out, not from the outside in. Our Lord's wisdom still works well today, because He is in authority over all our schools and private lives.

HOW FIRM A FOUNDATION?

It has been said in various contexts that you can't make a good omelet with rotten eggs. Along the same lines, C.S. Lewis stated that no matter how much or how good the wine is, if you pour it into a mud puddle, you still have a mud puddle. Jesus Himself referred to the same kind of predicament, i.e., wasting something valuable on an unworthy or unready recipient. He called it "casting pearls before swine."

Classical, Christian education is a valuable commodity and to gain the fullest possible benefit from it, students need to come to it with a home-developed foundation. Put another way, there are certain intrinsic characteristics of the families whose students do well in this kind of education. When these characteristics are absent, it is very likely that in spite of the best efforts of the school and teachers, the student will gain little. The following is not intended to be the exhaustive compilation of those characteristics, but they should serve as examples to illustrate the point. The order of their presentation is rather random, since they all relate.

"Moral training" is the big "E" on the eye chart of prerequisite characteristics. Children coming from homes where God's Word is honored and obeyed will see a profound similarity in the expectations at school regarding their behavior. Homes that identify sin as sin, expect cheerful obedience, and show love and forgiveness consistently will find the school's standards will reinforce those biblical principles.

But how does that kind of training *practically* look at school? What are some even more precise evidences of a firm foundation that enables a student to get the most out of the school's program? One very obvious evidence is the student's view of authority in general, and his parents' authority in particular. A good measure of the student's regard for authority is the love boys show to their mothers, and the respect girls display for their fathers. Listen to how students talk; if the subject of parents comes up at all, it takes very little astuteness to determine the health of the student's view of his parents.

Another related characteristic is old-fashioned etiquette or manners. In the past, good manners were referred to as the "oil" of maintaining good relations with others in public. It is not a sin, per se, for a boy not to hold the door for a girl, but it is probably an indicator that his training in being a gentleman is not complete. The way a child speaks to an adult, the way he sits or slouches in his desk, and other numerous little acts that show respect for others, especially the elderly, speak volumes about that student.

A firm foundation also shows up in the way a student "filters" the plethora of cultural messages. Is there evidence of growing biblically based discernment, or does the student generally accept almost every attractive, popular theme at face value? Legalistic rejection is not biblical discernment any more than is a wide-eyed, "I-wanna-be-hip" attitude. Biblical discernment takes a lot of study, time, and a willingness to stand alone at times. "Wise as serpents, innocent as doves" sums it up quite well.

A student's appearance billboards both his respect for others and his family's training in discernment. Even in the secular world, appearance is recognized as the message-sending device it is. Dress should not be *the* means to determine success, but it is a lie to tell children that it doesn't matter at all. Even young children understand the difference "dressing up" makes in how they regard an activity. All little girls want to look pretty at a wedding, and all young boys want to wear their team uniform with pride. A student who supposedly doesn't care about his appearance actually cares too much for himself and not enough for those who have to see him. This attitude profoundly affects his teachability.

A firm foundation provides a student with a solid work ethic, i.e., standards of doing a job well. This goes beyond just being honest and not cheating on the test. Doing their work "as unto the Lord" practically means they don't have a "is-this-going-to-be-on-the-test?" mentality toward the acquisition and value of knowledge. Most often the students with a strong work ethic, who sweat bullets for every B they get, will fair far better in the adult world than those gifted students who breezily accept their A's.

Finally, parents will improve their students' opportunity to gain much from a classical, Christian education by ensuring that they (the parents) understand, value, and teach the purpose of this education. It is not enough to send the kids and pay the tuition—the parents must be able to articulate the reasons they are doing this and help their children understand it as well. Otherwise it will only be one more program dad and mom sign their kids up for, like summer swimming or piano lessons. Do you want this type of education for your *grand*children? If not, or if it doesn't make any difference to you, then consider going with something cheaper and easier. If so, then it must be understood to be valuable by your children. They will pass on only what *they* value, for all else will drop away with the passing of their parents' generation.

How firm is the foundation? As I consider the hundreds of students I've known through Logos, there are evidences of many, many deeply sunk pillars, thanks to God.

LOVING THE STUDENT, APPLYING THE ROD

In *Bedtime for Francis*, one of the best children's stories I've enjoyed reading to my own children, Frances, a young badger, has been having a hard time staying in bed and going to sleep. Things in her darkened room concern her and she goes to discuss them with her parents. Her parents calmly and wisely address her concerns and send her back to bed. Finally Frances goes to her father in his bed and after waking him with her concern about the wind moving the curtains, her father replies.

"If the wind does not blow the curtains, he will be out of a job. If I do not go to the office, I will be out of a job. And if you do not go sleep now, do you know what will happen to you?"

"I will be out of a job?" said Frances.

"No," said Father.

"I will get a spanking?" said Frances.

"Right!" said Father.

"Goodnight!" said Frances, and she went back to her room. Frances closed the window and got into bed."

That book was published by Russell Hoban in 1960, back before the enlightened age in which we live that has come to see spanking as a Neanderthal means of discipline, if not actual child abuse. During my graduate work, I was the sole defender, among many school administrators, of this ancient practice. The others argued heatedly that "violence begets violence." When I pointed out that the most secure and well-loved students I knew came from homes that included spanking as a normal punishment, one administrator told me straight-faced, "Well, if children are secure, they can stand a certain amount of problems in their homes." Oh brother!

Our culture, Christians and non-Christians alike, used to be steeped in the biblical traditions and principles of raising children. "Spare the rod and spoil the child" was one verse (albeit paraphrased) every parent knew (Prov. 13:24). And, strangely enough, kids were better behaved as a result. I do not have the space or time to go into why this very healthy practice has become virtually a crime. The saddest aspect of its decline is that many Christian parents have meekly accepted the world's way of "disciplining" children and have abandoned the clear biblical imperatives. I don't know how many times, during a conference with parents of a rowdy student, I have heard the comment, "We tried spanking him, but it didn't seem to make any difference." "Tried"? Do we "try" feeding our kids to see if they grow? If we don't notice a significant change overnight do we stop the feeding experiment?

Logos School believed that God knows more about raising children than our current culture does. Therefore, I have had the honor of reinforcing, through the use of a wooden paddle in my office, the good discipline begun in many homes. Here are some characteristics of a good spanking:

1. It is never done in anger! Love and calm determination should exude from the parent/adult.
2. The actual strokes should be limited (I use three) and each one should sting. (It's all in the wrist.) A wooden spoon or paddle are my tools of choice. Using the hand has many drawbacks, not the least of which is that, with a child of large mass, it really might hurt me more than it hurts him! ("Him" is no mistake; I personally don't spank girls, other than my own. I ask a female staff member to fill in for miscreant young ladies.)
3. Limited crying is acceptable; wailing or screaming are not.
4. A quiet hug and prayer of restoration and forgiveness should immediately follow. (Since the child may not be a Christian he should not be pressured to pray vocally, but the adult should always pray for the child.)
5. A clear, verbal expression of love for the child should be conveyed. Then any directions for other apologies and restitutions should be given.
6. The parents are to be called that same day, usually in the evening, to explain the situation and consequences clearly. (The student should have been encouraged to tell his parents *before* the call from the principal.)

I have not included every aspect leading up to the spanking for the sake of space. One of the best indicators of a really good and proper spanking is that five minutes later, complete, restored fellowship is evident between the spanker and the spankee. I have experienced this countless times, when I encounter a student in the hallway who was recently in my office. The air is clear, all is forgiven, and we may hug again, or just say 'Hi' warmly.

God knows what He is doing. He honors those who honor Him and His Word. We took that seriously at Logos. We also take seriously the application of His Word about training children through spanking and other forms of love, delegated to us for a time, by our school parents. It works very well.

YEAR-END FIELD DAYS

As each school year wound down, there was a lot of necessary, rather frantic preparation for finishing well. Not only did report cards need to be calculated, compiled, and run off (on our new copier, a far cry from the first years of using a duplicating machine), we had Honor Rolls to construct and ribbons to give to the deserving students. Then there were the parents and staff members to recognize and thank. Heaven forbid we forget to thank someone or spell a child's name wrong on a ribbon or certificate!

I've often told folks that I think of the work to begin and end each year as somewhat like flying a passenger jet. (This is also known as hyperbole.) Before the plane takes off (so I've been told and trust), the pilots and ground crew take time to run over a thorough checklist of things that need to work well for the flight. There is no real panic or rush to get it done, thankfully. That's sort of like our having the summer months to get ready for the new school year: ordering texts, getting furniture, planning lessons, painting rooms, ideally having all the teachers we need, etc. Back to the airliner: after cruising at thirty thousand feet for a period of time, maybe with a bit of turbulence here and there, the end of the flight comes up. The jet has to essentially make a controlled crash, dropping through the sky to land on a narrow strip of concrete, slowing rapidly from 450 mph to fast enough to stay airborne, but slow enough to land and brake, very hard! OK, maybe it's not quite as exciting, but we have to plan and teach lessons almost up to the last minute of our nine month "flight," then quickly throw together plans and documents to have our own "controlled crash." As far as I recall, we never lost any passengers, er, students, in the process.

One of the events we did early on which, like almost all our 'firsts,' quickly became a tradition was our year-end field day. I might as well be honest. The field day was meant to be a fun time for the kids, certainly, but it was also a way to clear the school out during the last few days, giving the teachers a break from having to plan anything. The work and grades were pretty much done and figured, so we all needed a last blow-out!

Having buses at this point was a blessing, since we could haul the kids to wherever we wanted to have a picnic and play games. East City Park is a lovely, wooded ten-acre spot on the east side of Moscow, of course. There were picnic tables, a large covered shelter, and play equipment. It took about ten minutes to drive the buses there from the Church of God.

The Lord gave us rather warm weather in late May during our first years, so one spring I thought it might be a cool idea to have the kids bring squirt guns. Like I said, it seemed like a good idea at the time. To help them re-load (refill) quickly, we planned ahead and brought one of our thirty-three gallon plastic garbage cans. We filled it full of water from a park hose. Then all the kids had to do was to shove their empty guns in the can and, blub-blub, they were back in action!

What I pictured in my mind was happy squeals of laughter as the children ran in all directions throughout the park, squirting this friend or that, while being squirted themselves. A wiser adult, especially a male, could have anticipated what would happen in reality. I quickly found out. Sure, I had brought a gun, thinking I would join in from time to time, as I wished. Instead, I had barely given the instructions for re-filling, when I was suddenly surrounded on all sides by dozens of guns pointing directly at *me!* Yes, they squealed with laughter as they chased me throughout the park, soaking me thoroughly. Even my heart-rending pleas for a truce so I could re-load were met with maniacal laughter. Only by taking shelter under the... shelter, where food was stored, was I able to get out of the intense cross-fire. The other teachers were no help; for some sick reason they found the one-sided battle amusing.

OK, I learned my lesson. The next year I came equipped—I bought the largest, three-gallon-backpack water cannon on the market! I had my revenge that year. But apparently the Lord thought enough was enough and subsequent springs were so cool in May that a snowball fight wouldn't have been out of the question.

CHAPTER IV

THE ROLLER RINK

GROWING PAINS

As I mentioned earlier, Logos grew quickly and we met with the council of the Church of God to ask them if we could use the main floor Sunday School classrooms, too. This would mean sharing rooms and even taking over some wall space (for bulletin boards).

At the meeting with the church council, wise men like Jay McCoy and Larry Lacey supported the idea, but let us know we needed to actively seek our next (school-centered) home. We had known all along that the basement would be a temporary arrangement, but now the reality of seeking another, larger site was daunting, to say the least. Meetings were held with construction and realty guys to determine what we might be looking at if we built from scratch. Costs of at least a million dollars were presented, and that would be just to build a school to house the 120+ students we had by our fifth year.

I found those estimates to be rather discouraging, especially considering that our entire annual budget at that time was around $300,000. If not obvious already, my faith was pretty small at that time and it didn't take much to convince me that we were done as a school. Once again I recall praying and talking with Julie, sure that Logos was finished and I would need to find other work.

As we had in the summer of 1981, the board began searching throughout Moscow for another suitable location. Since we had no capital to buy land and build from scratch, we knew we had to find an existing facility. But it appeared that all the larger buildings were already occupied with either a business or a church.

Larry Lucas deserves the credit for having the vision for turning a roller-skating rink on Baker Street into a school. It looked like what it was: a large, rectangular, cinder block building. It was built in 1980 to be a skating rink, and that's what it was, with very few frills added. Located a few hundred yards off of what we locally refer to as our Moscow-Pullman highway (others would just call it a Miracle Mile), it appeared to me to be as attractive as an empty warehouse. I had taken my kids skating (and falling) there a number of times so I knew what the interior was like: a large, dimly lit room, with a yellow floor, a large disco ball in the center of the ceiling, and brown carpet wainscoting up the walls. Oh yes, and a snack bar area.

I was adamantly opposed. The rink's location and appearance were enough to repel me. Yes, it had nearly fourteen thousand square feet of open space and the price certainly was right; it was about a quarter of what we had been told it would take to build a school from scratch. Roller skating as a fad had fallen on hard times, so to speak, and the U.S. Government's Small Business Administration now owned the building and wanted to hand it off to just about anyone.

One spring evening I decided to drive to the building and actually walk around and up behind it. Well, what do you know? There was actually open land and even a lovely vista of Moscow Mountain from there! We could put a playground up behind the rink, something I hadn't imagined possible. From then on, I was all for it.

After talking with a banker and doing some math early in the summer of 1987, we held a dessert fundraiser, starting with an open house at the rink (including an impromptu game of floor hockey) and ending with pie and an appeal for a down payment. We needed about $48,000 to get the loan to purchase and remodel. It was raised that night, by God's kindness expressed through a handful of dear people.

We started demolition and construction in July. Out went the large disco ball and music speakers, along with the snack bar tables. In went lots of windows (cut out with a huge diamond-bladed saw, wielded by a guy whose arms were as thick as my thigh!) and lots more ceiling lights. The architects drew and re-drew plans to get the greatest use of the space for classrooms, offices, and an auditorium, not to mention hallways and space for lockers. Lots of interior walls would obviously be needed, requiring lots of labor for which we didn't have the budget. Hence, volunteer help was the word of the day. Evening after evening, Saturday after Saturday, school dads would show up to pound nails and, eventually, hang what seemed to be an unending amount of sheetrock. An earthmover was hired to level out almost an acre of land east of the building for our playground. For this playground, unlike our first one, we actually ordered and installed real metal play equipment, including a slide and swing sets.

Speaking of sheetrock, I had a close and uncomfortable encounter with it. The sheets were mostly twelve feet long and four feet tall, and came in varying widths. At one point, a large stack of them was leaning against one wall of a small hallway area when someone asked me to find a sheet of five by eight, I think. So, standing in front of the sheets, I started pulling them toward me one by one, looking for the correct one. The stack began to shift in my direction. A more experienced construction person (or perhaps anyone paying attention) would have realized this might end badly. It did. Just as it occurred to me that I had a great deal of weight pressing against me, the weight won the balancing act. I was thrust rudely and firmly against the opposite wall and pinned there quite securely. After meekly calling for help and being released by guys who didn't hide the pleasure they were getting from it, I was encouraged to find less complicated work to do.

But I wasn't the only one to experience a "downside" to the experience of building your own school. The ceilings of the rink were high, eleven feet to the false ceiling, and above the drop panel ceiling was an attic space about five feet high. Since the rink was a free-span (no supporting poles), the attic area contained all the beams, trusses, wiring, and duct work. We had to add a lot of wiring for the additional classroom and hallway lights, as well as wiring for our fire alarm system. Crawling around up there to string the wire required a person to carefully step from one wooden truss to another. Should you misstep, you would find yourself stepping onto the fragile ceiling panels. In other words, falling through to the floor eleven feet below.

Among those working in the attic to run wires one evening was Doug Wilson. I happened to be in the room that would become our library. Looking up I saw that some ceiling panels had been removed and Doug was sitting on a truss about thirteen feet up, pulling the red alarm wire. Starting back to my work, I heard a short yelp and looked up in time to see Doug falling through the ceiling! There was barely enough time for me to think: "Yikes! What should I do?" when with a loud thump he landed. Thankfully, his fall was largely broken by a pile of sheetrock pieces and insulation. Still, he hurt a finger fairly badly. Thus, in one way, the library was inaugurated.

Our grounds got a good bit of attention, too. We plowed up the front yard, planted new grass, and installed an underground sprinkler system with a timer. Then we planted a variety of young trees in the yard, and juniper bushes in the front bank of the school. The playground behind and above the school was also seeded and equipped with the sprinkler system. Fences make good neighbors and, besides, the city required them so we put up hundreds of feet of chain-link fencing around our campus perimeter.

By far the most popular features of our new school, at least to the students, were the dozens of tall, blue lockers we installed on both sides of the center hallway. Imagine a dad on Christmas Eve, staying up all hours putting together ("some assembly required") his daughter's first trike. Now imagine about 150 such trikes, each requiring the fastening of dozens of small nuts and bolts to hold them together. I was pleased they made the students so happy!

One strange side-note: When the rink first opened in the early '80s and Logos School was still at the Paradise Hills Church of God, I was earning summer pay by doing sign painting around Moscow. The Baker Street roller rink owners hired me to design and paint their business sign: "Rollin' Derby Skate Center." I did so on the front cinder block wall. Years later, in July of 1987, I found myself on a ladder painting out my lovely "artwork," just as the former owner happened to drive into the parking lot below me. I climbed down and we shared the moment of irony together.

School needed to start that September and we were far from ready to move in to the new site. So once again, the Church of God folks kindly let us use their Sunday School rooms, as well as our downstairs classrooms, to begin the year.

By October, the new home of Logos School was almost complete. On the exterior, the school sign was up, eleven classrooms, a library, lunchroom, offices, twenty-three windows, and one set of new doors had been added. One Saturday, while we were busily constructing, a group of would-be skaters came into the building to inquire as to times the building might be open for them to enjoy their favorite sport. Tempting as it was, I refrained from sarcasm and did not point out the obvious changes in the building's name and purpose. Nor did I charge them an entrance fee.

Finally in November, we were as ready as we were going to be. The floors were all still the original roller rink yellow (i.e., no carpet yet) and the playground was just mud, but it was our new home. We picked a day, arranged for several grain trucks to be available and packed all the desks, chairs, and other sundry school furniture across town to the former rink. Many families lent a hand, so the rooms were rather quickly put together.

The first school day at our new Baker Street home was very different than our first day of opening Logos, more than six years earlier. Our new school felt immense! The student population of about one hundred and thirty students could easily ramble around inside our almost fourteen thousand square feet of space. We started the day all together with a brief ceremony of raising the American flag for the first time on our very own flag pole out front! Then we prayed for the day, thanking the Lord for our new home, and got to work in our yellow-floored classrooms.

Later that month we held a more formal dedication service in our new auditorium during which we thanked the Lord, as well as several key folks and businesses who had given much in time and money to make a real school for Logos. The overall feeling among the families, staff and school board was…at last, we're home!

SPECIAL PROGRAMS: SPEECH MEETS AND SPELLING BEES

I already noted that we owe a great debt to the Association of Christian Schools, International (ACSI) for their practical help and encouragement in our early years. Two of the special and practical programs they offered their member schools were Speech Meets and Spelling Bees. Not ever having experienced either of these events in my growing years (not even spelling bees), when I first read about them in the ACSI materials, I was intrigued. They sounded like a good combo of fun and academic challenge for the kids. Both programs came with lots of guidelines to follow, including how to conduct an in-school competition, and then going on to inter-school events.

As we began to try these programs on for size, they rather naturally brought us into contact with the closest sister Christian school across the border in Washington: Pullman Christian School (PCS). I had briefly met with their founders as we prepared to open Logos. PCS had begun a year before us, in 1980, as a ministry of Living Faith Fellowship, a Pentecostal church, and they used the Accelerated Christian Education (ACE) curriculum and approach to education. The ACE program offered a pretty complete, self-paced curriculum for the students to follow. The teachers were there to assist and guide, but the students could proceed as quickly as they mastered each level.

The principal of PCS and I agreed to set up dates and times for our students to compete against each other in the inter-school level of speech meets and spelling bees. This obviously became easier and more interesting as both our schools grew in enrollment. To go into all the details of these programs might threaten the special bond between you, the reader, and this humble volume. Therefore, I will refrain and only give you the salient facts as they pertain to the affect they had on how Logos grew and changed.

The speech meets, at each level, were judged by a panel of three judges. Students were awarded on how well they met the criteria for the speech given orally. When we had inter-school meets, the panel was predictably made up of judges from both schools. Ribbons of blue, red, white, and green (in descending rank) were awarded at the final ceremony: blue was Superior, red was Excellent, white was Good, and green was for Participation. Yes, you read correctly—we gave out ribbons for essentially showing up, breathing, and saying something. Here again, we had to learn through doing it badly first that students don't value such meaningless awards as much as adults might want them to. After every such award ceremony, we would find a plethora of green ribbons decorating the floor, like so many fallen leaves. We got the message and the green ribbons weren't reordered after a while.

We would often ask some of the Superior winners to share their pieces in front of the gathered masses of students at the awards ceremony. The ACSI handbook didn't suggest this; we came up with the idea ourselves. By and large it was very well received. There was that one time when, after calling up a young lady with a blue ribbon to present her piece, it quickly became apparent to all concerned that she had received the wrong ribbon! Awkward doesn't begin to describe the sense all the adults felt.

This is as good a time as any to mention that the PCS students not only wore school uniforms, but the uniforms were red, white, and blue. To the Logos casually clad student body (in those days), the sight of these prim, patriotic-looking students arriving at Logos was a sheer delight. We had to work diligently to ensure that unkind comments, looks, giggles, etc., would not cause offense to our visitors. To my chagrin, it took Logos seventeen years to figure out that school uniforms were actually a very good idea for many reasons. It never occurred to me to ponder what preparations for politeness the PCS students were given by their teachers before embarking to come to the slum-school.

The PCS students also typically had more, well, serious and 'spiritual' speech pieces than we did. I never thought of Logos as liberal by any measure, but it can be safely asserted that we were less conservative and serious than our brothers across the border. With that as a backdrop, you might appreciate the following speech meet experience. And it was my daughter who was the orator on this occasion.

Carolyn was in sixth grade at the time and we had been doing inter-school speech meets for a good number of years by then. She had won a blue ribbon for her piece earlier in the day, and it was now time for the award ceremony. I knew what her selection was of course (although, being a natural actress, Carolyn hadn't needed a lot of help), but I hadn't really thought how it might come across in that particular setting.

So I blithely called her up to give her piece before the audience. She confidently mounted the steps to the stage and launched into her poem with gusto. It happened to be *The Highwayman* by Alfred Noyes. For those unfamiliar with this tale (as apparently was the case with the entire PCS delegation), it has to do with deep love, cruel British soldiers, a bold and daring highwayman, and Bess, the black-eyed innkeeper's daughter. Oh yes, and a musket plays a key role.

As Carolyn warmed to her tale, I suddenly remembered what was coming and knew there was no avoiding it; it was sort of like watching a crystal teacup fall to the floor: all you do is watch in horror and wait for the shattering. Sixth grade Carolyn burst out with:

> They had tied her up to attention, with many a sniggering jest.
> They had bound a musket beside her, with the muzzle beneath her breast!
> "Now, keep good watch!" and they kissed her. She heard the doomed man say—
> *Look for me by moonlight;*
> *Watch for me by moonlight;*
> *I'll come to thee by moonlight, though hell should bar the way!*

(Carolyn paused for effect, and then dropping her volume to a stage whisper...)

> *Tlot-tlot,* in the frosty silence! *Tlot-tlot,* in the echoing night!
> Nearer he came and nearer. Her face was like a light.
> Her eyes grew wide for a moment; she drew one last deep breath,
> Then her finger moved in the moonlight,
> Her musket shattered the moonlight,
> Shattered her breast in the moonlight and warned him—with her death!"

Carolyn certainly had everyone's attention at that point, no doubt about it. The entire room of saucer-eyed students sat in a thrilled, yet awkward silence. I do believe I saw a number of young mouths hanging open. From what exact cause I could not say for sure; I wanted to think it was because of the spell-binding poem or Carolyn's fine rhetorical skills. But most likely it was because these kids had never heard anyone, especially a young girl, shout out the words *breast* and *hell*, in a Christian school, of all places.

Spelling bees also became a traditional, annual event, which, I quickly discovered, happened with just about anything we tried once. This led to some long-term programs it took us years to change or remove. But spelling bees were sort of fun, if you don't mind the tension and weeping it can produce, and not just in the parents.

We learned a lot from the spelling bees. For instance, winning actually required that one be really good at memorizing many words and their unique letter order. Now, I realize that sounds obvious, but those skills don't have much to do with learning all the rules associated with spelling success. In other words, knowing that "when two vowels go walking, the first one does the talking" is all fine and good for lots of words like "speed" or "read," but it's worthless with even some normal words like "nation." And I don't recall any winners saying they were saved by remembering the right rule.

So, not surprisingly the Bee winners were usually students who loved to read and had read a lot of books, not just in school. The really exciting (and nail-biting) part of the bees came when the competition for the school winner got down to two students of similar ability. We had two such students, a boy and girl, go for over thirty rounds before a winner emerged! Whew! (They had blown by my vocabulary level back at round fifteen, I think.)

FUN THINGS TO DO, OR NOT DO, WITH OLDER STUDENTS

While not "official" programs, we decided to begin some special events just for the secondary (7th-12th grade) students. I admit that a major motivation for doing this was to try to "sweeten" their lives at Logos. Retaining these students was not only a challenge for us; in years to come, keeping and attracting older students would be very common problems for our sister ACCS schools. Older students needed different (and more complicated) activities to hold their interest than those we put together for the littles.

The reader might recall that we were down to five students in eighth grade, all that were left out of a class of twelve sixth graders two years earlier. Seeing as how these were our oldest students at the time, if we were going to build a high school program, we needed these students to stay with us. That was in 1987, the same year we moved from the Church of God to our new campus on Baker Street.

The board had its brass tacks meeting with the five families, where they told us they were in for the duration. To highlight the transition of these five eighth graders into the official start of their high school years (ninth grade), we threw a big party for them in the spring of 1988. We called it Eighth Grade Graduation, bought them all leather letterman jackets (complete with an 'L' that we bestowed regardless of the lack of sports), and generally made a huge fuss over them!

That program would mutate to Eighth Grade Promotion, and finally was phased out after many years.

But we wanted more than just an end-of-year ceremony to offer to these oldest students. So, thanks to some committed parents and faculty, we began offering some out-of-school trips: specifically rafting in the summer and skiing trips in the winter.

By "rafting" I mean the white-water kind, not the Tom Sawyer mosey-down-the-lazy-river kind. Once again, Larry Lucas led the charge and put together these trips for a number of years. They also involved camping, which has its own unique elements, particularly when you involve young teens. Tents, campfires, eating outdoors, sanitation: all become their own special set of challenges for the adults seeking to organize and execute a "great time" for the kids. Put more positively, let's just say each trip was a blend of delightful times in God's creation, combined with many opportunities for sanctification.

Not surprisingly, I recall one trip in particular since it altered my physical appearance to some degree. It happened our first evening down by the river. We were going to raft the confluence of the Salmon and Clearwater rivers, I believe (a confluence is where two or more rivers meet, so there are lots of rapids on which the rafts can rock and roll, so to speak). My oldest, Carolyn, was along for this trip and I was looking forward to experiencing the ride with her.

After we set up camp that afternoon, the guys, having some time on their hands, decided it was time to throw people into the river. I was chosen as one of those people, but I wasn't keen on the plan. So at the river's edge I managed to fend off most of my attackers. That is until a young, very strong boy named Joel got me in a head-lock. I jerked my head hard to break his grip; immediately two things happened at once: I got free from Joel, and my ear hurt terribly. I put my hand up to left ear where the pain originated—when I brought my hand down it was completely covered in blood. I staggered back up the beach and Bill Twigg (on site as a chaperone) came to my assistance.

"Bill, I think I need a doctor!" I told him.

"Yup. Your ear's about torn off," Bill calmly replied. He got me into a van with Tom Spencer driving and another parent, who happened to be a nurse. She told me to lie down on the floor and hold a towel to my ear. Being out in the wilderness of north Idaho, we had to go to two clinics to find one open at that hour. By God's grace, this facility had an excellent doctor who must have been studying plastic surgery.

It turned out that Bill's assessment was pretty close: I'd torn the fleshy parts of my ear into three pieces, requiring about twenty-seven stitches above and twenty-nine below my ear canal to reconnect it all. The doctor's summary as he finished was actually quite reassuring: "Well, Mr. Garfield, it looks like you have an ear again." He then swathed my ear with a huge bandage and, to hold it in place, wrapped several pieces around my head. Checking it out in the mirror, I halfway wished it was closer to Halloween; I already had a good start on looking like the mummy!

On returning to camp, Carolyn gave me one look and stated the obvious: "So you aren't going on the raft tomorrow, right?" Nope. But I didn't want to go home either, so I spent the next two days relaxing by the river's edge, sucking down Ibuprofen tablets and reading a good book on the Zimmerman Telegram (from World War I).

Not having cell phone service out there, I wasn't able to forewarn Julie to my appearance so it made for an interesting story at home. My ear healed just fine and Joel graduated a few years later; I heard he became a prison guard. Makes sense.

I never went on any of our ski trips, but the kids loved them. (Considering my experience with rafting, I could only guess what part of my anatomy would suffer on the slopes.) We got better group prices by going during the week so we let our oldest students take a day off of classes. (Such was our desire to have a unique program to offer Logos students.) We even enlisted our aged buses to get our skiers there and back again, which they did faithfully a good number of times.

But all good things come to an end sometime. I don't recall the last year we sent our kids off to ski, but the end came when we were getting too many older students to transport. Plus, it must be noted, we were less willing to take a day off of classes that were increasing in their value.

STAGING THE FIRST PLAY

Along with the all our new classrooms, we built what seemed to us at the time an immense auditorium. Essentially it was a fifty by fifty foot, tiled all-purpose room in the center of the south end of the school. On the north end of the room we built a small stage, three feet high, about ten feet deep and thirty feet wide. It even had a backstage door to the hallway. The stage didn't have curtains right away, but I was still anxious to put on a play, so we started rehearsing an old comedy: *The Mouse That Roared*. Most of the secondary students (about twenty-five) were in the cast or helped as crew members.

The play actually had a pretty fun story, based on Cold War fears and events. Considering we put it on in 1988, we managed to do this "period" piece just before the Berlin Wall came down in November of 1989! The story featured a very poor European country that needed a lot of money to help it survive. Its queen and her ministers come up with the clever idea of declaring war on the United States, then immediately surrender and seek financial help "rebuilding" their country, as the United States tends to do with all the countries it conquers. There are of course some unexpected twists, such as the tiny country having an "all-powerful" secret weapon (or at least the U.S. thinks it does), so it turns out the United States surrenders to the tiny kingdom.

There were some memorable, unexpected twists in our first major production at Baker Street, too, such as one of my leads not memorizing his lines until literally the night before we opened! Turns out his mother didn't know he was in the show until the evening before, so they stayed up much of the night working on his lines. My favorite recollection (and a lesson in directing) had to do with the young man who played our scientist, the one who created the "all-powerful" secret weapon. Initially he had all the stage presence of a pancake, but I was using any and all the secondary students who were willing to be in the show. However, on opening night, he underwent a classic transformation after hearing the laughter and applause of the audience. Acting can be intoxicating to the initiate, especially comedic acting, with the potentially disastrous consequence of an actor "milking" the moment and playing "to" the audience, versus playing for the audience. This young man became intoxicated on the sweet wine of audience approval. Every time he came on stage, his appearance became incrementally more bizarre (by his own doing). I managed to get backstage and speak some sobering words to him before his last and, no doubt, show-stopping arrival on stage.

NORTHWEST HISTORY TRIP

Tom Spencer and his young family had arrived in Moscow and at Logos in 1984. The board was very impressed with his obvious confidence and spiritual strength. They hired him to teach secondary history and some other courses. After the move to Baker Street and we began seeing the numbers of secondary students increase, I asked Tom to serve as my Vice-Principal.

Being a sharp fellow, although he accepted the position, he knew very well that it came with all the "glamour" of most vice-principal jobs. That is, though he wasn't the "principal," he had to deal with all the "vice." The older students were sent to him first for disciplinary problems, and then on to me, if necessary. But that wasn't all the joy he got to have: I also put him over the Logos Transportation Department, otherwise known as the four ancient buses we ran on routes. But he took all the responsibility and hassle with good grace.

Besides, not all the bus-related work was unpleasant: we had a number of very delightful parents who stepped up to drive the bus routes we had at the time. One particular driver, a school mom with a lot of gumption, Chris LaMoreaux, literally had to step up—she was so short that we had to put blocks on the pedals so she could reach them! "Desperate times, desperate measures." Another intrepid mom was Ann Casebolt. Ann's husband Dave worked for the U of I in their farm animal research area. What that really meant was the Dave and Ann lived on a sheep farm and had to deal with some pretty rough issues. So not much could bother Ann when it came to driving a bus. She and Chris went the "extra mile" to ensure our kids were picked up on time and delivered safe to school, and then home again. They made Tom's job much easier; the buses themselves, on the other hand, were often a nightmare.

Among the curricular choices we made for our secondary history program, we decided to ask Tom to teach our eighth graders the history of the Northwest. This specific class was chosen so the students could see history up close and personal in their logic (Pert) years. Logos School was smack dab in the Pacific Northwest: the closest significant museum was in Seattle, three hundred miles away. Besides, the northwest was the newest part of the United States, historically speaking. So where the east coast schools can take a day trip to Boston and tour the Old North Church, we still get moose that wander into town, thinking it's still their natural territory. Not that I'm complaining—I dearly love the Palouse, but when it comes to history, well, we don't go back too far.

The new class was to be taught in the spring semester and Tom came up with the idea of a Northwest History Trip: a three-day excursion that would take the kids to indigenous, historical sites particularly in eastern Washington, northern Montana, and northern Idaho. Tom did a good bit of research and phone calling to arrange interesting stops and accommodations along the way. The Lewis and Clark Corps of Discovery came out our way back in 1803–05, and their journey was well chronicled. Many of their campsites and descriptions of the terrain were in our neck of the woods, so to speak, so our trip with the kids would naturally include some of those sites.

We also managed to schedule visits to gold and silver mines. The former had become a tourist attraction, the latter was still a functioning mine (at the time). In addition to all these elements, it would be negligent of us to not include some history of the Indian tribes, battles, and culture that are all around this region.

From its maiden voyage, the Northwest History Trips was an immediate success! It would become one of the most memorable recollections of our high school students' career at Logos. Fun traditions sprang up, of course, that had to be done as part of every trip. For instance, the snowball fight in Lolo Pass was a must-do every trip (being at a pretty good altitude in the mountains, even in April we could count on snow). Parents were more than happy to accompany the kids, acting as chaperones, but also learning along with the students.

NON NOBIS

By 1989 Logos School was turning eight years old and we still hadn't settled on some of the most vital elements of the school. Things without which Logos could sink into a hazy, mediocre, ignoble existence. Even now I cringe with embarrassment to recall how long it took us to address our incredible lack. The reader may even have been growing impatient, wondering, "When in the world did they get their act together and finally pick a mascot, not to mention a school song?! Good grief!"

Well, we managed to tumble to both of these at about the same time. And it happened in 1989 thanks to Kenneth Branagh, the British actor and director. His movie version of Shakespeare's *Henry V* hit the theaters with gusto and great acclaim that year. It is still a fantastic cinematic accomplishment and does the Bard justice. The St. Crispin's Day speech before the Battle of Agincourt alone is worth the price of ticket: "We few, we happy few, we band of brothers...!" Whuff. If anyone can sit in their seat and not want to leap up, grab a sword and shield, and start hollering for some French blood...well, all I can say is that person has ice in his veins! (Note to my French friends: You know I'm not talking about you—or any of your ancestors, right?)

As history teaches us, and Branagh dramatically shows us, the Brits (with the help of their secret weapon, the long bow) not only win the day, they do so with incredible flying colors. Thousands of French knights were killed, compared to less than two hundred losses for King Henry's army. The king, out of great gratitude to the God of Heaven, orders that his men sing "*Non Nobis*," the song in Latin with the words to the first verse of Psalm 115:

> Non Nobis, Domine, Domine,
> Non Nobis, Domine,
> Sed Nomini, Sed Nomini Tuo
> Da Gloriam!
>
> *[Translation:]*
> *Not unto us, O Lord, O Lord*
> *Not unto us, O Lord*
> *Unto Thy Name, unto Thy Name*
> *Give the Glory*

The victorious Brits begin singing, just a few soldiers at first, as they wearily tramp through the mud, helping their wounded, lifting them out of the mire. The king himself leads the way, silently carrying the dead body of a young boy, one of those assigned to watch the soldiers' baggage—boys that were all killed by the French cavalry in a heinous, ungallant act during the battle. More and more soldiers join in the song, as the orchestral score underneath swells to greater and greater magnificence. Joy, sorrow, glory, and nobility all join together, as tears stream down the faces of the audience. Whuff, again!

I came away convinced that Logos School had to have *this* song as our school song! Nothing else would ever be so appropriate: the words were from Scripture, they gave glory to the Father, it was sung in Latin, and it was short! Perfect.

Oh yes; and we would be the Knights. I mean, who or what else would be more fitting to sing this song?

For decades to come we would teach this song to all ages of all our students. They would sing it at every assembly, of course, but it would also be sung by our teams after a tough basketball, lacrosse, or volleyball game, win or lose. It would be sung by teams before and after Mock Trial State and National competitions; by casts before drama productions; by the whole secondary following State Track wins or other major public recognitions. It would even be sung after hearing heart-breaking news that affected us all. Whatever we did that was worth doing was worth giving the Father the glory for it.

Non Nobis—only to God be the glory.

"YOU MUST HAVE BEEN A BEAUTIFUL BABY"

Without doubt the intentions (as usual) were sterling. Unfortunately the thinking was flawed, to put it mildly. One fall I read a news article about a local middle school that had gone through the expense and trouble to purchase a number of computerized, six-and-a-half pound "babies" for a health class. These were state-of-the-art, high-tech infants. They were programmed to cry at unpredictable times, and the only way to get them to stop was to insert a special key into their backs. The keys were attached to a hospital-type bracelet worn by the "mother" or "father" students. The bionic bambinos could even register any "abuse," such as being stuffed in a locker for an extended period.

The news article reporting this latest crusade against student promiscuity quoted the reactions of the students packing their plastic progeny. "It was fun at first," said one young lady. "But after a while I just wanted to throw it out the window." It seems that, just like the real McCoy, these toy tots would cry at night, causing frustration and irritation in many homes. Wonder what the parents of these short-term, young "parents" thought? One real mom was a bit put out at the loss of sleep, but figured "it's for a good reason." The "good reason" or intent, according to the teacher, was to let these kids know what it's "really" like to have a baby at their young ages. What folly! It is ludicrous to think that carrying around an electronically exasperating doll can teach young people anything about the love, security, and constant care real babies require. Nor can it teach them the heart-felt, often inexpressible joy that sweet-smelling, soft-skinned babies bring to a home. And, not surprisingly, no one thinks to bring in the idea that God ordained the structure of marriage and family specifically for the best nurturing of children.

But such a program is not a complete waste of time: it will teach the students one fundamental lesson. While it won't teach them to abstain from sexual activity, it will certainly teach them to "throw it out" should a baby be the result of their fun. This kind of program will do for the abortion industry what recreational dating has done for the divorce courts. Dating has virtually removed any concept of the commitment and covenant marriage requires, and replaced it with numerous, disposable relationships. Sex ed. classes, such as the one above, remove or ignore any reference to the biblical view of childbirth or childrearing.

Ironically, on the same front page featuring the fake baby story was an article on a local real-life tragedy wherein a young, angry father shook his three-month old infant to death. Perhaps this living child had also cried once too often in the middle of the night. This man is accused of murder, as he should be. But his criminal view of the inconvenience of children is being advocated and paid for by the same taxpayers who want to see him punished. Ideas have consequences, and bad ideas have bad consequences.

Logos School has always been and, I pray, always will be boldly affirming the view God has of children: that they are unique creations of a loving Father, and that only from *Him* can we and they learn the true value and purpose of life.

BOY MEETS GIRL

They were obviously a bit impatient, shuffling and yet tense, eager to depart the classroom in one explosive rush. But the teacher insisted they wait, even if it was a bit longer than usual. The last few girls were still gathering their personal items and heading out the door. Then, as the last young lady passed into the hallway, the teacher reminded the boys to "walk, not run" on their way to the lunchroom. They obeyed, but their steps were jerky, like a Ferrari having to drive twenty-five mph on an open stretch of highway. A good and necessary practice of self-control, with some outside encouragement, of course.

For several years before this particular observation, we had begun highlighting the need for upgrading the cultural aspects of our school. One significant form this took was in the area of etiquette. Put in biblical language, this was practicing love in the details. "Details" in this case meant the small opportunities we had every day to show consideration for others. Even more specifically, we were encouraging the children to make distinctions in how they show consideration for the opposite gender. The Bible is clear about these distinctions so we believed we should be also, regardless of our culture's never-say-die crusade to eliminate them.

So, for instance, in every grade, the boys were required to allow the girls to leave the classroom first. In the lunchroom, as they file in, the boys were to stand until the girls were seated. Young men were to hold doors for young women and ladies. (This has had the side-effect of young men frequently holding doors even for older male teachers.) During secondary assemblies, the young men were to watch for ladies standing in the back and assist in getting a chair for them. What were the girls and young ladies supposed to do for their part? How did they show consideration for their male peers? By treating the boys' deference to them with respect, not scorn or mockery. A thankful attitude was pretty much all that was required.

Were we just trying to hark back to the lost age of chivalry in some pathetic, anachronistic manner? After all, our mascot was a knight. Weren't we kicking against the current social goads, or even worse, not preparing the kids for the "real world" out there, where the sexes were really the same?

No, to all the above. For one thing, the age of chivalry was hardly one we'd like to emulate—it was largely adulterous and generally without a biblical foundation. As for the "real world," by whose definition? God made us male and female and until He rewires us, that's what we are.

Our goal in this, as with every other aspect of the education we provided, was to prepare the students to think biblically about all they would face before and after graduation. That included the rather critical, life-changing aspect of being married. To be clear: we were not getting into the realm of marital counseling, child-rearing, or even providing home management courses, per se. But a young man doesn't turn into a gentleman, knowing how to show consideration for a young lady, by merely turning eighteen, or twenty-one, for that matter. He becomes what he has been practicing to be since he was old enough to observe the model of older men. If he has never seen a gentleman in action or been required to act like one at five, twelve, and fifteen, he simply won't burst into one later, at the point when it matters to him. That is, when he meets a young lady to whom he does want to show special consideration. The ugly caterpillar won't become the impressive butterfly just by wishing.

To up the ante, God designed most people for the state of marriage. As Paul tells us, He grants a few folks a special gift of singleness. This means that the vast majority of those sweet little faces we saw coming to kindergarten each morning were heading for either a God-honoring marriage or possibly a series of heart-rending, self-centered relationships. That sounds kind of harsh, put that way, but the facts and figures of the "real world" bear this out.

The only question that we faced as a Christian school then was, in regard to those facts of life, what kind of behavior will we model and enforce for our students? Will we tacitly adopt the world's view and pretend that how boys and girls treat each other at school is of no consequence to marriage later on? Or would we, under the limited, delegated authority of our parents, seek to model and require the kind of countless, small considerations husbands should demonstrate to their wives and wives to their husbands? Which approach was really denying the reality to come in the lives of these students? Which approach encouraged the biblical mandate that young men are to treat young women "as sisters, in all purity and respect?"

There is a lot to how boys and girls are to interact, wherever they are or however old they are. Suffice it to say here, in all matters of the mind and heart of a student, the Scripture and its principles are neither inappropriate nor outdated.

TAX DODGERS?

You'd think our tenth year in business would have been quite a time of celebration. You'd also think we would have figured out most of the basics of running a business. Well, you'd be wrong. It might have been due to the fact that Logos hardly had any money for so long that we didn't seriously consider all the internal controls that small businesses should follow. Such as… it's always important to make sure you're paying payroll taxes… each month.

My first clue that we were a bit too casual on that last item was a registered letter I received from the IRS. Yes, that IRS. They formally and coolly let me know that due to our lack of consistently paying payroll taxes for some months (!), we had racked up a fine of about $20,000 in penalties. I've received a number of unpleasant letters in my career, but this was right up there with the worst.

Obviously I had to alert my board to the crisis promptly. That amount of money at any time isn't chump change, and for Logos back in 1990, it seemed catastrophic. For the first time in my life I offered my employer a letter of resignation. I figured that Logos was holed below the water line, it was my fault, we didn't have any way to pay the fines, and to top it off, what would this do to our reputation, to Christ's name? In short, it wasn't a fun time.

Once again, as they had when we were threatened with a lawsuit years before, the Logos School Board submitted to Christ and acted wisely. They directed me to inform our families of the situation and ask them to join us in a day of fasting and prayer. Classes went on, but each one spent time praying for provision and protection. By the end of the day, gifts had come in to such an extent that we could immediately pay the entire fine! (It wasn't quite the fun-filled event one sees at the end of *It's a Wonderful Life*, but sort of similar. I know I could relate to the emotional turmoil George Bailey went through.)

The board didn't stop there. They held a public meeting soon after and addressed parental questions and concerns straight up. Instead of throwing me under the bus, they owned the mistake and promised to make some bylaw changes, as well as internal controls. They also expanded the number of board members, creating three elected positions.

God had once again clearly carried us through a trial, demonstrating His faithfulness to us as clearly as His giving our fathers water from a rock in the wilderness.

THE JORDANS ARRIVE

Do you ever look back on your life and certain people that entered it and think, "There really should have been some special glowing light and/or blast of trumpets at the moment you met that person indicating *here* is someone very precious!" Well, I have. In reality, of course, that would be extremely weird and awkward for all present. But still...

Instead, those precious people kind of sneak up on you, get into your life and you get into theirs and before long it dawns on you—hey, these people are wonderful!

One such momentous meeting occurred in the summer of 1990. I can still picture it: Len and B.J. Jordan, with their children Mark, Angie, and LennyAnn came by Logos School and I met them in the auditorium. Their story was pretty remarkable. They lived in Elk River, a very small town smack dab in the timbered wilderness of Idaho about fifty miles northeast of Moscow. For quite a few years the small community of mostly Christian families had their children in one old, multi-storied, school building. The entire "district" consisted of about twenty-five students. So, while still a government school, classes were mostly taught by Christian teachers and aided by Christian parents. Len was the primary custodian, which was a full-time, sometimes round-the-clock job due to having to stoke the wood-burning furnace non-stop in the wintertime. (Elk River would get many feet of snow each winter.) To say the Jordans were a strong, God-loving, self-reliant (they shot or trapped what they ate), and close family barely does them justice.

So what brought this frontier family to check out Logos School, fifty miles from their home? The State education authorities had ordained that the Elk River school should close and the students be sent to a larger, certainly more secular, school district. The Jordans weren't going to have any of it. They were now ready and willing to drive about an hour and half each way to continue to provide their children a Christian education. Mark would be a junior, Angie a sophomore, and LennyAnn an eighth grader.

As it happened, we had an opening for a full-time second grade teacher. After some discussion and explanation of our mission and philosophy, I broached the idea of B.J. applying for the position. Initially she was reluctant due to not having completed college. I countered with the obvious fact that, in addition to working as a classroom aide for many years, she had managed to raise three clearly sharp and obedient children. She had three degrees, in my estimation.

Len approved, and so B.J. applied and was interviewed by the Logos board. After she left the meeting, the board discussed hiring her. Larry Lucas nailed what we were all thinking when he said, "There is a woman who is well-loved!" And it was absolutely true; B.J. was a strong woman in mind and body. But she was also very secure under Len's love and care. The vote was an easy, unanimous one and I was delighted to call B.J. to ask her to teach for Logos. Unknown to both of us, her acceptance would lead to a career of more than a quarter of a century teaching in Logos School.

The Jordans decided to move "closer" to Moscow and bought some acreage outside of Deary, about twenty-five miles from Moscow. They also began purchasing, raising, and breeding buffalo for sale. At that time I was still the elementary principal and we had faculty meetings most mornings before school. Every once in a while B.J. would come in late, not due to the distance she had to drive, but because one or more of the buffalo had snuck out of the pen. She had had to convince the immense beast (or beasts) to get back inside. Other times she would mention that she'd had a rough night due to needing to shoot a coyote from their porch. The critter had been getting at the Jordans' chickens or geese. In any case, I got used to the fact that at any given time my meeting might sound like a script for *Little House On the Prairie.*

A few years after the Jordans became part of Logos, LennyAnn, the quietest of the three, made an astounding shot while hunting. I don't believe the Jordans ever bought beef from the store the entire time I knew them. All their meat came from elk and/or deer they shot and butchered each fall. (Len made some amazingly tasty sausages!) All five family members would hunt and they were all good shots. However, this one hunting season LennyAnn had dropped an elk from about 445 yards! For those at home, that translates to hitting the animal from over four football fields away! Tom Spencer, the secondary principal, thought she deserved a medal so we had a special one engraved at the local trophy shop with the details of her shot and presented it to her at a secondary assembly.

Len was a logger and often spent the workweek out in the deep woods of north Idaho. But he also found time to help B.J. with special breakfasts for her second graders on occasion. Part of the second grade's curriculum was the study of Idaho history. What better way to help the kids learn how early trappers, loggers, miners, and hunters in this area lived than to give the kids a breakfast of elk sausage, scrambled farm fresh eggs, fried potatoes, and maybe even some pancakes? The mouth-watering smell would permeate the entire school and draw me out of my office, down to the second grade room where there was always enough food for drop-ins.

The Jordans had our entire family out to their ranch a number of times. My kids loved it—horse-back riding, feeding the buffalo (carefully), and great dinners. OK, they weren't all that crazy to see the shed where Len butchered the elk carcasses.

Sometime later, Len developed throat cancer and lost the use of his vocal chords. He learned how to talk using gulps of air and speaking in a whisper. Rarely did I ever see him without a kerchief around his neck (to protect his breathing port) and a smile on his face. He still managed to not only continue his rugged vocation, but he and B.J. built their dream home, made entirely of hand-picked, huge logs. It was essentially a magnificent home/hunting lodge, with a lovely wrap-around porch, stone fireplaces, and even a small waterfall over rocks into their bathtub! Stuffed animals served as accents around the vast, vaulted-ceiling living room. Naturally an immense buffalo head looked down from high above the fireplace. It fit their family to a T.

Then Len was struck with a fast-growing brain tumor. There was nothing the doctors could do for him. After just several bittersweet months spending precious time with his family and friends, Len went to his Lord on Christmas Eve, 2010. B.J. called me that day to let me know:

"Len's gone, Tom." She paused…"He told me he didn't want to go on Christmas, for our sakes. The Lord honored his desire."

A great crowd filled the Logos gym for Len's memorial service. Much like Theodore Roosevelt, Len had friends from every walk of life. Many spoke of his love for being out in the creation: hunting, gold-panning, fishing, but mostly just taking in the Creator's work all around him. One of my earliest memories of Len was when we were having dinner at their house shortly after we had hired B.J.. After we ate, Len and I were sitting in their living room. Len began to tell me about his seeing and hearing a bull elk one frosty morning out in the mountains. To this day I wish I had recorded it.

That was Len Jordan. I look forward to seeing him again, maybe he'll tell me that story again.

MY FAVORITE LATIN TEACHER

Dorothy Sayers, along with her brilliant idea of matching the methods of the Trivium with children's growth patterns, strongly advocated the teaching of Latin. We wanted the whole "classical" experience, so we figured that someone needed to teach Latin. Doug's college background in classical studies, plus his willingness to do it, made him the prime candidate. He brushed up on the ancient language and, as soon as we had third graders (by our second year), he popped in and had them *amo*-ing and *amas*-ing to beat the band.

Church responsibilities soon encroached on Doug's time and so we were blessed to find a single young lady named Martha Sebring who took up the banner. She, like Doug, had virtually no curriculum or materials to go by, so over the course of her years with us, she whacked out some worthy objectives. However, just as she was hitting her stride, in my opinion, Jim Wilson interfered. As much as I admired Jim, his match-making desires and activities came to be a thorn in my side. He seemed to regard our frequent hires of single gals as some sort of challenge.

It was always hard to argue with Jim, since God seemed to be on his side, so to speak. Such was the case with Martha. Jim and Bessie had a single nephew living in the south. A letter writing campaign began through some nefarious (again, in my opinion) means, and, lo, a match was the outcome. In her last year with us, Martha was kind enough to put her curriculum objectives in a neat and understandable form. At the same time, we began the search once again for a Latin teacher.

My Julie had always had a strong interest in foreign languages (I attribute it to her being both Norwegian and Swedish—languages that no one can honestly understand). The timing of the teacher transition was quite nifty actually: our youngest, Kathryn, was going to be in preschool the year after Martha left. So while Martha was wrapping up, Julie used that year to study Latin in a class Doug taught. The following year, 1991, when Kathryn went into our half-day preschool, Julie began her career teaching Latin.

I was still the elementary principal at the time, so not only did Julie and I share a workplace, I was her immediate supervisor. I even regularly evaluated her and was coldly objective and professional at all times. Since she was a natural and very capable teacher, I didn't actually have to be too cold.

Not long after Martha left us, she took the trouble to put her curriculum into actual Latin textbooks that she wrote. These were published by Canon Press and were an immediate hit with our younger, sister classical Christian schools. They became the basis for other published curricula in years to come. Eventually Julie was contracted with Canon to star in videos teaching Martha's Latin texts. Homeschoolers snapped these up with gratitude. So popular were these videos, that Julie became known as the Latin Lady to hundreds, possibly thousands, of children around the nation. How do I know that? Simply by being with Julie when we would travel to various places around the nation. Quite a few times we would be in some place, minding our business, when an excited woman would come up to us, exclaiming:

"Aren't you Julie Garfield, the Latin Lady?"

"Yes, I'm Julie," she would say, not necessarily encouraging the other tag.

"You're my Billy's Latin teacher! Billy, come here! Look! It's your Latin teacher from the videos!" And some small lad would come up and gaze at Julie in dawning recognition.

This even happened a couple times on the streets of our own town, Moscow. Julie was always kind and gracious and would introduce me to the starstruck parent and child. Then I would turn around so Julie could use my back for signing autographs. (OK, that's a lie. But I was often needed to keep the photographers at a respectful distance.)

Julie would be our only elementary Latin teacher for twenty-three years before we had the numbers of students to form two elementary classes from third through sixth grades, the grammar years. She eventually wrote her own series, *Logos Latin,* with new videos to match.

Was it ever a conflict of interest or a problem for us to share the same working environment? I can honestly say I don't believe it ever was; Julie, on the other hand, frequently threatened to report me for sexual harassment in the workplace. She never followed through, though.

MR. G. LOOK-ALIKE DAY

Our third kindergarten teacher was a gregarious and fun-loving woman named Linda Wagner. She was a fantastic teacher for the littles! I have used her as an example in many workshops when discussing how to teach to the frame of the students. I noted early on in my formal observations of her that Linda knew how to get back the attention of these easily distracted small people. If, as often could happen, they were one-upping each other with stories of cats, grandmothers, band-aids, etc., when they really needed to get back to phonics or math, Linda had a sure-fire technique. She would say in a very quiet, but clear voice: "And you know what…?" That never failed to not only quiet them, but get them all focused back on her. They all wanted to know the "what." From there she could and did get them right where she wanted to go: "Today we're going to find out what sound 'P' makes!" It never failed.

Linda not only was a very competent teacher, she was a natural encourager, sort of a female Barnabas, if you will. She often asked about my welfare and sought to cheer me up if she sensed that I wasn't as perky as I should be. That all needs to be understood as background for the kind of special day she planned apart from my knowledge, but with the obvious complicit help of the other faculty and the parents.

The first I knew that this one day was going to be different was when I walked in the school door and noted that one of the first students I met had a mustache. Now that would be odd on any day with any student at Logos, but this mustache was on a girl of about eight. Then as I saw other students wandering about, it was quickly apparent that mustaches were above many upper lips. Even my own children arrived at school looking like miniature versions of their father.

There was to be an assembly that morning and I didn't need a memo to realize that this wasn't going to be the assembly I had planned. As the children streamed in, Linda came up, also sporting a mustache.

"This is the 'Mr. Garfield Look-Alike Day!'" she informed me. Then it all started making sense, in a Twilight Zone sort-of-way. The students and even some teachers, male and female, were sporting mustaches, ties, jackets, caps; some had their hair pulled back to mimic my, um, "high forehead." Linda took over the microphone, asserting control over the proceedings unmistakably.

"And now we have some voices from your past. Can you recognize them?" Now one of the reasons I've never liked surprises very much is that I'm lousy at knowing what to do in the "moment." This was par for the course. Voices did come over the PA and it didn't take me long to recognize my parents' speaking. I assumed it was a tape, since they lived in Portland and were both working at the Conservative Baptist Seminary. This was a weekday, hence my assumption that they were dutifully at work. I should have known better; after a few moments my dad and mom walked into the auditorium with a mic in hand.

Obviously I was thrilled to see them. That is, until they began a slide-show of photos from my past, childhood included. The students were delighted, laughing with glee, especially when my folks got to my teen years, when I sported long hair and clothing of the 70s. Oh joy.

But Linda had also arranged a generous cash gift from the parents which paid for a lovely meal out at a restaurant with my family later that day. That eased the awkwardness a great degree.

All in all, it was one of the nicest events I'd had at Logos. And to make it even better, it was never made into a *Tradition*!

I CORINTHIANS 13 IN TRV (TEACHERS' REVISED VERSION... WITH APOLOGIES TO BROTHER PAUL)

1 If I speak with the tongues of Latin, Greek, and all other Romance languages, but do not have love for my students, I have become as the sounding of the class buzzer or recess bell.

2 And if I have the gift of knowing a student's chance of passing my class just by looking at him, and know how to explain all mysteries, even the purpose and working of the Electoral College, and all knowledge, without relying on my teacher's editions, and if I have all faith to remove the entire Department of Education into the sea, but do not have love for my students, I am nothing.

3 And if I give all my tape, chalk, and pens from my desk to help equip poor students and poor teachers, and if I deliver my body to frigid temperatures and high winds at recess duty, but do not have love for these precious students, all that sacrifice profits me nothing.

4 Love for my students is patient, enduring all sorts of strange behaviors; it is kind, not delivering an incredibly applicable, but nevertheless, snide comment when tempted; love is not jealous of my "private, personal" time; love for my students means I model humility to them, even though I do know more than they do, and I encourage them to be open to correction, too, for love is not arrogant.

5 Love for my students shows itself in my classroom decorum, it means I seek no glory for myself, it is not easily provoked, even by the umpteenth time that little guy has done that; it does not make a big deal out of what could be interpreted as a personal offense;

6 It does not rejoice in teaching about pain and suffering, even if the "bad guys" are the ones on the receiving end; it does rejoice in teaching about God's truth and real justice toward all.

7 Love for my students draws on God's grace to bear countless antagonisms, it believes the best is possible from any student, and does not doubt a student's word without good reason each time; it hopes that each student will succeed and endures many set-backs to that hope, without giving up on the student.

8 This love never fails, by God's grace alone, in providing the strength and stamina I need to show these students love; but if I rely on my top-notch, *Seven Laws* teaching ability or immense

knowledge of the subject, these will be done away with and probably forgotten by the students; if I rely on my quick wit and large vocabulary, they will cease with every dumb cold or sore throat with which I may be afflicted; if I rely on even my knowledge of how to integrate the material, even this will not last as long as love.

9 For all that we may know as teachers, we still know only part of God's revelation, and even in our best teaching times, we are teaching poorly and partially compared to the Master Teacher;

10 But when all truth and real knowledge in Christ is revealed in the Eternal School, our "best" teaching will be done away with.

11 I need to remember that I, too, was once a child like those looking up to me now. I, too, perceived life as a child, seeing my teachers as demigods; I spoke, acted, and, yea verily, even thought like these students; I grew to adulthood, these students, even the boys, will too. I did away with the thoughts, actions, and speech of a child, through the hard work and loving training of my teachers; these students, too, will one day lay aside these childish ways.

12 For the time being my students will see, as in a hazy picture, the Master Teacher teaching through me, but, Lord willing, when they come under His eternal, perfect education, they will see Him face to face; now I teach from my limited understanding, but then I will be able to learn much more and know, as I am now known by my Teacher.

13 But for this time the best characteristics of my teaching should be: my faith in my Lord and His Word; my hope in my students—expecting the very best from them, and my love for my students—as an obvious channel for God's love; these three characteristics, but the greatest of these is love.

CHAPTER V

DOUG WROTE A BOOK

By 1991 Logos School was turning ten years old and, like many children that age, we had found out a few things about life, but we still had a lot to learn! For instance, the philosophical bedrock we claimed—classical education—was still a little shaky. Why do I say that? Because many of our (still) weekly board meetings often had times when we debated among ourselves as to what we actually meant by "classical."

It seemed there were essentially two possible views we could adopt and pursue. One view, the one I had been trying to build our academic program upon, was a literal adoption of Dorothy Sayer's recommendations in her article, *The Lost Tools of Learning*. This approach relied heavily on using teaching methods that matched the three stages of children's growth. Sayers called these three stages: Poll Parrot, Pert and Poetic. She believed that the characteristics children exhibited in each of these stages would nicely match the kind of teaching used in teaching the "Trivium" used for centuries in the western world. The Trivium included Grammar, Logic (Dialectic), and Rhetoric. There's much more to this approach, of course, but the bottom line is that this view of classical education relies primarily on teaching methods that best match the frame of the student.

The other view of classical education we considered was still an adoption of the Trivium, but would put more emphasis on the actual material (curriculum) being taught. For example, the widely accepted Great Books of the Western World would be a significant element to this approach to classical education. In other words, the curriculum, i.e., the content, taught would be the hallmark of our classical education.

So the debates we had for about ten years were a back-and-forth of which view should be the one that would make Logos School's education distinctive. As noted above, I had been working with the teachers and building our curriculum with the idea that Sayer's approach was the one we had embraced: lock, stock, and barrel. So, to be honest, I found these times of debating rather distressing and not a little unsettling. Each time I wondered if the staff and I would have to go back to the drawing board, metaphorically speaking, and re-do much of what we had put in place.

I often came home from these board meetings with my stomach churning and thinking, "How are we ever going to move forward if we don't land on one view or the other?"

Well, in the same year we turned ten, Doug Wilson wrote a book that would not only settle our debates forever, but would kind of be the educational equivalent of the "shot heard round the world." That might sound like a bit of hyperbole, and perhaps it was, but that book would change many thousands of lives, including lives of people thousands of miles away from Moscow, Idaho.

Doug didn't write the book with the intention of settling our debate, and I'm sure he never dreamed it would have the national and international effect it eventually did. He wrote it because he had been asked by Marvin Olasky, who worked with Crossway Books Publishers, to write a book on education. The book would be the next volume in the Turning Point series which was made up of Christian books on cultural topics such as economics, the arts, and politics. Education was to be the next topic in the series.

Doug decided to use Logos School for his book as an example of one way to do Christian education. He appropriately entitled it *Recovering the Lost Tools of Learning*. It was essentially a philosophical and practical discussion of how Logos School had, since its inception, tried to flesh-out the model of education presented by Dorothy Sayers in *The Lost Tools of Learning*. In addition to some of our school policies and guidelines, he gave practical examples of the kind of curriculum objectives we used in the grammar (Poll Parrot) level with our youngest students. He described the way we tried to use debate, argumentation, and logic in every class at the logic (Pert) level. Our requirements for written and publicly defended theses done by our oldest students (Poetic level) were also part of Doug's description of classical, Christian education at Logos School.

However, the book was not meant to be simply a long testimony to what we had done at Logos. Rather Doug clearly laid out the biblical and pragmatic reasons for Christians to have their children in full-time Christian education. And that education should have a well-reasoned, philosophic basis that went beyond what most Christian school textbook publishers provided. Classical education, as a method, had proven itself successful for centuries, so why not "plunder the Egyptians," or in this case, plunder the Greeks, Romans, and Medievals, and pair a proven method with the content and purpose found in the infallible Word of God? Classical education would become the delivery system for helping the students "take every thought captive to Christ."

Upon its publication, in modern parlance, the book went viral! Being part of an established series, it was received by an immediate large readership. Many of these readers, as it turned out, not only had children, but had apparently been actively searching for a rigorous, thoroughly Christian education for their progeny. In short the book struck an empathetic nerve in numerous homes across the nation. Calls and letters starting pouring in to the Wilson's home, Doug's office, and to our school office. Typical questions were:

"How can we do what you're doing?"

"What materials do you have that we can get copies of?"

"Can you help us start a school like Logos in our town?"

"How do you get other parents excited about classical education?"

"Can you come out and help us get started?"

"Can you help us?"

"Do you have a radiator for a '66 Impala?" (OK. That wasn't one. Just checking to see if you were paying attention to the part about where we got our phone number.)

This was all very overwhelming to us! I mean, all these people were looking to us for help and I was keenly aware of how little we really had to offer. We were still very young ourselves and these people were treating us like we were some sort of experts in Christian education!

The saddest and most unexpected part of the phone calls, at least the ones I fielded, were the many, many tales of how disappointed parents were with their local Christian schools. I had always assumed that, in general, Christian schools across the nation were doing an adequate job and that we were just another, different flavor among the variety of Christian ed ice cream options. Instead, call after call revealed that sincerely searching parents had found their Christian school not up to the task of providing a thoroughly Christian education. At first I thought I might be just getting the malcontents whom no school could ever please. And maybe some of them were, but since I ended up meeting a fair representation of those searching parents in years to come, I know that crankiness was certainly not the issue in most cases.

The volume of interest in "this classical thing" didn't wane; if anything it gained momentum over the next couple of years. Doug came up with the idea of holding a conference on classical, Christian ed for folks that had the motivation, time, and sense of direction to come out to Moscow.

The conference was put together for the summer of 1993, having as its theme "Repairing the Ruins," with loads of preparatory work done by Doug and Nancy Wilson, as well as Chris LaMoreaux and many others. It was announced through *Credenda Agenda* (another locally produced Christian newsletter) since we had no real internet capability yet, and people from around the nation signed up. The conference was held at Logos School over three days. Over seventy delegates from around the United States came for seminars and workshops. Representatives came from schools and homeschools as far away as Texas, New York, Wisconsin, Minnesota, and Ohio. California, Washington, and southern Idaho were also represented. Seminars included topics addressing: "What is a Christian Worldview?"; "Biblical Discipline in the Christian School"; "What is Classical Education?"; "Assessing Student Progress and Learning"; as well as seminars in teaching Bible, Latin, Rhetoric, and Formal Logic in a Christian school. Seminar and workshop leaders were all staff members of Logos School—secondary teachers and school administrators: Doug Wilson, Tom Spencer, Wes Callihan, Jim Nance, Chris Schlect, and me.

Among the delegates present were Marlin and Laurie Detweiler who came all the way from Orlando, Florida. It quickly became apparent that they were there to learn as much as they could, as fast as they could. While Marlin sat in on the talks, Laurie spent a great deal of time sitting on my office floor, pouring over the catalogs I had and asking me a torrent of questions. It was their intention, they let me know, to start a classical, Christian school in their area. They wanted to open in September and, this being June, they figured rightly that daylight was burning!

Marlin was also instrumental in helping to officially form the Association of Classical Christian Schools (ACCS). He and Doug had had some previous correspondence, so it was appropriate that when the "founding committee" gathered one evening of the conference in the Logos staff room, those present consisted of Doug, Marlin, Tom Spencer, and me. We sat and discussed the primary mission of ACCS (no surprise—"the promotion of classical, Christian education"), and whacked out some initial bylaws, too. I remember it all struck me as somewhat similar to the informal, yet weighty feeling I had when Logos was nearly ready to open twelve years earlier.

I've been on a high dive only once in my life and it took the United States Navy to put me there at the tender age of eighteen. All I had to do was jump, not dive, into a pool about ten stories below (ok, maybe twenty feet, but still). Yeah, it was that kind of feeling, somehow knowing that with one small step, in one short moment, life would change forever.

The reviews of the conference were very encouraging. One person took the time to tell us:

"Thank you all so very much for the hard work and generous spirit that went into making such a rich, meaningful [conference] available to us at such a modest price. My husband strongly encouraged me to go... and I admit I was very hesitant. But now I am so thankful for the affirmation of our vision of what education can be, for the challenge to press on in biblical thinking, and for the great quantity and quality of practical assistance."

Two more ACCS conferences were held in Moscow in 1994 and 1995, with the last one attracting about 140 folks, so we held it at the local Best Western Hotel. It was during that conference that we were convinced by many kind-hearted folks to "take this on the road." But more on that later.

FIRST ACCREDITATION

As I earlier testified, the ACSI had offered much help to us in our first years. We had become members very quickly and appreciated all their newsletters, conferences, and spelling and speech meet programs. They also offered their members the opportunity to become accredited by ACSI, an accreditation which was recognized even by some secular entities, among them foundations that may offer financial grants.

However, more important than the possibility of receiving some extra funding was the biblical principle accreditation supported. Paul says that those who measure themselves by themselves are foolish. Telling our school parents that we were a good school was true enough, but we desired an "outside" assessment and thought our parents would also appreciate that, too.

ACSI's accreditation process wasn't a cakewalk. We had much to do to get ready for a six-person team to arrive on campus to examine our materials and observe all we did. After applying for and receiving the initial Candidate Status, we put together a Self-Study, the most important element of this process. We did all that in the fall of 1993. Then in early May, a team of Christian administrators from schools across the northwest came and spent three days carefully examining our school to see if it met the standards for ACSI accreditation.

Obviously we were all a bit on edge, even the students. The team did a very thorough job of looking through our school's files, procedures, and programs. I certainly didn't have any idea at the time that all this experience would be helpful in the future when ACCS would seek to build its own accreditation program. However, I did note some puzzling aspects to the team's scrutiny. At one point a team member was standing with me observing our lunch time. After discovering that we neither had a kitchen that could provide daily hot lunches for the students, nor had the desire to ever do so, still asked me:

"Have you ever looked into seeing if the local school district would provide your students with lunches?"

"No. As I told you, we have no desire to get into providing lunches on a regular basis," I replied.

"Well, if you don't want to use the district, you know, perhaps the local hospital might work with you."

Apparently I wasn't needed for this conversation.

Later in the team's report, among their recommendations was, you guessed it, the idea that we check into providing students daily lunches, perhaps with the help of the district or local hospital! Otherwise the report and subsequent accreditation approval were very encouraging and positive. At the same time, I couldn't help but notice that very little was said about our actual academic program, e.g., our curriculum choices or teaching methodologies. That wasn't entirely surprising; it hadn't been long after they arrived that the team had called me in to the library where they had their base of operations. They were understandably curious about our classical approach. I had done my best to give them a crash course in what we were attempting. They weren't dull-witted; they had just never come across a horse of our color.

Several years later that disconnect would widen and we found it best to allow our accreditation to lapse without renewal. Nevertheless, we are indebted to ACSI for all their help when we needed it most.

A LANDMARK GRADUATION

On Saturday night, May 21, 1994 in the University of Idaho auditorium, Logos High School held its sixth commencement ceremony. In addition to the unique aspect of this senior class being comprised of nine lovely, young ladies, this class also had the distinction of containing a number of girls who had been at Logos for ten years or more. But what made this a real landmark moment was that two of Logos School's first kindergarten class members: Jessica Lucas and Bekah Wilson, were graduating. Bekah was the daughter of Doug and Nancy Wilson and was very much the reason Logos School was formed.

As Bekah crossed the stage to receive her diploma I wasn't thinking of the profound changes Logos had gone through in thirteen years; I was picturing the little two-year-old who had named her goldfish "Tom and Julie," which warmed our hearts then and now. The Christian band, "Mountain Angel," in which Doug and I were two of the four members, met at the Wilsons' home for weekly Bible studies before practices. One night Julie and I forgot to say good-night to Bekah before we left. Nancy called us later so we could correct that faux pas.

But we wanted to make amends, so we invited Bekah over for dinner. Doug and Nancy approved. A few nights later, on a snowy evening, I walked the few blocks over to their house to escort Bekah to our home. Holding her hand, I walked the little girl back to our apartment where Julie fixed hot dogs. After dinner we showed her our Christmas tree ornaments. Then I walked Bekah back home, while she chatted virtually non-stop.

That was the memory on my mind the evening of the 1994 commencement, but it was certainly not one I was going to share during the ceremony!

SUMMER BREEZE

"That's not a barbecue, that's just grillin'!" Such was the opinion of not one, but all the Texans present at the meal. They weren't ungrateful for the burgers, mind you, they just wanted to make sure we used the correct definition. After all, these folks were classical educators, so correct definitions and terminology mattered to them.

This was just one cultural distinction among many that we, the Logos contingent of teachers, came to enjoy and understand by getting to know our peers from around the nation. This particular meal was under a pleasant, clear July twilight, where we were gathered in the courtyard of the local Best Western, feasting on a buffet that featured grilled (touted as "barbecued") hamburgers. This would be our last evening together after four full days of teacher training, sponsored by Logos School.

The hundred and sixty or so people who had come to Moscow, Idaho, of all places, from all points of the compass, had one more morning of workshops before they would disperse and wend their various ways home. They would eventually arrive in Virginia, California, North Carolina, Georgia, Maryland, Minnesota, Montana, Washington, parts of Canada, Florida, and, of course, Texas, to name a few locations.

What compelled busy Christian teachers and administrators to spend lots of money, time, and travel efforts to come this far for this particular training? The simple answer is to learn more about teaching classically. Good as the two-and-a-half-day conferences we had started doing in 1993 and 1994, they weren't meeting the demand for practical training in this teaching methodology. The annual conferences of ACCS had helped hundreds of folks get the vision for this type of education, but since most attendees were wanting to start actual schools, they wanted to know how it would "look" in teaching history to second graders, for instance.

However, there just wasn't time or enough resources during the conferences to meet this need. So, in July of 1995, Logos School offered its first week-long summer teacher training to classical, Christian educators. (We picked mid-July because that's when Moscow's summer is at its best!)

The idea was to invite attendees to come to an actual classical, Christian school and within its classrooms hear about and discuss teaching methods for a specific age-group and/or discipline. Three tracks were offered: Grammar, Logic and Rhetoric, and Administrative. There would be a general session, or plenary, first thing each morning during which the attendees would sing, and then hear a presentation on a broad issue related to classical, Christian education. The rest of each day would be filled with about four to five workshops sessions (usually offering three to four workshops each) in each track. The administrative track would have one workshop per session. As you might guess, the plenaries and the workshops were conducted by Logos staff members and Doug Wilson.

But it wasn't all just workshops and lectures. As time went by, other delightful traditions and events began to be a part of the week. A few classical materials vendors, including Logos, offered their wares in our auditorium. Each morning delicious breakfasts were offered to attendees by the coming senior class, as a fundraiser. Lunches, too, were offered frequently by one or more of the Logos High School classes. Evening events took shape in the form of two group dinners (one a sit-down buffet and the other a picnic in the park), concerts, summer plays, hikes, star gazing, and even trips to a buffalo ranch! Sprinkled throughout all these packed days were many opportunities for folks to just visit with other attendees or have a quiet chat with one of the Logos teachers.

Logos staff and parents would frequently have some of the attendees over for dinner or even stay the week in their home. New friendships sprang up and, since many schools began sending their new teachers as a part of their school's orientation, we saw some of the same veteran teachers and administrators return each year. Networking for folks seeking and offering teaching positions was a helpful part of the week, too.

We certainly did not set out, when Logos first began, to some day offer a week of training for other schools. This was something God in His wisdom brought to us and we sought to respond in obedience and faithfulness. Eventually other schools and entities also began to offer good training. That is a healthy indicator of good things happening, again by God's blessing.

IT'S NOT ROCKET SCIENCE

"But what will you do for science labs? The kids need all that hands-on practice, you know, experiments and stuff, to get into any university!"

That was one of the top five arguments we heard when we told folks we were serious about offering high school grades at Logos. Considering we were back in the church basement at the time this goal was first set, it was somewhat understandable to question our scientific resources. Yet, even while there, we made do with what we had. The church allowed us to use the kitchen off the fellowship hall for a variety of reasons. So our various science teachers (an admittedly generous title) really did 'kitchen sink' experiments. I recall one in particular: our oldest student, Jim, was receiving a tutorial on the pressure produced by a certain chemical reaction in a large, glass flask. The teacher had Jim test the pressure produced by covering the top of the flask with his hand as firmly as he could. I happened to enter the other end of the fellowship hall at exactly the same moment that the flask exploded. Glass shards landed at my feet. Jim and the teacher were frozen in their tracks; Jim still held the top of the flask in his hand.

This was another instance of angels watching out for us at Logos. No one was hurt. But we all concluded that there must be better pressure-testing experiments.

When we moved to the roller rink, we designated one of larger rooms as the science classroom/lab for the older students. We even piped in natural gas and water for labs. Well, two gas outlets and one sink. But it was a start. Now that we had "real" science classes, it seemed a natural progression to require individual or team science projects and then science fairs to judge and show off those projects. Many of our students not only benefited from these projects and fairs, but they also enjoyed doing them. But in the Garfield home, Julie and I privately referred to these events as "special torture!"

Perhaps it was because we were both humanities majors without a hard science bone in our bodies. Therefore, as Mendel would attest, our genes were unlikely to produce a child with a strong scientific bent. And we didn't. We did our best to put on happy faces when it came time for our kids to select a "science project." But our kids, while not engineers, probably sensed our fear and doubts. So each one of our four children went through the Purgatory of coming up with a viable hypothesis and then the process to test it, observe it, and finally come up with a conclusion about their hypothesis. Or something like that.

What's wrong with all that, one might ask? Sounds like a great way to introduce kids to the scientific method, doesn't it? Sure. Well, here are some actual hypotheses from the Garfield progeny which were put to the test:

1. *Will plants actually grow in the dark, as long as you water them?* (No, of course not!)
2. *How long does it take bread to mold, under different conditions?* (Who cares?! It will get thrown out as soon as it does!)

3. *How fast do marbles travel when going down a series of plastic tunnels?* (OK, that probably wasn't the hypothesis, but it's what I remember about it. And it was the cleanest project our kids did. Read on...)

4. *How disgusting is it to get up early, in the dark, to drive two junior high girls out to, of all places, the local sewage treatment plant and take water samples?!!* (That wasn't the hypothesis, either, but it should have been. The girls, one of them mine, could have pretended they had another reason for making these trips, for days on end, and actually be measuring my increasing levels of repulsion. They would have certainly won a blue ribbon in the science fair.)

Over time, and under the wise instruction of Mr. Wes Struble, our long-term, amazing science teacher, the science projects became reasonable and worthwhile. The fairs quietly disappeared—I don't recall anyone raising an objection. I know in our home, though it was too late for my kids, we acknowledged the end of the fairs by breaking out the champagne and moldy bread.

The elementary science program, while not needing the same level of sophisticated equipment as the secondary grades (i.e., the amazing cast-offs Wes could get from contacts he had at the local universities), it still needed a thorough examination. As I stated earlier, we had purchased, lock-stock-and-barrel, a popular Christian publishers' materials to use in our first years. But the longer we practiced the classical approach to teaching, the less we liked various curricular materials. Case in point: It appeared that the "Christian" approach to elementary science was to arbitrarily stick a Bible verse on a worksheet that otherwise was fairly similar to what you might find in a public school.

Other than coming from a creationist standpoint, our initial elementary science materials didn't have much to commend themselves.

Our first major permutation occurred when we decided to tackle this area and wrestle it to the ground. One of our school moms, who was a brilliant scientist and math person herself, offered to lend a hand in coming up with a revised program. With her assistance, we took a hard look at not only the Christian materials we were using, but elementary science materials published by secular companies, too. A glaring pattern emerged, one we felt displayed an amazing oversight by all the publishers.

To a publisher, Christian or secular, out of the four major fields of scientific study: Earth Science, Physical Science, Biology, and Chemistry, the elementary programs largely addressed only two: Earth Science and Biology. The laws of physics and the elements of chemistry were almost entirely ignored!

"Ah hah!" we all said at Logos. "We will design an elementary science program that balances studies of all *four* fields! We will even design really cool experiments, put together classroom kits of neat objects, and construct colorful charts of each area!" And we did all that. To illustrate, for example, that for every force exerted there is an equal and opposite force (or something like that), we designed an experiment wherein a student with a fire extinguisher would sit in a red wagon (the wagon's color is actually not important). Then when he triggered the extinguisher, the force of the CO_2 spray in one direction would propel the wagon in the opposite direction! At least that was the theory.

We attempted these types of physics experiments in the tiled auditorium. They rarely worked out as neatly as we hoped. The wagon experiment only worked well if the kid was rather small (something to do with weight and friction, I suppose). The problem there, you might anticipate. That's right; small kids and fire extinguishers aren't a real good mix. The kids weren't strong enough to hold it steady and, well, lots of things got sprayed and perhaps the wagon might move a bit, too.

Some experiments did work, such as some of the nifty chemical reactions. However, what the elementary teachers discovered (doing their own scientific study of the children) was that even with the colorful graphic charts and experiments with fascinating items, the kids weren't grasping the necessary *concepts*. They tended to just remember *what* they saw and did, versus *why* things happened, i.e., the 'laws' behind the experiments. Also, they could memorize chemical elements and even some compounds, but here, too, the *concepts* related to combining elements didn't register.

What finally registered with us was that we were forgetting all that Sayers had been saying about kids and concepts in "The Lost Tools of Learning." We could almost hear her upbraid us with her proper Oxford English accent:

"I say, you thick Yanks! I mean, really! What was the point of my rather keen speech if not to help you understand that you need to study the frames of these poor little tykes. You might recall, if it's not too much trouble, that I put forth the idea of having the children pursue collections and categorizing the various flora and fauna they see regularly. Surely such a locale as remote and uncivilized as northern Idaho must absolutely be overrun with every type of tree, bush, and wild creature! Now, do try to get it right this time!"

Well, she didn't have to take that tone with us, but we got the point. We did go back and study the suggestions she had made. And, what do you know, it was like she knew that by and large, chemistry and physics are more properly taught at the logic and rhetoric levels of instruction.

So we re-tooled once more. Out went the posters and kits, in came more fundamental curriculum objectives that included identifying the local birds and trees, as well as the geography we find all around us in the Palouse. In doing our research we discovered that in the "old days" students didn't study "science," they studied Natural History, which included the very things we were pursuing. I won't take the time or space here to include all that we put into our third version of elementary science; suffice it to say it has proven to be a grand success! One delightful example was seen in our kindergarten classes. The teacher at that time was given a large set of beanie-baby toy birds that, when you squeezed them, made the correct bird call. The children had been charmed and couldn't wait to learn more about "their" birds! Once again we confirmed that many times the old ways are the best ways.

In all our work with revising science, above everything else we wanted to foster the natural wonder and curiosity children have about God's world. What a delight to affirm with them that "this is my Father's world, and to my listening ears all nature sings and 'round me rings the music of the spheres!"

THE DEVELOPMENT OFFICE

Mr. Allen Cumings had introduced us to the idea of actually marketing Logos to the public through an attractive and informative newsletter. His consulting visit in our early years at the church was invaluable. Now that we were in our own place, we needed to take marketing to the next level: we needed someone to actually do it!

In our first years I was the primary guy to promote the school. In addition to writing the newsletters weekly (!), I knew we needed to get the news about Logos and enrollment opportunities out to the local churches. After all, it was from these churches that most of our families would come. So each spring I would contact the churches I knew had students already attending Logos and asked if I could make some kind of presentation about the school. For the most part, possibly out of curiosity, the churches were kind enough to let me come. Sometimes I even got to do a short bit in the morning worship service! Many times I used a slide projector (early version of power point) and showed slides of our campus and the kids enjoying the learning process at Logos.

But with over 130 students and our own building after 1987, I asked the board if we could hire a development person, even half-time. They approved and our first eager Logos School promoter was a lovely lady named Barbara Fountain. Her daughter was one of two girls in our junior class at the time, graduating in 1990. Barbara hit the ground running with ideas such as a Grandparents' Day and attractive brochures. She even put up with an "office" that was really just a desk in the short hallway from the auditorium to the utilities room.

Barbara was followed by another school mom, Trish Miller, whose family would become long-time friends with ours. At the time they lived just down the street from us so their kids and ours played frequently. Trish encouraged local businesses to become Logos Boosters and even get a printed display should they sign up. She also recognized that getting our mortgage paid off as soon as possible would be a good thing. So she began a campaign with the catchy slogan: "Debt Free in '93!" Sadly, not many folks were excited about giving toward a mortgage payment, but it was a positive effort in the right direction.

Trish made her greatest and longest lasting contribution to Logos not through marketing the school, but through marketing our library. It was she who had the vision for building a viable library out of an empty, dark room we had allocated for that purpose. We were out of remodeling funds by the time we made our move into the Baker Street home, so Trish came up with another means to fund a library—she came up with the annual Book Drive! This was a fun, competitive program among the classes that matched pages read with pledges. All the funds raised went into buying bookcases (rather important for housing books), as well as buying great children's literature. She also encouraged folks to donate old, gently used hardbacks to Logos. Over the years Trish managed to completely line the walls with lovely, tall wooden shelves displaying thousands of books for all ages of students. Carpeting and oak tables and chairs turned the once empty room into what I liked to call our school's "living room."

After Trish left development work, we finally bit the bullet and decided to hire a full-time development officer. This time our hire was a guy with a varied job background: Ed Van Nuland. Ed was a new dad to Logos. He had gotten my attention when, serving on one of our first auction committees, he stood up in a parent meeting and gave a great impromptu speech. He had been a radio personality as well as a local businessman so he knew many community folks already. This made it rather easy for him to hit the streets and solicit various kinds of support for Logos.

Ed would be our Development Officer for eighteen years, 1992–2010. Over that time he would actively raise several million dollars for Logos (he would know the precise figure). We became good friends and weathered many challenges together. Ed was always upbeat, but also very honest. His personality compelled people to like him so it wasn't all that surprising that he could convince many types of people to give to Logos. He believed in our mission passionately and never came across as a "salesman." Many times after our weekly meetings we would pray specifically for the needs of our donors, as well as school families. It was Ed who taught me that development was far more about relationships than about fundraising.

For many years Ed had the herculean task of pulling together our annual, grand auctions. This would take a minimum of six months of active planning and work. He would always form an ad hoc committee to help him, but there were times when a few of those folks let him down and he had to pick up the slack. The auctions were a delightful event and had a different theme each year. The students who helped with set-up and presenting the items for sale that evening had a blast! That's notable for a few reasons, not the least of which is that it would be those students who would become young parents in years to come. They would recall the excitement of our auctions and help bring them back when their children began attending Logos.

"Bring back?" one might ask. Yes, we stopped doing them after one particularly discouraging event. It should have been a grand slam of a night! The decor was beyond amazing: a French village surrounding the dining tables. A record number of fun items had been procured and even the meal was tasty. To top it off, though we hadn't planned this aspect, Idaho's Governor showed up and we auctioned off his tie. (There had been a Lincoln Day Dinner for the Republicans at the nearby Best Western. A politically active school dad brought the governor, the lieutenant governor, and one of our state senators over for the ending of our auction.)

Nevertheless, as the auctioneer later told us, the guests seemed to be sitting on their hands. When the dust cleared, our net revenue barely cleared our costs. Very discouraged, I told Ed that we weren't going to do this again for quite a while. He agreed and we switched to annual fundraising dinners, with some student and/or staff entertainment. It would take our next Development Officer, and the alum parents, to jump back into the pool.

NOW FOR SPORTS NEWS

During the '80s we had attempted to field various sports for the handful of secondary students at Logos. At one point we even had a flag football team. Once we moved into the roller rink, we started getting more older students. But the tile auditorium was our only indoor "sport" area. It was about two thousand square feet which gave us some space, but not many options. In addition to being our lunch room, it was a major passageway for anyone wanting to get to the offices, staff room, and most importantly, the bathrooms. That meant that either the game had to stop when other students or staff came through, or we had what the military refers to as "collateral damage."

At no time was this more apparent than during our winter sport of floor hockey. Even though the PE kids were using plastic sticks and pucks, the velocity of the pucks was impressive. I mean that literally: when the speeding puck made contact with human anatomy, it made an impression of some kind! So, it was very common to hear:

smack

screeeeet (puck sliding across tile)

SMACK

CLACK (puck hitting wall)

whack

"WAIT! Stop! Kid coming through!"

silence

"OK!"

SMACK

The above is an actual transcript since my office was on the other side of one of the auditorium walls. I also felt the tremendous THUMP as the frequent body slammed against my wall, my framed pictures shuddering and occasionally falling onto my desk. Even with all that attention to care, more than one teacher and student felt the sting of a puck by being in the wrong place at the wrong time.

We tried changing up the indoor sport to something less lethal. I don't recall who found it, but it was called Global Ball. It was pretty much like volleyball, only there were three large holes in the net through which you tried to hit the ball. We rigged the net across the auditorium and gave it a try. To put it mildly, it didn't catch on. The main reason? It was hard and boring. So we went back to Dodge-Floor Hockey.

Finally, around 1993, we had enough students to organize real teams and sports. Doug Wilson gets the credit for the importation of lacrosse to Moscow, and arguably, Idaho. The guys took to it immediately. It was originally an American Indian sport using sticks with nets, balls, and the frequent fatality. Sort of like rugby in England and soccer in Brazil. I knew about lacrosse from the little history I learned growing up in Michigan. The story I recall best is when a tribe (sorry, I don't recall the name) was playing lacrosse outside Fort Pontiac or Detroit, and the soldiers were watching them. The Indians "accidentally" lobbed the ball over the fort's wall. They then asked the soldiers if they could retrieve the ball. The soldiers, apparently never classically educated about Troy and wooden horses, graciously opened the fort and allowed the Indians to come in. Well, you can probably take it from there. When I first heard the story, I sort of admired the Indians and figured the ball had a higher IQ than the soldiers.

For many years our intrepid lacrosse team had only one opposing team in all of Idaho. They were from the Boise area (southern Idaho, where the potatoes are), so the teams would meet in central Idaho (there's one or two towns there) to compete. Depending on the outcome of that game, I could honestly tell folks that Logos was either the best in the state or second best. Over time, ok, about twenty years, the sport gained popularity and many more teams popped up. Still mostly in southern Idaho, but finally some were formed in the Spokane, Washington, area.

We needed a sport for the girls, so about the same time we formed our first guys' basketball team, we made one for the ladies, too. The following year, we discovered there was enough interest among the girls in volleyball. Being a fall sport, versus basketball being a winter one, we went ahead and added volleyball to our extra-curricular offerings.

Our first volleyball coach was a tall, athletic young lady named Jessica Puckett. She was not only a godly woman, she had played volleyball (and other sports) in college. Our oldest child, Carolyn, was a junior at the time (1995). Julie and I, not being sports people ourselves (some of our best friends have done sports), had sort of assumed we'd get our kids through Logos without having to do all the early morning drop-offs, buying the right shoes, as well as other more awkward sports wear. Not to mention the hours of bleacher-sitting, all the while hoping it's not our kid that loses the game.

So when Carolyn admitted that she wanted to be part of the first Logos volleyball team, we didn't leap about the room in joy. But we did want to support her, so we gave our permission and thus we quickly became a sports family. Eventually all three of our girls would play volleyball and Seth would play basketball. However, I remember Carolyn's first games vividly. Not only did I have to get used to bleacher-sitting, I was nonplussed by volleyball. From my vantage, the games seemed to go like this:

1. Our team crouches in neat rows, eagerly waiting for the other team to serve the ball.
2. The ball is served and sails over the net to our side.
3. Our team runs away, going to any spot on the court where the ball is *not* going to go.
4. The ball hits the floor.
5. The other team gets a point.
6. Repeat.

Carolyn, being herself, often seemed to wait until it was clear that the ball was going to hit the floor approximately 150 feet away from her. Then she would madly run and fling herself onto the spot where moments before the ball had landed. I knew I was missing something in my understanding of how the game actually worked. After a while I did understand and, it should be admitted, the team improved in their reactions.

Coach Puckett was a joy to get to know. I had foolishly obtained my CDL (commercial drivers license) and was thus one of the few people on the planet who could drive our team buses to away games. Actually I enjoyed doing it and was glad to volunteer for years to come. It was during those bus trips that Jessica would sit in the seat behind me and chat all the way to the game. Don't misunderstand me; she didn't blither, she just had a lot to talk about and was very interested in Logos. She also confided to me that she was prone to being car sick (which included buses), and talking helped keep it at bay. She quizzed me about classical education and I quizzed her about her life and experiences. It was all very pleasant and helped the trips go quickly.

More than once Jessica stated emphatically that *if* she ever got married, and *if* she ever had kids (God willing), she would for *sure* put them in Logos School! By God's kind grace, not only did she get married to a wonderful man (Ed), she did have children and she did put them into Logos School. She also went on to be our only volleyball coach for more than twenty years!

Eventually we added cross country and track teams to our sports retinue. It would be these teams that would earn Logos School our first State sport wins!

HELLO MR. WHITLING!

Our first decade or so of hiring teachers taught us quite a bit. It wouldn't be appropriate in this setting to give too many obvious clues and changing the names may not protect anyone. So, I will merely say that, when it came to hiring teachers, we learned at least the following:

1. Don't hire someone who includes as a personal reference a person who is dead...for three years!
2. If someone strikes you as, well, being a few fries short of a Happy Meal, even if they are nice, thank them for coming and move on to the next applicant.
3. If an applicant doesn't seem to have many social skills or good grooming habits, it means they shouldn't teach, anywhere.
4. A Christian testimony and sincerity are not the only prerequisites to consider when hiring someone. Especially if that person has truck loads of sincerity.
5. If we collectively had to gulp, hem or haw to get the necessary votes, it never turned out well.
6. Never put an ad in the local paper! Whuff.
7. Oh yes, and never, ever hire someone sight unseen, or coming from a long distance, especially California. (No offense to any Californian readers—you would understand if you'd been here.)
8. Hiring in August is almost always a very scary proposition—sort of fifth round draft choices, if you follow me.
9. The very best applicants come from the parents in your school, hands-down!

So it came to pass that around the summer of 1994 we found ourselves in need of a third grade teacher. We had put the word out locally with no viable applicants coming forward. So we expanded the search a bit, using our ACCS contacts.

Toward the end of summer, August I believe (see #8 above), we finally had two applicants come forward at about the same time. Our normal procedure for hiring faculty was to have them do a preliminary interview with me (and Tom Spencer, if they were seeking a secondary level position). Then if that went swimmingly, I would set up an interview with the board. For more than thirty years, the Logos Board held to the standard that every teaching hire had to be a unanimous decision. (When the board adopted the Governance Model, as described by John Carver, all the hiring was moved to the admin level.)

Thus I interviewed both applicants. One was a motherly woman of middle age, with some previous elementary teaching experience. She was soft spoken, but struck me as very confident and caring. My only concern for her was how quickly she would pick up the classical methodology. The other applicant was a much younger man, hailing from California (see #7). He said he'd heard and read about Logos School and desired to move to Idaho just to be part of our school. He had a young family and had some rather unpleasant teaching experiences in California. (No comment.)

I was rather torn as to which of the applicants to send on to the board; I thought the woman would probably be a better fit for third graders than a young man who looked like a poster boy for the U.S. Marines. But something about him impressed me; he seemed very wise, far beyond his years.

So I passed them both on to the board for their consideration and selection. Both applicants did well in the interview, but afterward in the board's discussion, they noted the same quality in the young man that I had seen. Still, was that enough of a quality to tip the vote in his direction, over a motherly woman? Yes, it was; that and the fact that the young man seemed to already have a solid grasp on our classical philosophy. He actually seemed eager to put it into practice.

Once the board made a hiring decision, it was my pleasure to contact the applicant to invite them to join our faculty. I was able to let the young man, a fellow named Matt Whitling, know before he left town to go back to California, that we would be delighted to have him come on board! He sounded equally pleased and let me know he'd be back with his family soon. That was a good thing since school was scheduled to start in a matter of a couple weeks!

If you are at all familiar with Logos School or ACCS conferences, you will have already said to yourself, "Oh! So that's where Matt Whitling came from and how he started at Logos School. Good grief, Tom, how could you have not *instantly* seen his amazing worth?" Or some similar wording. I have no excuses and it was tempting to say I did see great potential in that young man. My only refuge is to point back to the lessons learned and listed above.

Matt was a fantastic third grade teacher. He was so skilled that as soon as I could I asked him to move up to sixth grade to have even more influence on the kids in that critical transition year. Years later, after we separated out the elementary principal position from my duties, Matt was asked to take that half-time spot, and keep teaching sixth grade half-time. (After me, our next elementary principal was Dr. Larry Stephenson who, after a year with us, was asked to be the superintendent of a sister ACCS school in North Carolina.)

One legacy of Matt's elementary principal leadership will surely be his assembly sayings. At each of our bi-monthly elementary assemblies, Matt would teach new sayings and review older ones. For instance, he would say, "Leave it…" and the kids would all shout out together, "…better than you found it!" Or he'd say, "If you fall down…" and the students would respond, "...smile, keep on playing!" Some would be Bible verses, others were quotes from historical plays classes had done. Another favorite of mine, that even the older students daily applied in my own classes was: "After class…," and the reply "… thank your teacher, thank your teacher, thank your teacher!"

It didn't take long for Matt to also become a popular and valuable ACCS conference speaker. Initially he did only workshops, but the

ACCS executive director, Patch Blakey, saw how folks responded to Matt's talks and asked him to do plenary speaking as well.

Having worked closely with Matt for over twenty years, I've seen him in just about every possible scenario school life can toss up. The wisdom I first recognized not only was real, it continued to grow and mature, which only meant great blessings for Logos. I can't count how many times I went to him for help and advice in making an administrative decision. And also more times than I can count, he gave me sound, wise counsel. Sadly, even after all my years doing this job, I still had a tendency to shoot first and ask questions later. Especially when it appeared that a teacher had been maligned by a parent, or a student had done something particularly bad. Matt would be the voice that, like the Proverbs, urged me to get all sides of the story before rendering a judgment.

He lived whatever he espoused. He and his gracious wife, Tora, eventually had seven children: six boys and one girl. I have no doubt that each of them will grow up to either emulate their father as a man of God, or seek to find a godly husband like Matt. Even though my children were mostly grown by the time I really got to know Matt, I still studied what he did that worked so well with his kids. It wasn't hard to figure out: at home and at school Matt planned. He considered what might be coming and he planned what to do or how to prepare his children. For instance, instead of trying to discipline his kids during a church service for being fidgety or disruptive, he and Tora had the kids practice sitting still at home, on the couch. They made games for the kids to practice obedience. The kids would be out on the lawn, Matt on the porch. He would shout "Drop and roll!" The kids would all do it and at the same time holler out a chorus "Yes, sir! Yes, sir! Yes, sir!," etc. They loved it because they knew it pleased him and it was fun. All those obedience games were preparing them for more serious times when obedience would be necessary.

Matt could tell stories. That was also a skill he brought with him. And though he was raised in California, there was an Idaho boy waiting inside him. He took to north Idaho living like, well, like a shotgun to duck hunting. He quickly made many friends of school dads who showed him the tricks and treats of fishing, hunting, and just being in the outdoors. Matt also credits his dad with the love of nature and being creative with his hands. So between relishing all that the Palouse area could offer and having the skill to tell stories, Matt frequently regaled his ACCS and summer training audiences with real life stories that always had a message. I particularly like to watch the audience's reaction to stories of shooting rattlesnakes or elk's legs being brought into his classroom for Show and Tell. Priceless.

I discovered Matt's ability to tell stories early in our relationship. One time he and I had been asked to go to Mississippi to hold a small training conference for several schools there. We had a delightful time and I found out how catfish tastes when it's deep-fried. I also found that I preferred the shrimp. I had driven us to the Spokane airport, so when we flew home, arriving quite late at night, I joked to Matt that he needed to help me stay awake as I drove us back to Moscow. Matt strikes most folks on first blush as a strong and quiet type. That's because he usually is. But that night, he took me at my word and for the hour-and-a-half drive, he talked pretty much non-stop. And it wasn't ever boring. I learned about his folks, his growing up in California, his siblings, meeting and marrying Tora, and why he wanted to come to Logos, among other topics.

In 2005 Tom Spencer left Logos and would later work for ACCS. I took over the secondary principal's spot for three years. By the end of that time, I had to confess to the board that I was being overwhelmed and not doing either the superintendent's job or the principal's job very well. We briefly considered hiring another administrator, but then Matt came to my office and asked if we would be open to him being the K-12 principal. I know that the board's and my only concern was if the work would be too much for one guy. John Carnahan, our superb Activities Director, offered to take some of the secondary program's load. The deal was struck!

Not long after Matt assumed the full-time admin position, Tora was hired to help with the testing and other secondary programs. We also moved one of our newer hires, Loren Euhus, to become our Registrar, a critical position especially when we began using Renweb as a database.

Matt also took on coaching the boys' varsity basketball team, in addition to teaching boys' junior high PE and having a Bible time with the sixth graders each week. Somehow he managed to not just juggle all those responsibilities; he excelled in all of them.

Change is one of the few certainties we have, in addition to God's faithfulness and the Word. So I'm sure as Logos grows and becomes Logos 2.0, Matt's duties will morph as well. My prayer is that Logos learns much from his example and plans wisely for the future.

CHAPTER VI

A BIGGER MENU

1994-95 – A WITNESS TO THE CASE OF LOGOS MOCK TRIAL

Some of the greatest things that have blessed Logos School have snuck up on us, quietly and unassuming. In the late fall of 1994 a long-time friend, Mr. Dean Wullenwaber, approached us with the idea of forming a "Mock Trial" team. Dean was a Christian and an attorney (yes, there are some) living in Lewiston at the time. His family had been involved with Logos when they had lived in Moscow years before. (Lewiston is warmer and has year-round golf; those were Dean's reasons for moving from Paradise.)

What Mock Trial meant and required was not entirely clear to me initially, but I was delighted that we could have another unique extra-curricular program to offer our older students. As Dean explained it, the team would consist of seven or eight students acting as attorneys and witnesses. They would study a "case" made just for Idaho Mock Trial teams. Then the team would prepare both defense and prosecution sides of the case. We would go up against other north Idaho teams. The commitment for Dean was not small; he drove up from Lewiston forty-five minutes each way to run the weekly practices of our first team from November to February's Regional Competitions in Coeur d'Alene (a resort town eighty miles north).

I didn't attend that first Regional, but heard from Dean the next day. Our team didn't come in first or even second place, but we were selected on a draw to be the third of three teams from our region to advance to State Competitions in Boise. Now practices took on a more intensive aspect. Arrangements were made for the kids to travel the three hundred miles south to our state's capital for several days of competition in March. Fortunately, the Idaho Law Foundation helped cover the costs of the Mock Trial teams' travel and lodging.

Late on the evening of the final day of competition (which, to be honest, had escaped my notice), I was just dropping off to sleep when the phone by my bed rang and jerked me awake. I put the receiver to my ear and regretted it as someone began screaming, in quite a high register. It took a while, but I finally convinced the caller that not only could I not understand what she was saying, but that I was quickly losing my hearing. Finally she calmed down enough for me to catch the words.

"MR. GARFIELD, WE WON, WE WON!!!"

"Uhm...you won?" I replied, still trying to figure out who this was and what had been won.

"YES! WE WON STATE! CAN YOU BELIEVE IT?"

Brain click. It was Jessica Moore, a student with an amazing vocal projection and, more to the point, a member of our Mock Trial team.

"Wait! We won State Mock Trial?"

"YES, YES! CAN YOU BELIEVE IT? We're all going kind of crazy, but WE WON!"

And so we were hooked. We went on to win State again the next year, which not only obviously pleased us, it demonstrated that the previous year wasn't a fluke. After a few years, Dean had to curtail his trips to Moscow and so the gavel, so to speak, was picked up by Mr. Chris Schlect, one of our part-time secondary teachers. Chris had young ones just joining Logos after some years of homeschooling.

As I learned more about what went into preparing the case for competition, the dramatic skills needed by our 'witnesses' intrigued me.

Loving drama as I did, it didn't take much convincing from Chris to get me involved helping the witnesses with their characters.

Carolyn, our eldest, was also fascinated by the program and became part of the team in her last two years of high school. So now I had even more reason to attend the competitions. What I saw went far beyond a debate using legalese, though the use of the rules and evidence were extremely well executed by our lawyers. I was struck by the contrast between our kids and the other teams' lawyers and witnesses in the Logos students' obvious ability to speak and carry themselves well. Our students were confident, poised, polite, relying more on memory than on notes in hand, winsome, and just very persuasive. They spoke articulately, using complete, well-crafted sentences and looking the jury members in the eye. They used logical arguments and actually responded to the other side's points, instead of ignoring them or just asserting an unproven point, as other lawyers did frequently.

But they were also real kids; after a stiff competition, they wanted nothing less than lots of food (ideally burgers and fries), while they and their coaches analyzed the judges' scoring sheets.

National competitions began in 1998, but we couldn't have gone in any case since we didn't take State that year. However, we did win in 1999, which meant we had a berth at Nationals. However, not only was the cost a factor; we just didn't think we could stand up against the best of teams from states with much larger populations (i.e., almost all of them). But we received funds and our team went to St. Louis where Nationals were being held that year. It was pretty much as scary and different as we had expected, but it was also a great deal of fun. The other states' teams of students were welcoming and friendly.

The victories in Mock Trial came to mean a great deal to me. Why? It became quickly apparent that this extracurricular program, more than any other, was a uniquely appropriate showcase for displaying what we were striving to inculcate in these students from kindergarten through high school.

As a school we could talk all we wanted to about the niftiness of the centuries-old Trivium (grammar, logic, and rhetoric) approach to teaching, but if we weren't daily applying its rigor in each classroom year after year, our kids would have a hit-or-miss record in rhetorically demanding settings like Mock Trial. Instead, on one extended run, our A teams took the State title ten times consecutively. When we finally lost in the final round of our eleventh straight shot at State, it was to a sister ACCS school, Ambrose, from Boise. Our two schools had dominated the state competition for many years and a great relationship had grown between the teams and coaches. The Logos kids often stayed overnight on their campus while in Boise.

Put simply, I came to regard Mock Trial at Logos as the canary in the mine of our rhetoric program. Should we ever start losing in this program, it would mean one of two things:

1. The Mock Trial program itself had changed and become more politically correct, or
2. Logos School was not doing its job in classically educating our students.

It is my fervent desire that neither of these sad circumstances will occur.

LOGOS SCHOOL VISION STATEMENT

After meeting weekly for many years, the Logos School Board determined to scale back that schedule and go to meeting once a month. They also decided to hold an annual board planning meeting. This initially took the form of a sort of retreat, sometimes it was even held out of town. I had stopped being a board member after about eight years and was actually much happier—I was no longer my own boss!

It was during one of those planning retreats at a hotel in Coeur d'Alene in January of 1997, to be precise, that the board determined to construct a more fleshed-out version of the mission of Logos School. Even though we were already sixteen years old, or perhaps *because* we were now sixteen years old, the Vision Statement was one of the most timely and well-crafted documents we ever fashioned, by God's grace. (It has since been picked up and adopted by many ACCS schools.) Here is the original which served us for going on twenty years, as of this writing:

Our Students:

We aim to graduate young men and women who think clearly and listen carefully with discernment and understanding, who reason persuasively and articulate precisely, who are capable of evaluating their entire range of experience in the light of the Scriptures, and who do so with eagerness in joyful submission to God.

We desire them to recognize cultural influences as distinct from biblical and to be unswayed toward evil by the former.

We aim to find them well-prepared in all situations, possessing both information and the knowledge of how to use it.

We desire they be socially graceful and spiritually gracious; equipped with and understanding the tools of learning; desiring to grow in understanding, yet fully realizing the limitations and foolishness of the wisdom of this world.

We desire they have a heart for the lost and the courage to seek to dissuade those who are stumbling toward destruction; that they distinguish real religion from religion in form only; and that they possess the former, knowing and loving the Lord Jesus Christ. And all these we desire them to possess with humility and gratitude to God.

Our staff members:

We likewise aim to cultivate these same qualities in our staff and to see them well paid so that they may make a career at Logos.

We desire them to be professional and diligent in their work, gifted in teaching, loving their students and their subjects.

We desire they clearly understand classical education, how it works in their classroom and how their work fits into the whole; that they possess a lifelong hunger to learn and grow; and that they have opportunity to be refreshed and renewed.

We desire to see them coach and nurture new staff and to serve as academic mentors to students.

We look to see them mature in Christ, growing in the knowledge of God, their own children walking with the Lord.

Our parents:

We aim to cultivate in our parents a sense of responsibility for the school; to see them well informed about the goals of our classical and Christ-centered approach.

We desire them to grow with the school, involved in and excited about the journey.

We aim to help them to follow biblical principles in addressing concerns, to be inclined to hearing both sides of a story before rendering a verdict, and to embrace the Scripture's injunctions to encourage and stir up one another to love and good works.

Our community:

Finally, in our relationship with our community, we aim to be above reproach in our business dealings and supportive of the local business community.

We further seek to exemplify the unity of the body of Christ, to develop greater fellowship and understanding with the churches, and to bring honor to our Lord in all our endeavors.

CLASSICAL & CHRIST-CENTERED...COMPUTER...EDUCATION?

By the mid-'90s, computers were clearly making an impact on all of American culture, not least in education. Around 1996 I received two pieces of correspondence at about the same time, and addressing the same subject, only from two completely opposite views. The topic they shared was the use of computers in education. The one strongly advocated our buying into a proposed online classical education. It came by fax, not surprisingly. The other came from *The New York Times*.

"Computers in education," as a concept, was a step beyond the initial concern back in the '80s of "computer education," which primarily was about teaching students to master and possibly even program these machines. By the '90s computers had become as commonplace in schools as no. 2 pencils, if just a tad more expensive to obtain. At Logos we had wrestled with how to approach this overwhelming phenomena ever since the days of buying our first (and only) Atari 400. Would we let this fascinating and growing technology guide our educational philosophy? Would we be doing our students a disservice in their education by not having cutting-edge equipment in each room? How much should we use computers to teach the students, if at all? Are computers critical or just helpful to a quality education?

The article I received from *The New York Times* said things about using computers in school that I hadn't read or heard anywhere else. It addressed many of those nagging questions with which we wrestled. That being the case, I wanted to include excerpts from it:*

> What's most important in a classroom? A good teacher interacting with motivated students. Anything that separates them—filmstrips, instructional videos, multimedia displays, email, TV, interactive computers—is of questionable value.
>
> Plop a kid down before such a [computer software education] program, and the message is, "You have to learn the math tables, so play with this computer." Teach the same lesson with flash cards, and a different message comes through: "You're important to me, and this subject is so useful that I'll spend an hour teaching you arithmetic."
>
> Computers promise short cuts to higher grades and painless learning. Today's edu-tainment software comes shrink-wrapped in the magic mantra: "makes learning fun."
>
> Equating learning with fun says that if you don't enjoy yourself, you're not learning. I disagree. Most learning isn't fun. Learning takes work. Discipline. Responsibility—you have to do your homework. Commitment from both teacher and student. There's no short cut to a quality education. And the payoff isn't an adrenaline rush, but a deep satisfaction arriving weeks, months, or years later. [...]
>
> One of the most common—and illogical—arguments for computers in the classroom is that they'll soon be everywhere, so shouldn't they be in schools? One might as well say that since cars play such a crucial role in our society, shouldn't we make driver's ed central to the curriculum.

I just love that last line. Stoll (a published astrophysicist, by the way) concludes that excessive reliance on using computers as teachers can encourage the students to assume that:

* Clifford Stoll, "Invest in Humanware," *The New York Times*, May 19, 1996.

> the world is a passive, preprogrammed place, where you need only click the mouse to get the right answer. That relationships—developed over email—are transitory and shallow. That discipline isn't necessary when you can zap frustrations with a keystroke. That legible handwriting, *grammar, analytic thought and human dealings don't matter.*" [emphasis mine]
>
> Looking for simple ways to help in the classroom? Eliminate interruptions from school intercoms. Make classes smaller. Respect teachers. Protest multiple-choice exams which discourage writing and analytic thinking.

Bottom line: We greatly appreciated and used computers at Logos School. But amazingly helpful as it was, even the wonder-tool of the century needed to be kept subservient to time-tested, good teaching by living and loving teachers.

"ONE FISH, TWO FISH..."

You would think I could have picked up on the idea far earlier than I did. I certainly had enough clues presented to me, especially by my own progeny over the years. It should have been obvious when Carolyn, at only three years old, "read" aloud the entire story of Sleeping Beauty into a Tape player. She was able to do this after hearing her mother and I read it to her for about a zillion nights in a row.

Even with succeeding years and children, I was slow to comprehend the idea. Certainly I should have grasped it when child after child beat the tar out of me at the "Memory Game." Good grief! Why couldn't I remember where the matching animal babies were under those cards? Yet, there I'd be with my children accusing me of not trying and "letting" them win. Of course I would swallow my pride, and as a mature adult confess to them that...well, yes, I *wanted* them to win sometimes.

By now you probably know the idea or phenomena to which I am alluding: the incredible, but innate ability young children have to memorize relatively easily and recall repeated information. Actually, my poor powers of perception notwithstanding, most people recognize this characteristic of young children. Nursery rhymes, the alphabet song, and countless other childhood ditties have been passed along from generation to generation. And for countless generations of Europeans and Americans, it was *the* tool used by teachers to pass on knowledge to young students. However, for the past several generations in the United States (since about John Dewey's time) applying this God-given gift to educate children has been denigrated and disused. Repelled as anathema or at least as anachronistic, "rote learning," like corporal punishment, has been tossed on the trash heap of "outdated" teaching methods by modern educationists.

Nevertheless, soon after World War II, Dorothy Sayers observed this about the marvelous memorizing ability children normally have: "The Poll-Parrot stage is the one in which learning by heart is easy and, on the whole, pleasurable; whereas reasoning is difficult and, on the whole, little relished. At this age one readily memorizes the shapes and appearances of things; one likes to recite the number-plates of cars; one rejoices in the chanting of rhymes and the rumble and thunder of unintelligible polysyllables; one enjoys the mere accumulation of things." Otherwise known as the "Grammar Stage" of the medieval Trivium, in a child's life this period seems to last from about age four to about eleven years old. Look at Miss Sayer's description again. Doesn't that sound familiar? Consider just one aspect of her statement—the enjoyment children have in silly sounds. Perhaps Dr. Seuss understood this peculiar love children have, too. In any case, he certainly charmed, and continues to charm, millions of children with his wonderful-sounding, multisyllabic words and strange stories.

As you know, Logos has been committed to implementing the Trivium since we began. However, in the early nineties, we had a renewed vision of what was academically possible with the little ones. We had chanted Latin endings for years in third through sixth grades with great success. But then, with the adoption of some new, Poll-parrot style English grammar materials, and several other teacher-created applications of rote learning, recitations, chants, and songs, we saw tremendous results in the kids' abilities to recall the material presented!

For example, our second graders' grasp on parts of speech, attained through constant, clever recitations courtesy of the Shurley Methods, amazed even our older students. Our third graders began doing "State

Facts," as designed by Matt Whitling, several times a day. The teacher would announce, "State Facts!" Immediately the students took turns popping up and shouting out special facts about each state studied to date. It took just a few minutes, but they obviously got to know all the facts by heart and enjoyed the exercise.

These improvements and innovations charged me up like few things had. We continued to make these and other new grammar methods a lasting part of our elementary curriculum. It only made sense: God has designed the world in such a way that when we use anything the way God designed it to be used, His blessing is usually obvious in the outcome.

SECRET DECODER RINGS AND NANCY DREW

"Now it's time for Little Orphan Annie's secret message just for you kids that have one of Annie's secret decoder rings!" Many young adolescents in the 1930's listened eagerly for this message on the weekly radio program. My mother admitted to having one of Annie's secret decoder rings. What was the appeal to these kids? Was this just a unique sign-of-the-times for Depression-era America? Or was this just another manifestation of a universal urge and interest of kids in that age-group?

Quite a few years later, another generation found the first Nancy Drew mysteries to be great, non-stop, page-turning reading. Again, the age group most attracted to these short books were the young adolescents of the time. The books were not exactly the height of Western literature, yet they were extremely popular probably due to the stock formulas in each: the young sleuths beating the bad adults (and thinking faster than the good adults) at a "game" of clues. Again, was this just a passing fancy?

The traits mentioned above—the fascination with puzzles, the desire to "beat-out" adults, the urge to figure it all out—are not unique to any generation of people. They do seem to be most evident in children of a certain age-group, however. Little children and older teens are not as enthralled with the above kinds of activities. Generally speaking, it appears that kids from about ten or eleven to about fourteen or fifteen are prime for what Dorothy Sayers calls the "Pert Stage." Here is how she described them in "The Lost Tools of Learning":

"The Pert age, which follows upon this [the Poll-Parrot Age] (and naturally, overlaps it to some extent) is characterized by contradicting, answering back, liking to "catch people out" (especially one's elders) and in the propounding of conundrums. Its nuisance-value is extremely high. It usually sets in about the eighth grade."

At Logos, we discovered that this Pert age frequently set in earlier than eighth grade for most kids. Perhaps that has to do with the overall shortening of childhood we see in our culture at large. In any case, the Pert age seemed to correspond nicely with our junior high program (seventh and eighth grades). These students wanted to know the whys and wherefores of the material, and they had a propensity to argue and debate. Therefore, we sought to channel their desires to our own ends. We taught them formal Logic in eighth grade to give them the necessary structures for sound arguments. We planned debates (watching for hurt feelings) that rehashed historic and/or spiritual issues. These students also possessed vast stores of energy. Therefore, in the daily classes, we often used role-playing to help the kids exercise their thinking and oral skills on their feet. The junior high drama productions were also a great place to see these characteristics put into practice. Other applicable and successful teaching methods for this age included puzzles, review games, position papers, hands-on projects (such as maps and displays in geography, or experiments and demonstrations in science), and good old Socratic questioning techniques.

The goal, as with the Poll-Parrot and Poetic, the other stages of learning, was to take advantage of the natural, God-given traits students had and match them to the time-proven process of teaching and learning, i.e., the Trivium. Done well, this method of learning was at least as interesting to the kids as a decoder ring, and frankly a lot more useful to them in later life.

WOODSTOCK AND PAUL THE APOSTLE

"Going up to Yasgur's farm. Gonna join a rock-and-roll band. Got to get back to the land and set my soul free." So sang Crosby, Stills, Nash, and Young in celebration of the biggest, muddiest camp-out ever seen. Over a quarter of a million young adults spent three rainy, drug-hazed days in a field in upper New York, having their hearing and most other senses threatened, if not destroyed, at the rock concert of the century. (And, no, this isn't the voice of experience.) Woodstock was held in August 1969, symbolically the nadir (or zenith, depending on how you look at it) of the hippie movement that began in the sixties and burned out in the early seventies.

Aside from the plethora of bizarre and immoral manifestations of that era, some observations can be made about the basic, similar characteristics of those young people. I would submit that the majority of them (us) were smack dab in the midst of what Dorothy Sayers would call the "Poetic Age." I know I was—and I don't think I was alone. Harken unto Miss Sayers' description: "The Poetic Age is popularly known as the 'difficult' age. It is self-centered *[!]*; it yearns to express itself *[My, my generation…]*; it rather specializes in being misunderstood *[People try to put us down…]*; it is restless and tries to achieve independence *[Born to be wild…]*."

But there's hope: "And, with good luck and good guidance, it should show the beginnings of creativeness, a reaching-out toward a synthesis of what it already knows, and a deliberate eagerness to know and do some one thing in preference to all others." She goes on to say that a fair amount of latitude should be given these students to pursue an area of special interest, while encouraging them to see the overall integration of knowledge. Individual subjects, as such, now meld into a wider view, a biblically based view, of the world.

It is during this age, then, that Rhetoric—the skill of speaking and writing well and convincingly—is so suitable for mastery. Every former "subject" becomes a form of grist for the mill of expression. These students now delight in expressing their thoughts and opinions. It was the work of prior teachers and training to equip them with ability to recognize supportive facts (Grammar), and the appropriate connections of those facts (Logic). Then they were ready to use that prior work and skillfully express a synthesis of knowledge. At Logos, during their Rhetoric classes, our juniors and seniors were required to research, write, and then defend several theses in front of a committee of teachers. They were assisted in the construction of the papers by those teachers who had expertise in the topic chosen by the student. But the topical premise had to stretch across more than one subject or field.

In Acts we see Paul the Apostle using his rhetorical skills for the glory of God: "And according to Paul's custom, he went to them, and for three Sabbaths reasoned with them from the Scriptures, explaining and giving evidence…and some of them were persuaded and joined Paul and Silas" (Acts 17:3, 4). Our senior elective Apologetics course was a very popular class. It very nicely combined the skills of rhetoric with the knowledge needed to proclaim the truths of Scripture, as Paul did. Some of our graduates have remarked on the applicable benefits they have used in the "outside" world, from the skills and knowledge they obtained in their Rhetoric and Apologetics classes.

In addition, while the school maintained a standard number of required credits for graduation, in order to allow them to make "some one thing in preference to others," the seniors were allowed to choose among a number of classes. This choice included the option of university classes and/or an approved independent study. Many of the independent studies took the form of apprenticeship with professionals in the community. We heard many positive comments about this aspect of our high school program, from students, parents, and the business community.

So, the Woodstock generation notwithstanding, there is a lot to gain from and offer to students in the Poetic Age. We were very delighted to see that our graduates regarded and emulated Paul the Apostle more than Peter, Paul, and Mary!

"INNOCENTS ABROAD"

After three smallish, but enthusiastic ACCS conferences were held in Moscow, we decided to take the advice of many folks and, well, take it on the road. The first two annual conferences, held in June of 1993 and 1994, were conducted at Logos School. The third, in 1995, with about 150 folks attending, was in a venue more in keeping with such conferences, the local Best Western hotel.

But time after time individuals from the farther corners of this great nation urged us to put on the conference closer to…they didn't actually say "civilization," but that's what they meant. Anyone living in Moscow, much as we love it, knows that it's a pain to get to and get back to. So we certainly understood that moving the conference to the east coast would probably attract more folks. And it did, about four hundred folks!

I'm not sure why we decided to go for Raleigh, North Carolina, but you can't get too much further east than that without getting wet. One reason I know we chose that site was that a sister school was nearby and able to help with some of the on-site preparations. The hotel we had booked was large enough to have the conference held in its ballroom, but the sister school was able to give the hotel people more details about our needs.

Those of us presenting talks determined to fly out together. Thus it was that we all experienced entering the hotel at the same time. I say 'experienced' because I'm pretty sure most of us had never been in a hotel that nice or that big! Talk about clichés. We were gawking unabashedly as we entered the massive lobby and took in all the lovely accommodations. The rooms were palatial to those of us whose traveling typically involved Super 8 and Motel 6.

The entire experience of that first "away" conference was downright heady. At one point I found myself sitting in an overstuffed chair on a stage, along with Doug Wilson and Tom Spencer for an evening Q&A time. Hundreds of people sat in front of us, peppering us with questions about practically implementing this "classical thing." We passed a microphone between us as we attempted to give brief, but hopefully helpful answers. Hands-down Doug was the most articulate among us, but Tom and I chimed in with administrative tips, such as only admitting students who won't be a threat to you or the other students.

OK, we may have given even less obvious suggestions.

The ACCS board not only grew in numbers at that time, which for many of us was the beginning of some long-time friendships, but the board also decided to ask Mr. Patch Blakey to be the first ACCS executive director.

A quick note about Patch's character: He and his family moved to Moscow to put their kids in Logos after he finished his Navy career as a captain. While this gave him a pension, he still wanted to work. He heard that we had an opening for a janitor so he applied. When I discovered that he was a former captain, I confess to being nonplussed. On one hand I knew he would certainly have the requisite work ethic. On the other hand, from my naval experience, captains were pretty much like Pharaoh. Could I really ask a captain to clean toilets? Patch made it easier on me:

"Tell you what, let me work for a week and if you like my performance, you can start to pay me!"

Of course I hired him!

It's not often that our former janitors go on to become CEOs of organizations, but Patch had the humility to do the former job and the wisdom to perform the latter. The ACCS Board was delighted that he accepted the post. He also immediately began serving as master of ceremonies for the conference. Patch went on to serve ACCS faithfully for twenty years, after which he was recognized and thanked officially at the conference in 2015.

Many of the folks we met at the 1996 conference either already belonged to new ACCS schools or would become the founders of such schools. As such, they would also become friends we would see at many future conferences. I grew to love and look forward to the summer conferences partly just to see those special people again—a family reunion of sorts. (I am blessed to come from a strong Christian extended family so my memories of reunions are happy ones. I mention that because I know that's not always the case.)

HAVE BRIEFCASE, WILL TRAVEL

Once ACCS was formed, and especially after the 1996 conference back east, the demand for practical, on-site help came to a boil. Folks were so desperate that they began asking me to come to their hometowns to give them a hand. That meant paying to fly me from Moscow to wherever they were seeking to construct a classical, Christian school. I was very honored to be asked, and so began many strange and usually delightful trips around the country. Yes, I meant to say "strange" because, well, some of the trips just were...different, as compared to the kind of life I lead in the hinterlands of north Idaho.

The requests I got fell into about three main categories:

1. Meeting with a steering committee or first board to address start-up questions,
2. Training for teachers new to classical education (i.e., pretty much every teacher),
3. Speaking to a group of parents about classical, Christian education,
4. Any combination of the above.

My very first trip was sort of a combo of all three categories. You may recall the Detweilers I mentioned earlier. Marlin and Laurie had come to the first ACCS conference we held at Logos. They were living in the Orlando area of Florida at the time. Being the movers and shakers they were, they wanted to start a classical school in August of 1993, two months after the first conference! Not only did they glean as much as they could from us while they were in Moscow, they called me later that summer to come down and do some teacher training for the four teachers they had hired.

Being all kinds of new to this sort of thing, I readily agreed, missing some key warning labels, i.e., August and Florida. I flew into Orlando at about midnight, apparently in the middle of a hurricane, judging from the turbulence. Then, feeling sicker than I ever had in the Navy, I staggered into the jetway. I noticed that everyone raced ahead of me down the sleek passageways. Following more slowly I soon discovered the reason for their haste: we weren't actually in the main terminal; there was an automated shuttle that ran every few minutes to whisk people off to the real terminal. I had missed one so I had to wait for as long as three minutes for the next one. Alone in my personal shuttle, a friendly recorded voice let me know that Orlando has the busiest airport in the universe and that Disney World is Mecca.

I spent about a week in the Detweilers' home, using most of each day to work through basic teaching ideas and methods with the new teachers. At one point I had a break and, feeling a bit house-bound, I decided to take a walk. No one was around to dissuade me so I popped outside and headed up the lovely, palm-tree lined street. The sky was a brilliant blue and the sun shone brightly…so brightly that barely had I gone a block before I began to wonder if I could make it back to the house on my hands and knees before I disintegrated into a Tom-shaped puddle, which would quickly steam away into the blue sky. Hot doesn't begin to describe it. Orlando had to have been originally part of the Sahara. Except the Sahara doesn't have any humidity, so even it would have been preferable to the thick air I had to slice through to return to God-blessed AC!

But it wasn't all work and potential death by heat. One evening the teachers and I were invited to have dinner with R.C. Sproul (Sr.). He was a delightful host and a very wise man. He was also serving on the new school board of what would become Geneva Academy there. In spite of his wide renown and reputation in the evangelical world, he was very genuine and charming. However, I did find it somewhat humorous when, after delivering quite a long, strongly worded opinion on a topic the new school might face, he paused and seriously said:

"But, you know, I'm only one board member."

One last recollection of that first trip has to be my ride to the Orlando airport to catch my flight home. Marlin wasn't able to take me, so he'd asked a friend to pick me up. This guy's mom was flying in so he was headed to the airport anyway. As I waited and my ride still hadn't shown up, I passed the time with some vague attempts to catch one of the hundreds of scurrying little lizards in the backyard. I had some notion of taking one home to Seth, my son.

Finally the car pulled up and we began what I like to call the Ride of a Thousand Angels. That's how many angels I believe had to be on duty to make sure we didn't die in a fiery wreck as we raced through traffic in a manner that would have done Bruce Willis proud. And all the while the driver was doing the following:

1. Asking me about my life (which I was sure would end any moment),
2. Answering his cell phone (everyone in Florida already had one by 1993),
3. Eating.

We literally squealed to a stop outside the terminal. The driver looked at his watch and actually said, in a calm voice:

"It was nice to meet you. You'd better run for it."

I did.

Another time I was asked to help troubleshoot a Canadian Christian school that had been in existence for about one hundred years. Really, one hundred years. The terms *trouble* and *shoot* really should have tipped me off that this would not be a happy trip. My first realization that I was in for a bumpy ride occurred within ten minutes of arriving at the school. The stern, female administrator showed me around briefly, then sat me down in the staff room and said:

"When we heard you were coming, I thought we should put up more God posters in the hallways." She was serious. Cutting to the chase, among other suggestions, I recommended to the board that she be fired. She was.

But another Canadian trip actually was fun, if a bit bizarre. I usually mention to my hosts that, if possible, I'd enjoy seeing some of the sites of their area. I mentioned that idea on this trip and was given a whole day of touring sites, in the company of two blond school moms. I mention the blond aspect because, well, they were, and they both had fun, quirky personalities to match. On what was a very cold winter's day with mounds of snow everywhere, we saw Niagara Falls (partially frozen), toured a butterfly "aviary" (if that's the term), drove into a closed historic fort (where we got stuck in the driveway—I "rocked"the transmission while they pushed—it was their idea!), and we ended up having a great dinner, overlooking the Canadian side of the Falls. (The American side was lit by spotlights that changed pastel colors every few minutes. Not tacky in the least.)

One of my favorite trips was back to my home state of Michigan. As it happened, some of the faculty of a sister school from the Great Lake State had come out to one of our earliest summer training weeks. When I discovered that they were from Michigan, I asked them to come to our home for dinner. The administrator was a gracious and very intelligent lady named Vicki Church. She told us that she and her husband Bill had helped found the school back in Rochester (north of Detroit). Bill was in lumber sales and they had three children. The oldest was planning to attend NSA in Moscow after high school.

Not long after that initial contact, Vicki asked me to come and do a short training conference at their school. I jumped at the chance to see my old stomping grounds. They also paid to have Julie come and, after the conference, we toured Greenfield Village with the Churches. Henry Ford built the village back in the 1920s, using his millions to literally dismantle, move, and re-install famous American structures to his huge estate. For instance, the Wright brothers' bike shop was there, along with Thomas Edison's (a good friend of Ford) original laboratory and Walt Whitman's home. There was also a massive Ford Museum which housed classic cars, trucks, trains, and countless other memorabilia. I had been there many times as a youth and loved it every time! It was even more fun as adult and knowing something about American history.

Our friendship with the Church family grew and, as the Lord likes to tell good stories, our youngest daughter, Kathryn, married their son, Mike, in 2007, so now we share grandchildren.

Over the latter part of the '90s, I went to many states that I'd never visited. During each visit, I collected souvenir key chains for my kids and magnets for Julie's fridge. (She never seemed to like them as much as I did.) However, out of all the states, Texas seemed to take to this education like it was some new brand of cattle. In one year I went to no less than five different places in that great state. I came to admire it and really enjoyed the folks I met in each spot. One of my first impressions of Texas was that they truly love their state flag. I have never been in any state that displays its flag like Texas does: it's everywhere you look. On my first visit I assumed from all the flags along the streets that a state holiday was at hand. I inquired of my host. He said no and wondered why I thought they were celebrating anything. I pointed out the flags and he had a good laugh—Texans like to laugh and they do it very loudly.

On another occasion, on the long drive from the airport, my host pulled over to show me a large statue of Sam Houston (guess where I was) near the highway. It was very tall, perhaps sixty feet or more. As we walked around the base, I pointed out this feature. My host proudly exclaimed:

"Yes, sir. This is the tallest free-standing statue in the United States!"

Now, I may have not understood him correctly. Or perhaps he meant the tallest, *male* statue in the U.S. Being an American History teacher, I knew that the Statue of Liberty was a great deal taller than Mr. Houston, but as I reflected that I was in the heart of Texas, I kept my counter-point to myself.

On yet another occasion I didn't endear myself to my hosts with my opinion. But, in my defense, they did ask. See, I really, and I mean, intensely, dislike Mexican food. I don't have any poor opinion of those people (apparently the majority of Americans) who enjoy it. I just never want it to ever have a close encounter with my personal taste buds. Yes, I do mean any form of it. I can't recall how many dear, well-meaning friends (and even strangers) who have said:

"But have you ever tried 'X' [meaning some Mexican food substance]? You might like it!"

No. I have not tried every possible food item from the category identified as "Mexican." Why would I do that? If the food item has earned the label, there is a reason. That reason, be it the ingredients and/or the way they are combined, is adequate to serve as a No Trespassing sign for my digestion.

So, that food exclusion being part of my DNA, during one Texas trip I found myself in a large pick-up with several Texan men around lunchtime. One of my newfound partners asked the group where we should stop for lunch. The exact way he put was:

"So which Tex-Mex spot should we hit?"

Seeing as how there were about as many Tex-Mex eateries in that town as there were Starbucks, the options suggested came fast and thick. Then, as I knew would happen, one of the guys, being polite, asked me if I had a preference.

"Well," I said hesitantly. "Uhm...I don't really have an opinion on any of those restaurants."

Something in my voice must have tipped one of the Texans to ask:

"You do like Tex-Mex, right?" he asked, with the same look and tone he'd use to determine if I respected my mother. Or maybe his mother.

"Heh. Well, I think I'd really like 'Tex', but if it's all the same to you guys, I'll pass on the 'Mex.'"

They all had a good laugh, which I took as a sign that Julie wouldn't be getting a phone call late that night from the Texas Rangers to say they'd found my body hung on a cactus far out in the desert, my mouth stuffed with cilantro.

One of my favorite memories of a Texas trip started with a lot of trepidation of my part. I flew into a fairly large Texas city late at night (a pattern I discovered when going east). My hosts had mailed me (not much internet yet) a package with instructions and a map. I was to rent a car and drive about 80 miles out into the scrub-land to get to their home. So I rented a car and, without any hint of GPS to help me, drove out into the Texas landscape by the light of the full moon. I grew very fond of the moon that night as I drove along an apparently deserted highway, except for the occasional coyote and deer (no antelopes) randomly dashing out of the dark. Had the moon shone less bright, I may have turned one of those suicidal animals into a hood ornament.

But I finally arrived at the address of the ranch, which was an oasis to me by that point. I pulled into the driveway in the wee hours of the morning. The instructions told me that they had a guest house that would be all mine. I saw the guest house and all the miles of fear and wild life faded. It was a log cabin, complete with a homey lantern lit on the porch and some lights on inside. As I made myself at home in the upstairs bedroom, with its stone fireplace and huge, log-framed bed, I knew why I liked Texas.

ONE NIGHT IN MEMPHIS

The success of the 1996 ACCS conference convinced the board that we should stick in the eastern part of the U.S. for a while. We were also seeing a lot of interest in classical education in the south, too. So for the 1997 conference we decided to go to Memphis, Tennessee, where a member school was located. The hotel-conference center was located in the heart of Memphis, which made getting to some of the famous spots very easy. Beale Street, the Pyramid Museum (which had the Titanic artifacts on display!), and, of course, the Rendezvous restaurant, famous for its incredible ribs! The vent from the kitchen propelled its mouth-watering smells into the streets, pulling in innocent bystanders from blocks around.

Logos was by now being asked for more and more of our in-house materials. What had begun quietly with folks asking for a copy of our handbooks or policy manuals, ramped up to many requests for our curriculum guides and pretty much anything else we had to offer. Initially we just charged for the copies and postage, but business-minded friends encouraged us to charge a bit more for the work and thought, not to mention experience, that went into our materials. Thus began our Marketing Department. In other words, my secretary was paid extra to come in on Saturdays and run off what folks were ordering.

For the Memphis conference, Julie and I took turns manning the "vendor booth" Logos had in the hallway. It was pretty much a table with our items stacked on it, nothing compared to vendors' displays in years to come. Oh yes, and a cash box.

The end of the conference came at noon on Saturday and I tried to say goodbye to folks and package up our remaining items at the same time. Our flight would leave in the morning, so Julie and I hit the hay early, rather exhausted from all the workshops and conversations we'd had for two and a half days. As I was putting our stuff in our suitcases in preparation for an early start, I couldn't find the bundle of cash and checks from the cashbox.

You know how panic begins: the cold pit in your stomach, then the cold sweat on the forehead, the hands start shaking, breathing becomes shallow and fast, your mind races in every direction at once, and pretty soon you can't remember your birthday. Yeah, that pretty much describes my growing anxiety. I knew I had bundled the money but could not for the life of me recall where I'd put it.

Julie urged me to stay calm, but that train had left the station a while back. While I was wracking my brain, I was also trying to calculate how much money we'd had. (No, there was no laptop with recorded sales or even written receipts.) I went down (eleven stories) to our rental car to unpack all my carefully packaged boxes to see if somehow I'd dropped the bundle in one of them. Then I went back to the conference center to search the halls. By this time it was past eleven at night. My mind told me:

"Well, nimrod, if you'd left it on the table, there's probably one very happy janitor somewhere in this building!"

I went back to our room (eleven stories up), defeated. Julie and I finally got around to praying (yes, it had come to that!). I also decided to ask Patch Blakey to join us in praying—which meant calling and waking him up, but he was kind and said he and Deb would pray.

Then I lay back and began to relax. Loving all things Sherlock, I remembered one of his tips for finding lost things: mentally reconstruct everything you did with the object. So, I saw myself hastily packing boxes, filling last minute requests… using a nearby large envelope to…

I shot bolt up in bed with a shout—causing Julie to nearly scream in terror!

"I remember where it is!" I leaped from the bed to my suitcase and, burrowing deeply, pulled out the large conference materials envelope… wherein I had thrown the bundle of money, along with some other items.

Though I felt like sacrificing two bulls and a goat in thanks to God, we just prayed again.

And the next year I made sure we hired a competent person to do sales! His name was John Carnahan. He would be with Logos, in some capacity, for the next twenty years. He not only handled marketing for us (having been a savvy business man in Boise), but he taught a number of secondary classes and was our very capable Activities Director for many years. Most of all he was a very good friend who had the gift of encouragement when I (and others) needed it most.

When John turned more to teaching, his marketing position was assumed by Scott Oplinger, a very organized man who I believe was part German. He was organized to beat the band and grew our marketing department into a revenue source that brought in more than a hundred thousand dollars to Logos each year for a while! (As other classical curriculum businesses grew, our status as the only source changed and our sales began to understandably decline after a few years.) A number of our teachers were encouraged or just offered to write more materials, both for their classes and for publication. As we sold their materials, they received royalty payments, a win all the way around!

BLESSED BY THE AFFLICTED

"Sing, O heavens, and be joyful, O earth; and break forth into singing, O mountains: for the LORD hath comforted his people, and will have mercy upon His afflicted" (Isaiah 49:13).

Nathan was a bright, strong lad of ten when his family moved to Moscow from Maryland in 1997. They had been active in another classical, Christian school back there. Nathan's folks wanted him to attend Logos in second grade, but they were unable to find an aide to be with him while at school, so he was home that year. You see, while Nathan's mind was alert and sharp, for some reason known to God, his muscles did not always do what he wanted them to do. That included the muscles and connections that regulate speech. Nathan, therefore, needed physical assistance constantly. He communicated in writing through a special computer board on which he typed. He could walk and even run a bit, but he had to be closely monitored lest he stumble into someone or something. Sometimes his head needed to be physically pointed at whatever he was to pay attention to. His excitement and frustrations frequently came out in either happy squeals or deep moans.

Two aides were found in preparation for Nathan entering Logos' third grade, but I confess I had a good deal of concern and hesitation as I considered accepting him for the few hours each day that his folks requested. Would he be too great a distraction to the other students in the class? Would his needs, even with the aide present, draw too much attention from the tender-hearted teachers? And would his time in school really be of any benefit to Nathan himself? Finally, with the encouragement from one of his former teachers in Maryland, my friend Leslie Collins, I accepted him. To be brief, it was one of the smartest decisions (by God's grace) I have ever made. His parents sent us the following letter after the year was over and they were preparing for their planned move to Bellevue, Washington:

> We would like to take this opportunity to express our deep gratitude to Logos School and to you, the Board of Directors, for allowing Nathan to attend your school this last academic year. Through your generosity, the Lord saw fit to bless Nathan and us

in many ways. Nathan had one of his best years in terms of academic improvements. He was able, with assistance, to complete the Third Grade math curriculum, and showed us that his ability to work with these concepts continues to improve. In addition, we saw a marked breakthrough in his ability to use his computer with greater independence. But this was even more pronounced in the reading curriculum, where Nathan began spelling words, one letter at a time, while totally independent of any assistance.

While this work was achieved through the services we provided with an aide and additional work in the home, we believe that much of this would not have occurred without the help of Logos School. We saw Nathan's countenance and enjoyment of life increase this last year as he found friends who would reach out to him at school. Both in the classroom, as well as in the lunchroom and at recess, Nathan was rarely left alone. This simple integration motivated Nathan to strive to do what others around him were doing, whether that was playing freeze-tag or silently reading at one's own desk. In addition, church became a place of greater fellowship for Nate because so many kids (and adults) were used to seeing him every day.

We are certainly aware that Logos has no intention of becoming a 'full-inclusion' school, and we do not buy the egalitarian nonsense either. However, this effort to reach out to our family and to Nathan, as well as to provide an opportunity to other kids to serve someone like Nathan, has produced blessings that will multiply for years to come in many lives. But it required a substantial risk on your part, and for that we are very grateful.

We have often heard many reports of what a blessing Nate was in the school. If, however, you did ever receive complaints or concerns, they were never passed on to us. If you have any concerns that would be of help to us in future settings, we would appreciate your comments. Thank you for your patience with us and with Nathan. (Matthew 25:34–40)

We missed Nathan (and his family) but stayed in touch with their ministry on the west side of Washington. Nathan and his younger brother were two of the most well-liked students in the elementary. Their parents' no-nonsense, biblical approach to their son's affliction was truly a lesson for all who saw them love and train their son at school. And all the elementary kids saw this happen at some point.

God does indeed often choose to glorify Himself through those we deem humble and afflicted. But for those who love as He does, He blesses them *through* the humble and afflicted. Yes, we certainly had a blessed year!

WHAT TO CELEBRATE:

In keeping with our virtual complete cluelessness as we began, we didn't give much initial thought to the kind and amount of things we'd celebrate as a school. The biggies were easy, of course: Thanksgiving, Christmas, and Easter. (For quite a few years, our seniors took it upon themselves to make a great lunchtime feast for the staff on the half-day we took Wednesday of Thanksgiving week. It was delightful, but it meant the staff would have two large meals in a row, Wednesday and Thursday. We let it faze out.)

But beyond the obvious holidays, it took us a while to figure out what else we should highlight for the kids and families. Our culture wasn't much help, considering that the Federal government recognizes more holidays than the Catholic church has saints. Not to mention that apparently every month of the year is Something Awareness Month.

Then there were the special days we wanted to designate ourselves. Days that we would celebrate, not by having a day off from school, but which would change our normal routine.

One of first in that last category was Grandparents' Day. While not unique, it was nevertheless very worthwhile. Admittedly, when we started setting aside a day in spring and having grandparents roll in to spend time with their little grands, it didn't occur to me that I might one day join the silver-haired ranks and have my own littles to dote on.

Another day we set aside that was indeed rather unique was Knight Day (catch the clever double meaning?). We earmarked the Friday before Spring Break as Knight Day and designed it to be kind of a mini-conference day for the secondary students (7th-12th grades). Now if you've been to a conference you might be thinking this sounds like special torture for children. But, nay, it was nothing of the sort. First off, we chose that day since the kids tended to be a bit distracted before the break anyway. So that meant no regular classes—a plus in their books already. Second, we offered special themes for our plenary (group) talks, as well as fun workshops throughout the day. Not to mention a pizza or sub sandwich lunch. Not your typical conference, is it?

One year the theme was Music and we had a plenary presentation done in the gym by my daughter Kajsa and her operatic husband Bray. They briefly ran through the history of opera and musicals, during which I was watching some seventh grade boys in the bleachers. They were polite enough, but their body language clearly indicated they wouldn't have minded being elsewhere. But when Bray launched into some samples of opera, with Kajsa accompanying on piano, well, those boys couldn't help but sit up and pay attention! Bray's voice literally filled the gym with a quality few of the kids had ever heard first-hand.

Another year we had FBI agents do a presentation on solving crimes. We had workshops where the kids did fun things like learning to juggle, or tie balloons into animal shapes, or bake a multiple layer cake. Informative workshops ranged from how Napoleon lost at Waterloo to the sinking of the Titanic to missionary trips and more.

Eventually we rolled Knight Day into our Knights Festival. But for many years we kept our Trivia Day on the Friday before Christmas break. During the morning the students finished their last final tests for the semester and then cleaned out their lockers and the classrooms. In the afternoon, we divided the kids into teams, mixing them up so each team had every grade represented. The Trivia questions came from the secondary teachers, so in essence, the whole afternoon's game was one big review period. But no one minded and the winning team got candy. We added our Alum Day to this event and that made it even more fun as many of the more recent alums came to compete in the Trivia game again! We'd end the day with Christmas carols and then send them home to celebrate the Incarnation with their families. (I've included our actual Holiday Guidelines in the appendices, for your pleasure.)

THE "PROVERBS" (AS LEARNED FROM LIFE AT LOGOS SCHOOL)

CHAPTER 1

1 Some proverbs of an administrator, the son of an administrator:

2 To know a few good ideas, but mostly to understand various accumulated opinions and experiences of dubious worth, gathered over time by the son of an administrator, and maybe to gain some sympathy, if not agreement in passing them along to others.

3 As rain comes in the spring, so snow will come immediately after paying for a new load of gravel for the driveway.

4 Like vinegar to the back teeth is a copier that breaks down as soon as it is desperately needed to run off a last-minute paper.

5 He who once gives a foot ride to a first grader will find he must do so daily.

6 As pearls carried in a paper sack is a lovely girl in a T-shirt and old jeans.

7 The fool says in his heart, "I don't need to study tonight; the test isn't until two days from now."

8 Grass will be able to grow where there are no children playing, but much joy comes from watching children play.

9 Like discovering you have lost five pounds is the gladness that comes from a student's sincere compliment.

10 Expediency is a tyrannical master, listen not to him when hiring a teacher or other staff members.

11 Many are the ideas education colleges give new teachers, but few are of value to the biblically minded teacher.

12 The righteous father does not hold back spanking from his son, nor does the righteous mother withhold chocolate-chip cookies from the administrator.

CHAPTER 2

1 D.A.R.E. is a mocker and provides no limits to a student's evil desires for blowing his mind.

2 The sluggard student leaves his jacket on the floor and remembers not where he put it.

3 Four things an administrator hates; five incur his displeasure: a lying tongue, a hand that is quick to strike others, a bus that will not start on a winter morning, anything coming from the N.E.A., and yet another jacket lying on the floor.

4 The Lord blesses even little schools in Moscow, Idaho; who can understand His ways?

5 A capable, friendly secretary is a gift from the Lord, as are competent teachers.

6 Look to the kindergarten teacher, O you teacher of higher learning, and see how productive she is and the work her students produce. Be like her in your energies.

7 "Remain in school!" cries the fool, yet he looks not at why his schools continue to empty.

8 He who greets a staff meeting with a loud voice early in the morning, it will be counted to him as a curse, though none would actually say so.

9 Where there are many founders of a new school, sin and disorganization will be present shortly. Good leadership lies with the few of one mind.

10 A foolish student seeks for a lost paper in a trashed locker and finds it not; A wise student finds his paper in an organized notebook.

11 The fool thinks education is like computer technology; only the newest innovation will do. Look back, O man, to how the fathers taught for generations; there lies education.

12 Three things are wondrous to behold, yea four are the delight of the administrator: A student who loves school, a father who leads his home, a staff working well and harmoniously toward a goal, and a person who prays for Logos School.

CHAPTER VII

FURTHER UP AND FURTHER IN

EXPANDING?

By the winter of 1996–97, the Logos School Board had been wrestling with a quandary regarding our campus for several years. We were filling up the former roller rink and some form of expansion would be needed rather soon. So maybe more classrooms? At the same time, we had a viable extra-curricular program that needed a home, i.e., a gym for our sports teams and a stage for our drama program. We had gone begging many seasons to find gym space for our volleyball and basketball games. The Moscow District and the U of I were as accommodating as they could be, but their events would sometimes have to 'bump' ours.

So the choice before the board was pretty clear: acquire more land east of the school building and add either a wing of classrooms *or* build a field house/gym.* The board determined to make a decision at their annual planning meeting in January. In the meeting's discussion, the board considered the pros and cons of each option:

* Many folks use *field house* and *gym* interchangeably. To me the former connotes a drafty old building that gets used for anything and everything, whereas the latter sounds like a facility with a clear purpose. As it would turn out, our gym would actually be used for everything under the sun, but I still call it a gym. Sue me.

- Classroom wing: The pros would be obvious—more space for expanding our enrollment, which would also increase our revenue. The cons were also obvious—more students would put additional pressure on our common areas (hallways, bathrooms, auditorium). It would also mean continuing to struggle along in our extra-curricular program, discouraging families from participating.
- Gym: The pros were clear—we would be able to house our own teams, have home games and put on larger drama performances. The cons were mostly in the realm of assumptions—some folks might assume we had "sold out" to the pressure of making sports too important. The old "tail wagging the dog" danger. We didn't take that possibility lightly; Logos lives in the shadow of the U of I, where sports draw many more alum dollars than the arts program. (To be fair, considering the nature of the arts program, this is not all bad.) Many fine schools, lower and upper ed, have looked to sports as an easy way to fund their other projects. The catch is that usually academic rigor is sacrificed so that the athletes can play and still graduate.

So the board wrestled with its options, but to be honest, not very long. As we tried to do in every challenge, we went back to our philosophy of education, as well as our covenant with the families we had at that time. It was determined that our first duty was to these families, not potential ones. That meant providing the kind of campus and facilities that would best meet the needs of our existing programs. To wit: a gym was needed.

Wisely, at the same meeting the board determined to preempt the tail-dog accusation by upping the ante for students going out for extra-curricular activities. Specifically, the required GPA (Grade Point Average) to be eligible to participate went from 2.0 to 2.5, or the equivalent of maintaining a B average. With Logos' academic rigor, this requirement actually had teeth.

That proviso added, the board then gave the green light to moving forward with the gym plans.

Of course, saying is easier than doing usually. The first order of business was obtaining more land. To build a gym on our current property would basically take out the playground area. Or it would have to be a fairly small building that would just cover our outdoor concrete basketball court.

Well, the Lord opened the land "door" in a rather unique manner. At that time, it was our understanding that the property adjacent to our playground had been sold. It would have been ideal in size and situation—it fronted on A Street, a new east-west corridor immediately north of our campus. That was why we began considering ways to build on our existing playground. Then one afternoon I got a call from one of the architects we had used in remodeling the roller rink into our school. He was very excited to let me know that, while in City Hall, he had overheard that the A street property was going back on the market! Knowing our desire to build a gym, he strongly recommended we get on the stick and get an offer into the realtor.

I immediately let my board know the news and the opportunity it offered. They didn't dither and, after due diligence, closed on the deal! This doubled our property east of the building and would be the logical home of our new gym.

THAT BITTERSWEET MOMENT

In the spring of 1997 Julie and I saw our first child, Carolyn, graduate from Logos School. We hadn't had a preschool program when she was that age, so we enrolled her in the Logos kindergarten back in 1984. By her senior year, she was one of a class of ten students, some of whom had been together since kindergarten. Carolyn had gained much from being at Logos and she had certainly plunged into all she could, extracurricular-wise. She had done drama every year from junior high through high school (not sure where she got that gene), went out for and played on the first Mock Trial and volleyball teams, and even got a part-time job at Arby's while in high school to earn some cash.

At the commencement ceremony held in the rich Gothic architecture of the University of Idaho's Administration Auditorium, Carolyn and her dear friend, Kim Rigg, sang a special number. The song was "His Eye Is On the Sparrow" and I found it very hard to stay composed, which was awkward being on stage and everything.

It was an incredible blessing to have all of Carolyn's grandparents in the audience. Julie's mom had graduated from high school on that same stage a fair number of years before.

Carolyn would go on to New St. Andrews College, a local classical, Christian school Doug had also been instrumental in starting in 1994. Carolyn would thrive there, as it prepared her for what would be a nine-year teaching career before her marriage in 2010. In her final semester at NSA, as part of the then cooperative student-teacher program between Logos and NSA, Carolyn was able to be an aide to me in my history class!

As it happened, her graduation song's theme, God's care even for sparrows, came back to me in a very different context not long after Carolyn's graduation...

JIM AND THE GYM

Shortly after the board approved the idea of "looking into" a possible field house in January, 1997, I was given the name of a man who might be able to give me information on large steel-frame buildings. Construction guys have always intimidated me by the large amount of practical knowledge they have, compared to the paperwork and often elusive ideas I deal with. When these guys complete a job, very often the skyline is changed. That's impressive! So, it was with some trepidation I found myself opposite Mr. Jim Yates, a builder of steel buildings, at a table in a local Bonanza.

Not surprisingly, Jim looked like a man who had spent more than half-a-century doing hard, manual work with his beefy, calloused hands. He spoke plainly, and with a slight Western twang he got right to the point. But he also had a wry, often self-deprecating sense of humor and a love for the Lord that put me at ease immediately. It wasn't long before Jim was using a napkin to make a sketch, the first of many in months to come, illustrating the gym he wanted to build for Logos School.

We continued to meet for lunch at Bonanza so often that the folks behind the counter knew our names and probable orders. (Jim liked a diet Pepsi with a chaser of water, for instance.) But one day, after we had discussed the gym plans for the umpteenth time, I got around to asking Jim about his own family. Jim then told me the story of his daughter. I don't know how long we were at lunch that day; I just know I was spellbound as this father recalled the way his daughter, who was afflicted with diabetes, had been held mentally and spiritually captive by a group of New-Agers in Texas. They didn't believe in modern medicine, but rather worshiped idols of healing crystals and gems. They nearly killed Jim's daughter through their godless beliefs and practices. It was an incredible tale of God's redeeming and timely grace, as well as this man's love for his daughter and God's accomplishing what man deems impossible.

Jim told me about one time, while eating at his favorite restaurant, he saw a sparrow slam into the window, killing it instantly. It reminded him of the statement Jesus made about His Father's knowledge and care of even the multitudes of small, seemingly worthless sparrows. Jim began a ministry of carving and sending miniature sparrows, along with a letter of encouragement to those he knew were in pain or otherwise experiencing hard times. He also wrote a book about his daughter's experiences entitled *Flight 654 From Austin*. Its publication put Jim in the public eye. He was asked to appear on a Christian television show, as well as make other public appearances to tell his story. He met and got to know Joni Erickson, another Christian whom God has used mightily through a hard providence.

Jim didn't want to talk about his story nearly as much as I did, but he did give my family a copy of his book after having dinner at our home. All of us read it and were blessed by the glory it gave to God.

Over the months following that talk, without any commitment, much less compensation from Logos, Jim came up from his work and home in Clarkston, Washington, countless times to talk, plan, pray, and generally encourage me. Honestly, he had more faith that this was going to happen than I did. The Scripture says that a brother is often found in times of adversity. The process of putting together the plans and then the funding of the gym were frequently filled with temptations to discouragement and frustration. Jim never wavered in his trust that God would do what was right.

"If you're not supposed to have this thing, then, by George, He's got something *better* in mind for your school!" he said on many occasions.

There were a plethora of aspects to this huge project. But one of the greatest blessings God gave Logos and me was the opportunity to meet and work with Jim Yates. Not only did he give his expertise and time free of charge, he made sure the building would bless the kids as much as possible. In the great scheme of eternity, the gym may not be dissimilar to the brief life of a sparrow, but not only was God aware of it, He used it to bless His people and the work of His kingdom in Moscow.

I JUST LOVE A STUDENT IN UNIFORM

For me, the tipping point came when I saw one of our high school boys, a cheerful big kid, show up for school one morning wearing a white T-shirt, coveralls with one shoulder strap hanging loose, and flip-flops (without socks, of course). "Good grief!" pretty much sums up my thoughts and feeling at the time.

For the first seventeen years of its life, Logos School had a dress code that was pretty simple: students were to be "Neat, clean, and modest." The assumption had been that the parents, knowing our standards, would happily comply and clothe their progeny accordingly. End of story. Lest it be thought that this was just an easy, off the cuff (so to speak) policy, prior to the opening of the school the Logos School Board did not have just one, but many serious discussions about student apparel. More specifically we debated the question: Would the students be allowed to go barefoot, or would we require at least sandals? No, that last sentence was not a misprint—we truly spent serious time on that very issue.

One must remember the era our culture was slowly climbing out of by 1981. Hippies were still waking up to the need to cut their hair, take baths, and get jobs. Three-quarters of the Logos School Board were baby boomers in their twenties. That means something: we were culturally clueless, by and large. For us, it was the rather conservative view to require sandals. Had someone walked in off the street, interrupted our meeting, and suggested we look into *student uniforms*, of all things...well, the expression "laughed to scorn" comes to mind. I'm pretty sure even Doug wouldn't have seriously countenanced that idea then.

On the other hand, one must also consider the nature and look of Christian school student uniforms of the early '80s. Not a pretty sight. Those poor kids in the uniform catalogs. Not to put too fine a point on it, the companies must have done a casting call that included the requirement of being the school pariah. The best you could say for the starchy, beyond-modest uniforms was that they were patriotic: red, white, and blue.

So back to 1998. By that point, the idea of making some serious changes to our student culture, starting with our dress code, was a drum beat that was increasing in volume and urgency. Oh, we had made some brave forays into the sensitive area of the students' appearance. At one point we tried insisting that the boys tuck in their shirts. (I'm still not exaggerating.) That met with mild disregard to outright disobedience, and very little parental support. It did serve to let me know that

1. any real improvement would need to be pretty drastic; and
2. the Civil War might look like a mild disagreement compared to what we would face.

But face it we did. A committee was put together to research possible uniform options for the youngest students. The committee's recommendation was that we not require families to buy from one source, but rather give them guidelines for the desired clothing. That way they could go with a uniform company or just pick similar items from Walmart.

Meanwhile, we researched the benefits of uniforms. There were many; even some inner city schools had found that having students wear uniforms seemed to have a strong correlation with lowered misbehavior. We were slowly discovering a maxim that not only private schools, but many other wise folks knew: how one dresses affects how one acts. Sports teams have uniforms for that reason, among others. Same with the military. Shoot, same with McDonald's and most other fast-food restaurants. Weddings, funerals, job interviews...you get the idea. So, if we wanted to have the students at Logos treat school as their work place, which it was, they should dress for the occasion.

Well, of course knowing and sharing all sorts of great reasons still doesn't calm every fear. What fears? As we spread the word that uniforms might be coming, I received an interesting assortment of communiques from parents. One dad, who had more degrees behind his name than I knew one was allowed to have, sent me a four-page letter. (I mention the degrees to make it clear he wasn't reacting due to low IQ.) In the letter, among other things, he let me know I was following the same thinking as Chairman Mao of Red China. Yes, I was encouraging the children to be little commies, since they wear identical outfits. Other fears I heard mostly had to do with the children losing all sense of identity, or that they would grow up ignorant of how to dress themselves, or that their self-esteem would suffer irreparable damage.

Finally, the watershed board meeting arrived. After a *great* deal of discussion, yea, verily, even debate, the board passed a motion by the margin of one vote. The motion was that we would require the next year's kindergartners and first graders to wear the chosen school clothing ('uniform' only in name). All the other grades, i.e., the vast majority of the students, would be grandfathered in and would stay under the old guidelines. As the first graders grew, we would require all students coming in after them to have the required clothing, sort of like a slow tide rising. In other words, we were going to wait over ten years to have *all* the students in a uniform look.

Even with that rather generous amount of time and the exclusion of most of the current student body, I still heard from unhappy parents about the board's decision. To be clear: I heard from parents whose children would never have to comply with the new dress code! Sigh.

But, to be honest, I wasn't all that provoked or tempted to respond to even outlandish complaints and concerns. That's because I knew, without a doubt in my mind, that when those kindergartners and first graders showed up in the darling little outfits the next fall, the battle would be over! We had landed on the beaches of Omaha; from here on out it would still be a fight at times, but we were on our way to victory in the Culture War, Lord willing.

MOTHER BEARS

"Let a man meet a bear robbed of her cubs, rather than a fool in his folly" (Prov. 17:12). Scripture makes it clear that there are indeed worse things than coming face-to-teeth with a mama grizzly who thinks you've been messing with her kids. But keep in mind it is a relative comparison, as you see in the above quote. In fact, the relative undesirability of being in company with a fool is quite heightened by the comparison, in my opinion. True, I have never actually been closer to a bear than when he's safely behind the bars of a zoo, but I have read too many of those Drama In Real Life Stories in *Reader's Digest*; "His teeth were as big as railroad spikes, crushing my head with the power of a hundred vises! I knew I was going to die!" Right. If I ever had had the desire to backpack in the wilds of Yellowstone Park, those stories would have cured that impulse very quickly. In fact, I take walks near our home only during the day.

Nevertheless, in my own little way, I believe I have had more than one encounter with "mother bears" right here in Logos School. My tangles have left only a few mental and emotional scars on my psyche, but they haven't been real pretty sights, either. Hackles raised, blazing eyes boring into mine, claws at the ready, growls barely restrained under the surface of her strained voice, mothers of not a few students over the years have held me at bay. Under my calm demeanor, sweat glands and heart were at maximum pumping power, and I mentally thanked Providence that a rather hefty desk was between me and certain destruction. Lacking any real firepower at hand, I have had to rely only on my own wits and the power of calming rhetoric: "Now, Betty, I understand exactly how you feel, but you have to see it from my side, too. If you kill me now, my own four children will be really disappointed! You do see that, don't you?" I have also discovered that my rhetoric can be enhanced by my kneeling behind my desk.

How do these situations come about? I frequently ask myself that same question. In fact it often comes to mind when I find myself kneeling behind my desk, pleading for my life. Actually, these situations, unlike a real bear hunting trip, often spring upon me without much warning at all. I mean, when one heads into the woods with some anticipation, and better yet, some preparation for such an encounter, then the bear arriving on the scene should cause little more surprise than seeing another actor come on stage at his cue. "Oh, there you are," the hunter might even say, "It's about time! I was beginning to wonder if I had the right forest!"

But I don't enjoy such deliberate anticipation or planning. No, usually the first I know of these life-threatening experiences is when my office door bursts open, and hovering over me is a seething mother, often with semi-crumbled school papers in her paw, er, her fist. Then, if I am lucky, instead of instantly shredding my sensitive emotions with her razor-sharp remarks and accusations, she holds herself in check and asks if I have a "few minutes" for her to ask me some questions. Often those situations can hold out the hope that life may go on and we can come to some reconciliation.

However, appearances can be deceiving and, though outwardly calm with me, she may have committed some bloodletting before she got to my door. I have had occasions when I thought we had separated with all my limbs still functioning as they should, only to find, upon tracing the mother's tracks through the school building, a teacher bleeding profusely from multiple wounds. The teacher is not really close to death, she just has the look of a wife at the site of a mining accident: barely holding herself together, and obviously suffering from shock and disbelief. So we work through it—her telling me that after twelve years of teaching she now realizes that she is a total failure and should take up garbage-collecting; me telling her that she is not a failure and that Logos, yay verily, the entire Christian school movement in the United States of America needs her to stay in teaching.

Godly perspective, as always, is the key to these situations. The "mother bear" moms usually calm down and come to see that we are truly sorry for causing mental anguish for her cubs, er, kids. And we usually come to see that we may have been hasty in assigning blame, or too many homework pages, or whatever. Dads, like softening music when present, often play a key role in providing that calming effect on upset moms: "Martha, you heard Mr. Garfield say he will review the test with Mrs. Johanson. OK? Now, let's go home and maybe he'll come down off the bookshelf."

OPEN FOR BUSINESS

Not long after my Memphis debacle, in which I thought I had lost several thousand dollars at the close of the ACCS conference, I was able to persuade the board to hire a real Marketing person. What had started literally as a back-room (ok, staff-room) copy-and-mail operation, selling some of our in-house documents to sister schools, was getting to be quite a demanding task. We hired a sequence of some part-time people fill in, but our sales (and product quality) really took off when we hired a retired Army officer, Scott Oplinger.

Being a Navy guy myself, Scott and I had the occasional military trash-talking episodes, but mostly he was all business. He and I met weekly for the eight years he was our Marketing Officer. I enjoyed our times of discussing the cover of this workbook or the filming schedule of that series. He took the 'look' of our ACCS vendor booth to new levels, also.

Logos rented a single-wide office trailer and parked it on the end of our outdoor basketball court. It contained our Marketing office and inventory, as well as Ed Van Nuland's Development office. He and Scott got along famously; they weren't exactly the odd couple, but they did have rather different personalities. As our sales and inventory increased, Scott asked for and got a wider, longer trailer to move into. He and Ed initially wondered if I could do something about how often a ball would bounce off their trailer during recess, but I managed to convince them that it was just one of their perks.

Though we didn't know it at the time, Scott was with us during the "golden age" of sales for Logos. Being the first, and for a number of years, the *only* source of uniquely classical curriculum and administrative materials brought in orders from far and wide. He was also there in the early part of the new century when a local hubbub broke out between the local homosexual forces and Christ Church. Our friendly connection to the church (and particularly Doug Wilson) brought Logos into the cross-hairs of the contrary members of our fair community.

During the War Between the States, General Robert E. Lee was such a Christian gentleman that he never referred to the Union forces as "damn Yankees." Instead, he would refer to them as "our friends from the North," or "those people." So in keeping with his spirit, I will refer to our opponents as 'those people,' too.

One of the primary movers among those people was a lesbian whose daughter I had taught in my student teaching days. She did me the courtesy of letting me know during a phone call that they were gunning for us, specifically to challenge the income we were getting from our sales of materials. She believed that it fit in the category of "non-related business income" and therefore violated our non-profit status.

Their first assault was at the county commissioners' level. This was the authority to which I annually submitted our formal request to remain exempt from property taxes. Up to that point each year's submission had been a rather perfunctory process. This time we asked our parents and friends to show up for the hearing, knowing full well the other side would have representatives there. They did. But the packed room was largely due to our wonderful families, even some children. It was not a public hearing in the sense of lots of witnesses speaking, but rather just a representative of those people challenging our appeal, and me, defending it, in public.

After the three commissioners heard our respective sides, they deliberated (sweated) also in public. I actually felt sorry for them; these were good men, mostly retired, who after running a farm or a business, were there just to help the community. Now they were being asked to vote on an issue, knowing they were going to make some folks unhappy no matter what they did.

Finally, they publicly stated that they weren't sure of all the tax-related issues, but it seemed to them that we weren't doing anything wrong. They quickly added that, should anyone want to appeal their decision, they could do so to the Idaho State Tax Commission. They even helpfully wrote the address on a nearby whiteboard.

Well, those people took note and filed an appeal to the next level. This meant that we had to get some more of our ducks in a row and have good, documented evidence that what we were doing was totally in keeping with our original stated mission.

The Commission held their hearing at the local Best Western and it had all the formality of a court case. There were four men this time, sitting behind tables and looking very stern. They also had a tape recorder going. Those people showed up, as did we (Scott in the audience with some parents and me at the other table). As those people arrived, they made some small talk, which kind of puzzled me. I didn't want or expect to fall to instant fisticuffs, but discussing the weather struck me as odd. I mean, if they got their way, Logos would lose many thousands of dollars each year for the foreseeable future. Whereas, if we won the day, nothing much would change, and those people would walk away; no harm, no foul.

The hearing took longer this time. I had no idea if I was making any headway, the judges kept the same faces as each side was heard. If I ever played poker, I wouldn't want to do it with them. I explained that our purpose in making the materials was to not only help our own school, since the materials were written by our faculty members, but also to help other schools like ours.

We took an intermission and all stood up to stretch and relax as much as possible. One of the judges, the guy on the end manning the recorder, came over to me.

"I just want you to know," he said quietly, "that my wife and I homeschool our kids and we use your materials. We think they're just great! Thanks for making them!" Then he slipped back into his seat.

As we began Round 2, I was rather encouraged by those comments, though I had no way of knowing if he was allowed to share that info with his fellow judges.

The testimony part finally ended, but this time the judges didn't deliberate in front of us. Rather, they told all of us that they would render a written judgment and send it to both parties. Oh goodie. I just love waiting.

But they didn't make us wait long—their summary report came within the week. I opened the letter with some trepidation, though I should have been more trusting in the Lord's way of doing things. In short, the conclusion of the Idaho State Tax Commission was that not only was it okay for Logos to make and sell our materials, it was a very wise thing to do to help fund our school!

I don't know if I did a little dance; I don't usually, but I was rather pleased and very thankful. After informing my board, I made a few dozen copies of the letter to keep on hand should those people try for another charge up Seminary Ridge, or Little Round Top, for that matter!

Our Logos Press "store" would stay open for business for many more years. During its time it would bring hundreds of thousands of helpful dollars to our annual budget. We developed a large catalog of materials that we used as well as sold: spelling and math programs, plays, admin handbooks and Latin charts, State Facts and poetry and grammar workbooks and more. Finally, after about eighteen years of making and selling curriculum materials, Logos Press was sold to Canon Press in 2012, where our materials could be made and distributed much more efficiently.

"DON'T KNOW MUCH ABOUT HISTORY"

Speaking of the items we made and eventually sold, this seems as good a place as any to explain how we ended up teaching history the way we did. You have to remember that, like Indiana Jones (probably a lost reference), when it came to planning, we were making it up as we went!

You might recall that we had abandoned a Christian school publisher's materials early on and decided to just make up our own curriculum guide. But our guiding light, if you will, was Sayer's *Lost Tools* article. We (our first teachers and I) knew that whatever we cooked up to teach, we had to build it around the frames of the children we were teaching. That actually helped quite a bit. For every discipline, e.g., math, English, science, etc., we attempted to break it down to its grammatical or basic elements and add to the material in logical, sequential steps as the children grew.

Therefore, when it came to the study of history, we simply considered Sayers's recommendations for the early (Poll Parrot) years. We didn't follow everything she suggested; we took a detour from her suggestion to memorize the kings of England, for instance. But we liked the idea of starting with the building blocks/categories of history: Important People, Places, Events, and Dates. Well, what are all those to a five-year-old? Following the same order, we came up with: "My Family, My Home, My Owwies, My Birthday (and Christmas), as starters.

And we built from there. Kindergarten History would focus on our homes and families, our wonderful town of Moscow, trips to the fire station, knowing our president's name, our birthdays and other important days, like Easter. We would also seek to integrate disciplines wherever possible: in early math we learn about money with coins that also have Washington's and Lincoln's faces on them, as well as famous places in Washington, D.C.

Building a history program that 'expanded' as the children grew in their ability to understand time and distances seemed obvious to us. So that by the time the students were in sixth grade they could grasp concepts like five hundred years or five thousand miles away, a bit easier than a first grader could. At sixth grade, then, world history makes more sense.

It wasn't until the ACCS grew and other classical, Christian publishers arrived on the scene that we became aware that there were other "schools" of thought on the teaching of history in the grammar years. At our summer training weeks we started having attendees ask us why we didn't teach history in chronological order, i.e., the way it happened? That was how a very popular publisher was doing it and many sister schools were buying that publisher's history materials. Finally, since we were having to explain our approach again and again, I decided to write an apologetic, explaining our thinking.*

THE BIBLICAL BASIS FOR EDUCATION

Please don't immediately or unconsciously reinterpret the title above as "The Basis for Biblical Education." There is a profound difference. (Also please note that I didn't say, "The Biblical Basis for Classical Education," even though I think that argument can be made without much effort. But that's not my point here.)

* See Appendix C.

So, what's the difference? As always, it comes down to what we believe about the world. If we believe that "knowledge," i.e., all the stuff we all need to learn, is somehow neutral, then Christians should just take a number and wait their turn for presenting a case for "Christian" education. However, if Genesis 1:1 is true—God really did speak the heavens and earth into existence—well, that changes everything. Literally every thing.

Many years ago I was asked by a friend who was a university education professor to speak to his beginning ed class. He was a Christian and knew what I did for a living, so when he said I had carte blanche on what I'd say, I was delighted. I began by praising the students for their courage to enter the ministry and teach religious tenets faithfully every day. Since we were at the local secular university, I'm pretty sure the students thought I was either very confused or had brought the wrong speech.

Warming to my theme, I pointed out that as they were embarking on a teaching career, they must certainly be aware that they would be dealing with very religious themes. Regardless of what grade or subject they would be teaching, they would daily be instructing their pupils about the obvious conundrums of life:

- Why am I here?
- Who made me?
- Does my life have any meaning?
- Where did this world come from?
- What or who defines *right* and *wrong*?
- Do I have any responsibility toward others?

From the dawn of time, philosophers and religious leaders of every stripe understood these questions as not only being profoundly "religious," they cannot be avoided in any formal or informal education system. In fact, historically education was all about these questions. Hence, it's not a question of *if* religion will be presented to children being educated, it's a question of *which* religion will be presented as truth.

How does this actually work out in reality? Consciously or not, the parents of every child born on planet Earth immediately begin answering those questions for their sweet, little bundle. As every child grows and expresses vast amounts of curiosity, parents don't stop answering those questions, but they may delegate others to help provide the answers, usually by enrolling their child in a school of some sort. There the child will hear a story told by his teachers. The story will seek to answer all those questions. Again, this is *unavoidable*, regardless of the school's location, curriculum, size, or even its stated mission. A story *will* be told that will seek to answer those questions.

This naturally leads to what should concern every parent, particularly Christian parents...will their child be told a true or false story? "In the beginning God created the heavens and the earth..." This passage is not only the answer to the debate between the Creation story and evolutionary theory; if Genesis 1:1 is true, then the story will have a direction, purpose, cohesion, and even a happy ending. All those questions above will get true answers. But what if Genesis 1:1 is presented as false, or up to interpretation, or just considered unimportant? Well, then, the story will give varied and conflicting answers, which are not answers at all, to those questions. Literally, anything could happen and might. Life is chaos and chance accidents. There is no wrong or right. We might as well eat, drink, and seek our own pleasure, or misery, because death awaits us all. All is vanity.

There is no neutral, third option. The story we and others tell our children will either be true or false. Our children will grow up believing the Truth or a lie.

Obviously the Bible has more than the first verse...but on it everything else is built. Because God made the world, the Bible not only answers the questions about who we are and where the world came from, but it tells the most wonderful part of the story—it tells of Christ, the Author and Finisher of our faith. In Christ our lives and those of our children have eternal meaning. Only in Christ do we understand and teach that we live in a true *uni*verse—all that we see, touch, taste, hear, and even smell tells a compelling and cohesive story. A story being told by an Author who knows our frames intimately.

Sadly, Christian schools too often tell a watered-down, incomplete story to children. They acknowledge that God created the heavens and the earth, but then treat all other consequential knowledge as some kind of bland oatmeal. This oatmeal, they believe, is commonly accepted by all educators, secular or Christian. So it's up to us Christians to flavor the oatmeal for our students with "Christian" condiments: Scripture as brown sugar and hymns as raisins! "Silly pagans, they just give their students bland, cold oatmeal. They probably even use 1% milk—we use the cream of daily prayers!" What nonsense.

"God's mystery, that is, Christ Himself, in whom are hidden *all* the treasures of *wisdom and knowledge*" (Col. 2:2, 3; emphasis mine). It's not "oatmeal," it's Christ! In Him, we move and breathe and have our being, in Him all things hold together. If that means anything at all, it means that the story we, parents and teachers, tell to these precious children must be Christ and His Kingdom. So it's not an option to seek to reveal Christ in history, in art, in math, in science, in manners, in eating, in music, in drama, in basketball...in our lives, lived before these students.

"For God, who said, 'Light shall shine out of darkness,' is the One who has shone in our hearts to give the light of the knowledge of the glory of God in the face of Christ" (2 Cor. 4:6). This is the story, this is true education.

GIVING AWARDS: NOT WHETHER, BUT WHY AND WHICH

As I read the long list of names, and the group of elementary kids up front grew to a fair sized crowd, I marveled, not for the first time, at the sheer number of students earning the awards. The next day Tom Spencer went through the same routine for the older kiddos: his lists were long, too, and many people attending the secondary awards assembly just shook their heads in wonder at the number of awards. In addition to the honor rolls, many other rewards were distributed, recognizing various hard-earned achievements.

Why did we go through all this? Didn't it make some students feel bad if they didn't receive an award? Most importantly, was it consistent with biblical standards and practice? Our so-called secular educational establishment asks the first two questions and comes up with one of two answers, generally. One answer in regard to rewards is to lower the bar, so to speak, low enough that just about anyone breathing can "earn" a reward and then, the theory goes, no one will feel bad. Perhaps you've seen this at high school graduations where there are more valedictorians than there are people in the audience. The other popular answer is to try to eliminate all competition en mass. Competition, it is said, is bad since it necessitates that somebody is not going to do as well as the others, and...you guessed it...that somebody will feel bad. They even try to eliminate striving for a goal or standard that might earn a prize, since, again, everyone might not make it.

So, the popular philosophical options on rewards seem to be: give it to everybody (making any award meaningless), or give it to no one (making any effort meaningless).

Does Scripture address this topic, and if so, what does it say? It does, and it says quite a bit! Here is an abbreviated list of applicable scriptures and principles:

1. Rewards are promised by our Lord to believers: Matthew 5:12, 10:42
2. Rewards are related to the work of the competitor: Psalm 58:11, II Timothy 2:5, I Corinthians 9:24
3. Rewards are not to be an end in themselves: Isaiah 1:23
4. Rewards, when kept in a right perspective, initiate tangible consequences: Proverbs 22:4, 23:29

In our school context, then, we regarded rewards highly. Yes, it is true that those students who did not earn any rewards, for whatever reason, were tempted to feel badly, or even to feel sorry for themselves. When Matt Whitling became our principal, I greatly appreciated his practical and wise counsel to the kids on how to receive rewards, i.e., with gratitude, as you would receive a gift. Because the rewards were indeed gifts: any abilities the students had were gifts, any physical abilities the students had were gifts, all from a loving Father. If a student didn't get that gift (or a reward), feeling sorry for himself was actually a form of pride, not humility.

We also believed that what we awarded and why we esteemed that work taught all the students valuable lessons. For example, we didn't award students with cash gifts for academic work, lest they be tempted to violate principle number three above. Also, among our various rewards we included the recognition of improvement, in light of principle number two. And, even in our current culture, good grades (representing real standards), and their recognition produce tangible benefits, e.g., scholarships for high GPAs or valedictorian* status.

In Philippians 3:23 Paul says, "I press on toward the goal for the prize of the upward call of God in Christ Jesus." Our most important principle regarding rewards was that good work brings glory to God and to the parents of the students. While they are students, they experience the joy of pleasing their parents whom they represent in their work. We prayed that, in their future, as adults, they would experience the joy of pleasing their Lord whom they would represent in their lives.

PARTY LIKE IT'S 1999!

American confidence and trust in technology was badly shaken toward the end of the twentieth century. We had come to rely greatly on the seemingly flawless and remarkable computer chip, developed in the eighties. But as we approached the year change to "00" after midnight on December 31, 1999, the same computer experts who had developed the marvelous chip started to give us dire predictions of a coming catastrophe. Their chips might just flip out when the date changed. And since those chips were in just about every significant electronic devise, from missiles to stop lights, if they failed, mass pandemonium was predicted!

Many people began to stockpile food and emergency items, in case the worst happened. Large companies, particularly in the U.S., spent billions on upgrading their computers to avoid the "Y2K" meltdown. Out here in northern Idaho, we already have a fairly high number of folks who want

* Our process for selecting the highest award (Valedictorian) and the second highest (Salutatorian) to be given to our graduating seniors was based only partially on their GPA. We met as a secondary faculty usually in late April and used a matrix to select the two students who would give the valedictory address and the salutatory (greeting). There were four categories we weighed for each qualified senior: GPA, Character, Honors, and Extra-curricular Activities. We actually assigned numerical values to help us come to a consensus. When the numbers didn't give us a clear choice (that we also felt good about) and we had to decide between two individuals for the top award, we would give even more attention to the Christian character and leadership each student demonstrated while at Logos. Community and church activities, if known, were also considered.

to live off the grid. This development not only gave them another reason to stay tucked away in the hills, it created many new converts to that line of thinking. Survival mentality became rampant. Generators, guns, ammo, and huge canisters of dry goods flew off the shelves in Costco.

At Logos we weren't planning on an apocalypse, but we didn't want to get caught unprepared either. With the support and advice of the board, I wrote a letter to our families and staff. It outlined three potential scenarios for Logos. Since we would be on Christmas break when...well, when whatever might happen, happened, I proposed that one of three situations might occur:

1. The date changes and not much else happens. In that case, yee-haw, a wipe of the sweat off the collective brow and we soldier on.
2. As the clock strikes midnight, portions of the power grid go down, with a moderate affect on our campus. In that case, we see what still switches on and proceed accordingly.
3. As the date and time changes, all the chips go whack-a-do and fry themselves into bits of smoldering plastic or metal (I think they're plastic, but not really sure). Chaos breaks out, there is no light or heat to be found in Latah County. Black helicopters fly overhead with snipers to take out looters, zoo animals run amok in the city. Scratch that, Moscow has no zoo. OK, then all the traffic lights fail (all six or seven of them) and drivers take side streets, instead. In other words, complete mayhem and madness!

In that case, the students should stay home, I advised with Solomon-like wisdom. Logos doesn't have all that many candles and it could get kind of chilly in our cinder block building. (Some students have always maintained that I didn't heat the building as it was. Not true. We had eleven-foot ceilings and the heat ducts were located in those ceilings. How often does warm air go *down*? I rest my case.)

It should be noted that, true to form, Christ Church decided to throw a New Year's Eve party in the Logos gym. They weren't being cavalier; the church officers had seriously discussed various scenarios as my board had done. I think the idea was that if the power grid was going to fail anyway, wouldn't it be fun to have everyone together? Or something like that. So they had a huge party, with live bands, food, dancing, and I was asked to give short snippets of history from the twentieth century at intervals.

Then, at midnight (in the respective time zones) across America, everyone held their corporate breath as the clocks ticked off the last seconds and then...nothing happened. Actually Australia was the first to experience the non-event, so by the time it turned midnight in the Pacific Time Zone (three hours after the east coast), we kind of already knew it was ok. Some old PCs (especially in Russia and Logos School) did revert their clocks (ours went to 1980!?), but hardly anything else occurred. The stockpiling folks now had months of dry goods to eat up, which kind of made me happy.

ARROWS FLYING AWAY

Once we crested the tipping point in the 1999–2000 school year, survived Y2K, and returned to school in January, things went on pretty much as before. But that spring semester went all too fast for my taste. Time really does fly by during any school year, but this one seemed to accelerate to light speed. No guesses as to why: Seth's class was graduating in May. Being a male and eighteen, he was naturally chomping at the bit to be done with school, yes, even Logos. Even so, I knew, and he began to realize, that he would miss his friends, some of whom had been with him since preschool.

Many times during that last year in Logos with him, I found myself mentally recalling the days, weeks, and months Julie and I had prayed, wept, and waited for him to come home from the hospital in Spokane. As a three month preemie, he had weighed in at only 2 lbs., 3 oz; an emergency delivery on a sunny July day. Two and a half months later he did come home, in the same autumn Logos School first opened.

Now he was graduating from the school that shared his age. He planned to go to the U of I, but wasn't entirely sure what he would study. A generally quiet, but kind young man, he knew how to help others, which was very appreciated by the patrons of the Safeway grocery store where he worked. Many Moscow folks knew him from his time there; so many in fact, that years later, after he had married, worked for a local software company, and then moved away, it wasn't uncommon for people to stop me and ask about his welfare.

The work at Logos had been difficult for Seth, as it was for many students. Nevertheless, he went out for basketball and even helped me in a few plays. It took a while to figure out, but eventually Seth found that he was good with numbers and business, as well as having great people skills. Accounting and working with a firm's customers eventually became his vocation.

But that spring of 2000, all I could think of was how proud I was of him and how much I would miss him when he flew away. Yet that's what arrows are supposed to do. I could only pray that to some extent I had helped sharpen him for whatever target he was to hit.

The next year, 2001, it was Kajsa's turn. With Julie as a mother, it wasn't too surprising that some of our children would love music. Julie had a lovely soprano voice which she used in a number of choirs and musical groups. It was also one of the many things that attracted me to her in 1977, but that's not the point of this story.

Kajsa, our token Scandinavian, blonde and gregarious, loved the arts and the social benefits of school. She did rather well in all her studies, but made and kept many friends among the students. To my great joy, she also loved drama and even took roles I knew she wasn't thrilled about. Her favorite role came early when, as a freshman, she was cast as Beatrice in *Much Ado About Nothing*. The director was a good friend of mine, Donna Grauke, in her varsity level directing debut. Kajsa was magnificent, if I may say so.

We sought to teach all our kids to play the piano, just to value music, if for no other reason. Kajsa took to it quickly and her ability was obvious. A number of years into her lessons, we discovered she had perfect pitch, which delighted her and Julie. (I had no idea what this was, though I tried to act excited for Kajsa. Julie privately explained it to me later.)

One of my favorite photos of Kajsa defines her perfectly. It was taken in her sophomore year (I was blessed to teach all four of my children U.S. History in their sophomore years) and it was on school picture day. Mark LaMoreaux, our favorite school photographer was still up on a ladder in the auditorium, talking with me. Just then Kajsa entered and crossed the room. Mark stopped her and said, "Hey Kajsa! I have just a few shots left. Let me get some of you!"

Kajsa immediately stopped and assumed the classic dramatic pose, head turned, arms thrown up, receiving the adoring applause of an invisible audience. Mark snapped it and later gave me a copy.

That year sped by as well and Kajsa went to the U of I to study musical accompaniment. She met a handsome, godly, young tenor there, Bray Wilkins, and was married after her junior year. They followed Bray's operatic ambitions, which eventually took them far away to New York City, the epicenter of grand musical productions. For a time, Kajsa taught music all day to a wide age-range of students in a sister classical school in Manhattan.

Another arrow gone with our prayers and aching hearts.

NOT VERY STREET SMART

"Behold, I send you out as sheep in the midst of wolves; therefore be shrewd as serpents, and innocent as doves." Matthew 10:16

It most likely happened in the wee hours (what makes them so small?) of a Saturday night in May of 2001. Of course, we didn't discover it until Sunday morning when one of our teachers arrived at school well before the church services held on our campus. He called me at about 7:30 am. I in turn, called the police and met them at Logos. According to the officers of the law, it appeared that at least one (!) person had taken a baseball bat to our glass front doors and, not thinking that enough fun, had also smashed portions of our stained glass windows on each side of the front doors. All the glass in the doors was shattered in very small pieces that had flown inwards for thirty or more feet. Quite the homer!

However, for some strange reason, the perp(s) did not actually go through the now glass-less doors and into the school. Had he (they?) done so, the large, glass trophy case just inside the foyer would doubtless have made for additional exciting batting practice. Therefore, the officers suspect the person(s) may have been interrupted in the act and left the premises in a hurry.

This actually was the second act of vandalism we had experienced that spring. Less than two weeks before our front doors were shattered, someone had used many of our classroom windows facing Baker Street for paint-balling practice, breaking two outside panes in the process. Was it the same unknown person or persons? Did we have someone out there who didn't like us, or maybe just our windows? (Maybe they accidentally ran into a school window as a young child…? That would be paneful! Sorry.) Anyway, we had no leads to offer the officers in either situation.

All this made us feel rather vulnerable, though. Were there any measures we could or should have taken that would have made these incidents less likely to happen? Well, no, probably not in these cases; although I had long entertained a secret fantasy of having several, large, extremely well-trained, sharp-fanged Dobermans prowling the hallways of the school all night long. The key there being "well-trained." (*"Logos School has an immediate opening for a second grade teacher due to our late teacher's unfortunate attempt to retrieve items from her classroom at 1:00 a.m."*)

But there were numerous, less violent ways we were vulnerable to being abused, or at least taken advantage of as a school. We were not very "street smart" when it came to preventing a host of small crimes, such as: items being taken from lockers (we didn't have locks on them); students lying about why they were in the halls during class (we didn't use hall passes); students' absences from school for questionable reasons (we deferred to the parents' statements and just kept records). Our basic system of discipline throughout the school was founded on one very intangible element: *trust.*

We certainly knew the Adamic nature we shared with all the students. We knew that we all sin in many ways. And we knew not all the students were Christians (as though that would negate them sinning). We simply didn't have the desire or know-how to build a system worth living and working within that was based on anything less than trust. Would we have been shrewder, as our Lord defines it, if we did have locks, bars, security cameras, even police officers in the school? Was "shrewdness" better served if we assumed guilt on the students' part when there was *any* doubt, or require more proof of their innocence? Should our administrators have had the street smarts and hard-boiled savvy of some TV-world, NYPD detectives?

By the nature of my questions it is probably obvious that I don't believe the above approaches were what Jesus would consider obedience to His command in Matthew. Paul has a parallel command in Romans 16:19—"but I want you to be wise in what is good, and innocent in what is evil." Wisdom and shrewdness, biblically speaking, certainly don't require us to be blind to or ignorant of the forms of evil, but our thought life is better spent dwelling on what is good.

Trust is good. Turning the other cheek is good. Even being defrauded can be good, rather than returning evil for evil. So, instead of growing hard and seeing the students in the school as little sinners just waiting their chance, or viewing those outside the school as only potential enemies and vandals, we knew we had to trust the sovereign Lord of the universe to do what's best. What can man do to us outside of His will?

DELIGHTFULLY DIFFERENT!

The solid thump of shield against shield was almost palpable for those watching. Swords swung and crashed again and again as the opponents fought with increasing vigor. They circled each other, looking for a weakness, a letting down of the guard. Then, the quick thrust and an exposed side was struck! It was the third time he had been hit and that finished him. He sank to his knees exhausted and raised his hand, the match was over. The crowd roared their approval of the strength and honor shown by both opponents. Not bad for two seventh grade boys.

But these were just two of the approximately thirty boys, from seventh through twelfth grades, who had taken part in the sword fighting. When the entire tournament was all done, Daniel Miller (8th) was the champion of the younger division (7th-9th) and Jacob Spencer (12th) was the champion of the older division (10th-12th). Each was given a full-sized, stainless steel, replica sword in a leather sheath. They couldn't have been more delighted.

Neither could I. This tournament took place in our gym, among our guys, and was an eagerly anticipated part of our newest, soon-to-be annual tradition of a Knights' Festival. This program, the replacement for what was becoming a too-worldly Spirit Week, was the product of creative thinking on the part of a number of secondary staff, but largely our secondary principal, Tom Spencer. We knew that removing Spirit Week had met with some concern and disappointment on the part of the students. So anything replacing it had two strikes against it already. The key theme became a medieval-style festival, with attendant sword-fighting, feasting, dancing, speeches, and oratorical debates. Each day had a theme: Remembrance, Thanksgiving, and Celebration. Throw in poster-making, speeches, and some displays of talent and we had three full days!

The feasting and dancing were on the last day, and also held in the gym. The entire secondary student body and staff sat together at candle-lit tables, placed in a large semi-circle, and consumed grapes, sausages, sparkling cider, bread, cheese, and cookies. After some talent numbers, the back half of the gym was used for some ball dancing, while Celtic music played.

This whole event was particularly gratifying in light of our efforts to turn our cultural ship around, so to speak. We didn't want to just react and simply halt certain worldly patterns, leaving a vacuum of cultural input. Instead, just as our Father invites us to celebrate, feast, and delight in His presence, we wanted to offer something good and beautiful for the students in place of the false and ugly which the world offers. God says yes a lot more than He says no, and we wanted to emulate His graciousness.

One of the very best things we ever did at Logos was to introduce the kids to the joys of dancing. But, unlike so many "boomer" dances, we didn't just turn down the lights, turn up the rock and roll, and let nature take its course. No, good dancing is a wonderful and often complex means of expressing joy physically. The Bible endorses dancing in some form in many places. We know King David danced before the Lord at least on one occasion. To do it well, the students needed to be taught the steps and how to keep rhythm with the music (often Celtic, waltz, or swing). We began to teach them from early grammar years (during PE and music classes) how to do some basic dances. By starting that soon, any weirdness about holding a girl's hand or spinning her around was avoided. The older students, who were learning these steps for the first time, were quickly taught that the point is consideration for and delight in your partner. In other words, good dancing taught the students a lot about real life together and particularly how to enjoy the opposite sex in a very healthy situation. This was a Creational view of dancing and the students couldn't get enough of it!

The idea of godly and fun dancing came, I have to admit, as somewhat of a watershed for me (and others I know). American Christians have a hard time getting their thinking around the idea of dancing being a positive thing for students. Why? Largely because our culture has captured and warped so much of what used to be pure and delightful. In much the same way Christians have surrendered what used to be a true and godly overall education for their children. God is not silent about how children are to be taught—in *His* world! They can and should be taught that He is One and that He still speaks. Or they can be taught that He doesn't exist or at least that He doesn't matter. The former education is like dancing before the Lord. The latter is like, well, groping in the dark. I want to see children dance!

So I believe, in a small way, we began to recover godly celebrating through this first Festival. The kids and staff loved it and everyone felt it hit just the right note. I looked forward, by God's grace and leading, to more of this sort of cultural revival. Further up and further in!

(By the way, the "swords" were foam-padded PVC pipes, just in case you were left wondering.)

"WE LIVE IN NORTH IDAHO, AND IT SHOWS"

That was the tag line for a local sporting goods and hardware store, Tri-State, "Idaho's Most Interesting Store," just down the street from our Baker Street campus. A few minutes walk from Logos would put you into the store. It really did represent Idaho quite well; about half of the large retail area was crammed with hunting, fishing, and camping equipment. The other half was mostly hardware items, with some household materials in nooks and crannies.

Having lived in my adopted state since 1977, I have come to love it very much. Though I am not a hunter or a fisherman, I have a profound respect for those that do those activities. The rolling hills, fields of wheat, ridges of evergreens and just the general wildness comprise a profound beauty that surrounds Moscow on all sides. It is best seen to be truly appreciated.

The farmers, loggers, ranchers, and even miners that helped make Idaho what it is today are not long gone. Many residents of the small communities in this area are related to some of the founding families who came here by wagon or train. Idaho history is easy to find; it's still in the hills and by the rivers. Abandoned mines, ghost towns, battlefields of the Indian wars, graves of the first settlers, even some of the first brick buildings are within easy driving distance.

IDAHO LIFE EXHIBIT NO. 1: FIREARMS AND THEIR USES

Like all regions, the lifestyles and attitudes of many who live here reflect our surroundings. Living this close to a wilderness, where the occasional moose wandering into town is no more noteworthy than a traffic accident, it shouldn't come as any surprise that we view guns and their use a bit differently than, say, New Yorkers.

So, for instance, when we had Cowboy Days (to highlight the letter C) in Kindergarten, the kids read and heard stories about cowboys and dressed up like Matt Dillon (even if they didn't know who he was). Toy six-shooters were thrust into the gun holsters of the miniature cowpokes. Once in a while I was invited by the teacher to come and show the kids my Colt .45 "Peacemaker" (a realistic replica, since I couldn't afford a real one).

One time I was asked by a curly blond Calamity Jane, "Is this where the bullets go in my gun?," holding up her cap pistol, which actually had a cylinder that rolled out. I confirmed that, yes, that was where they went. The class shared some stories of how they had either seen or used real guns with their parents or grandparents. Such was the trust these little ones had in those adults who loved and educated them, that I didn't hear one comment of fearfulness, much less that guns were "bad." Just that the kids were to obey their parents in all things, and not touch real guns, unless their parents said it was okay. Oh yes, and that the cowboy guns are good for shooting rattlesnakes.

In my sophomore class on U.S. History, I would show the same Colt .45, as well as a replica of the derringer used by John Wilkes Booth to kill Abraham Lincoln. As we got into the World Wars, I was able to show them the real German bayonet I was given by my mother-in-law. Her uncle has served in France during World War I and picked it up, along with a German helmet.

One year a dad of a student in my class asked if I'd be interested in having him invite a friend to bring in some World War II guns he'd collected. I was delighted by the idea and assumed the friend would maybe have a 1911 .45, or perhaps an M-1 rifle. Instead, when he arrived, he backed up his old station wagon near the school's back door and began unloading his collection. Or, rather, part of his collection, as he told us later. We put down four cafeteria tables upon which he proceeded to lay out weapons from every war since our nation's founding! Smooth bore muskets were placed beside cavalry officer's pistols from the War Between the States; a German luger nestled next to a BAR (Browning Automatic Rifle); near a Thompson submachine gun (Tommy gun) was an actual modern sniper rifle, to name just a few of the weapons displayed. The historic value of the pieces was beyond my comprehension!

The students gathered around as the collector explained the features and background of each weapon. Then he graciously allowed us to carefully pick them up and hold them. I didn't need to encourage the boys, but I made a point of telling some reluctant girls that this was a once-in-a-lifetime chance to touch history. I let them all know that the only other way any of them would ever see some of those pieces was behind glass in a museum! They got the point and pretty soon were holding the M-1 (which he had, too) or the Springfield rifle from the late 1800s, among others.

How did all this exposure to actual weapons fit in with our Christian or classical philosophy? Or did I allow it only because we lived in north Idaho and it showed? Well, I admit that part of my motivation was certainly due to admiring weapons. But more importantly, as with anything worth studying at Logos, our approach had to do with honestly and respectfully examining the value and nature of the subject. With guns, as with electricity, fire, chemicals, and cars, to name just a few things that can be lethal to innocent parties if used unwisely, we wanted the students to understand the nature of what they were handling. A very practical application of Paul's admonition to the Thessalonians to "examine everything, and hold fast to that which is good" (I certainly wanted to hold fast to the Tommy gun!)

On another level, guns have been treated by the liberals just as alcohol was treated by the Christian Women's Temperance Union a hundred years ago. The result then was Prohibition, a social experiment in which objects (alcoholic beverages) were blamed for the evil that men do. Our Lord said nothing is evil in itself; evil resides in the heart of man. Changing the objects to guns makes no difference in the folly that is the Social Gospel. That was also something we wanted the students to understand.

Applying Scripture, logic, and rhetoric standards to all the hype about guns proved valuable exercises for the students.

One final note worth mentioning on this topic: In response to the increasing number of tragic school shootings, combined with the limp wrist response by the government at the time ("blame the guns"), I was all the more proud of my school board's response. While we didn't believe we had any reason to fear our own students or families, we were not as sure about our local, college-age neighbors. So the board directed me to identify certain responsible staff members who would get qualified for a Concealed Weapons Permit and have them carry small arms on campus. I also instituted "Safety Drills," which other schools called Lock Downs, wherein I would call all the classroom phones, like a PA system. The teachers and students practiced bolting the door from the inside and putting down the blinds. The armed staff members were trained to police assigned portions of the campus. In the event that they found an intruder with a weapon, well, you get the picture. The same staff members received weapons and safety training from a local professional trainer.

And we prayed that we would never have to face the situation for which we were preparing.

IDAHO LIFE EXHIBIT NO. 2: MR. CARNAHAN AND THE SKUNK

Every once in while during my many years of working with Matt Whitling he would surprise me. He was always calm, godly, and wise; that never surprised me. No, he surprised me by doing something that, well, I wished *I'd* done! Like the time he put a dead skunk under John Carnahan's desk. OK, to be precise, his son Cotton did that actual placing, but he had his dad's blessing.

The first I knew of it was when Matt came and got me to show me what was awaiting John. At that time John was our Activities Director (AD) and had a back office on the north end of the school, right behind the bookkeeper's office. Obviously John hadn't arrived for the day yet. Matt explained, on the way to John's office, that his boys had found the dead skunk by the road that morning. It had been killed by a passing car during the night, no doubt, but hadn't been run over and…uhmm, you get the idea. So it was in pretty good shape, all things considered.

Matt's boys had even washed the skunk to knock down some of the pungent smell. Now it should be noted at this juncture, for those few who haven't had a close encounter with a live skunk; had the skunk sprayed before he died, well, no one would have gotten within ten feet of the thing. As it was, he apparently had been caught unawares by the car that knocked him dead, so no time for spraying. Even so, he was not without the fragrance fondly associated with his kind.

The door to John's office was closed, and Matt thought it wise to keep it that way. "But you can see it under his desk if you look through the window," Matt assured me. So I looked through the door's window. Yup, there was the little fellow, just poking his dead nose out from under the front of the desk.

Now the problem one often encounters with practical jokes (what makes them "practical" I've never figured that one out) is that innocent parties, otherwise known as "collateral damage" in military terms, get caught in the crossfire. Such was the case here. Our dear bookkeeper, Ginny, came in before John and, seeing his door closed, assumed he was in a meeting. However, she quickly noticed that the normally fresh air in her office was not as fresh as it should have been. In fact, it smelled like…skunk!

Thus it was that, upon investigating further and finally glancing in the window of John's door, *she* received the delightful jolt Matt had hoped John would receive. She didn't scream—Ginny had grown up here. After the initial shock, her next thought was that perhaps it was a live animal, in which case the door should certainly stay closed.

Finally and disappointingly, like the actor who's missed his cue, John entered. Ginny tipped him to the fact that his door was closed for a good reason—his office contained a guest. John therefore approached the door already warned. Glancing in he, too, wasn't sure if the animal was alive or dead. But he was no dummy; he mentally put the pieces together and figured that either I or Matt was responsible for this circumstance. So he came down to our offices and calmly inquired who had placed the aromatic creature in his office. Matt is nothing if not honest, so he confessed immediately (I would've tried to blame someone else). Together the three of us went to retrieve the beast, Matt bringing the work gloves and plastic bag used earlier to bring it in.

We opened John's door and immediately wished we hadn't, or at least not without gas masks. The bath the Whitling boys had given the little guy had had no affect on his postmortem, nasal assaulting, eye-watering powers. Whufff!

But Matt was right, he still looked pretty good.

CHAPTER VIII

THE NEW MILLENNIUM

AN EMPTY NEST

The graduation I dreaded for years inevitably came to pass. 2005. Kathryn's class was going to cross the stage and get their diplomas from Logos High School. Our youngest child was not a child anymore. She had actually become quite an accomplished and, more importantly, a gracious, godly young woman. Kathryn had thrown herself into everything she could do while in Logos. Close to my heart, she had done drama since seventh grade, portraying a variety of roles and even doing stage managing a number of times; without doubt the worst job in theater. But she excelled in every role and for her senior year, swan song production, I cast her as Emma in our show of the same name. If I may say so, she nailed the role!

Kathryn also followed in the steps of her two older sisters and did both volleyball and Mock Trial all through high school. She was the youngest (freshman) attorney that Chris Schlect, our Mock Trial veteran coach had picked. Having had to hold her ground as the youngest of our four children, and especially having Carolyn as her oldest sibling, Kathryn was ready for the courtroom. She was able to deliver a deadly cross exam on the toughest witness on any competing team!

Though rather diminutive in size, Kathryn sought out and tackled many challenges. She ran for Student Body President and, though she lost, she put in a good campaign. Well-liked by her peers and teachers, it was still a surprise and overwhelming honor for our entire family when the secondary faculty selected her to be Valedictorian of her class. Selfishly, I wondered if I would be able to hold it together, sitting on the stage behind her as she gave her speech. (I didn't, but nobody could see me.) She did a splendid job of praising her Lord and thanking her school.

After graduation, Kathryn and several of her fellow grads had the great opportunity to spend almost two weeks touring Greece and Italy. What made the trip even more special was that it was coordinated with three classical schools, one of them being The Oaks in Spokane, where Carolyn worked. In fact, Carolyn was the prime organizer of the tour and lead the kids through the amazing sites in those ancient countries.

For a while Kathryn considered attending the University of Idaho, but New St. Andrew's College gave her a very generous scholarship. We were all very thankful since that's where she had really wanted to go. The classical, Christian program there fit her very well. And, as God had done with Kajsa at the UI, it was at NSA that Kathryn was found by the good man she would marry. That man, Mike Church, was the son of dear friends, Bill and Vicki Church, who had moved out to Moscow from Michigan (home turf!), after helping start a classical, Christian school there.

"THE CONTROVERSY"

Now if you're like me (no show of hands, please—that's not necessarily a *good* thing), you might forget a few things from the early parts of a book you're reading. So, when the author assumes that you've been paying rapt attention and throws out a casual reference to an event or person from a hundred or so pages back, well, I know I normally have to stop and retrace the story line. Tom Clancy is the worst for doing just that, in my humble opinion. And I've read quite a few of his books. But my word! He expects all his readers to follow and retain about twelve sub-plots, forty-five different characters and understand all the technical references he makes to weapons systems. Give me P.G. Wodehouse *any* day—his plots and characters I can keep track of, no problem.

So, by way of reminder, the controversy I referred to earlier in this book had to do with the local gay community getting quite upset with Doug Wilson. To get back at him for his continually referring to Bible verses in various contexts that condemned the homosexual lifestyle, they went after our church's annual history conference around 2003. The church had asked Pastor Steve Wilkins to come and speak. Steve was a PCA pastor from Louisiana. And, as we all know, southerners are, to a person, racists by birth. So, the anti-Pastor-Wilson forces put out the (very false) rumor that the history conference was about the legitimacy of slavery, of all things.

All heck broke loose. Hundreds of college students and many liberal townsfolk got wind of that rumor and, just like Ephesians in Paul's day, they began shouting "Great is Artemis of the Ephesians!" and throwing dust in the air! Or at least the equivalent in letters to the editor and then even a march on the campus.

Anything associated with Pastor Wilson and Christ Church was painted with the same tar brush, including Logos School. Even several local conservative pastors couldn't distance themselves fast enough from Doug and Logos. They, too, wrote letters to the paper stating that in no uncertain terms 'real' Christians don't ever condemn anyone or anything.

At one point I thought it might be wise to ask a (formerly) very supportive church if I could come and answer any questions their congregants might have about Logos in all the hubbub. They let me come one evening and I addressed a group of about twenty people. Pretty quickly it became clear that they weren't particularly concerned about Logos, but they did want me to try to distance the school from Doug Wilson. He was just too controversial. I was dumbfounded. As calmly as I could I said:

"You should know that Doug has been my friend for over thirty years. He has been my pastor since I moved to Moscow. He was hugely instrumental in starting Logos School. There is no way on earth that

I would ever advocate what you want. We don't abandon our friends because our *enemies* don't like them. And, by the way, my daughter is engaged to one of Pastor Wilkins's sons; in short, you are really talking to the wrong guy!"

Doug and the elders of Christ Church, in an effort to show they had nothing to hide and were more than willing to address any concerns, called for a public town meeting. It was held in one of Moscow's two, old downtown theaters. A couple hundred folks arrived that night. A mic was set up so people could come down and, civilly, ask Doug and the elders anything they wanted to ask. After a short presentation by one of our elders who, as it happened, was a missionary to a Tribe in western Africa, the citizens were welcomed to take the mic.

Things actually were going quite cordially, with people calmly asking things like was Christ Church and/or Doug supportive of slavery or racism, and being told, no, they weren't. Then Erin Brockovich (not her real name) came striding down the aisle, carrying several large binders (which she never opened). Her purpose in being there, as she said when she impatiently got the mic, was to let the community know how heinous Logos School was.

She had been a single mom at our school for about four years, during which our relationship with her sadly went from very cordial to sour, for a number of reasons. She had left us some months ago. Now she was going to tell the world how awful we really were. She gave a short, spiteful diatribe then turned to what I assume she thought was on topic for the evening: how racist we were.

"That school even has a portrait of Robert E. Lee hanging in their fourth grade room!" she shouted, with all the fervor one would associate with Senator Joseph McCarthy in his heyday.

The reaction she thought might come probably didn't include laughter, which is what erupted. Don't misunderstand; the crowd was indeed largely made up of a mix of unhappy and just curious folks (Christ Church members had been urged to let other community members get the seats). These people included down to earth, hard-working farmers and businessmen. And they weren't dumb. Unlike Erin, they didn't put Robert E. Lee in the same class as Hitler.

Perceiving a dud on that shot, she shifted tactics.

"They actually spank children at that school! Yes, children are actually brought to the office and Mr. Garfield spanks them with a wooden spoon, just for misbehaving!" Again, the impression she wanted to give was that this amounted to pretty much the same thing as my tasing the kids.

And, once again, to her dismay, there was laughter, this time particularly from the males in the audience. They hollered out to let her know that they, too, had been spanked as kids and certainly deserved it at the time. Others were getting tired of her derailing the purpose of the meeting and called for her to take a hike. I was actually feeling sorry for her by this point. She only escalated things, though, when she turned on the audience members, accusing them of going to Christ Church.

That didn't go over well, either. People stood up and let her know that she was quite mistaken, but they said it in salty terms I can't repeat here. Finally it was necessary for a couple of men to gently, but firmly, remove her from the theater. After that, there was kind of a strange camaraderie among us all, as though we'd come through an artillery barrage together. A few former (i.e., expelled) Logos students went to the mic and let us all know that they, too, had been spanked and also certainly deserved it. I sat there, amazed at how the Lord had shut the lions' mouths, so to speak, and it looked like we were going to get out of this den after all.

GIVING WHAT YOU DON'T HAVE

"The student is not above his teacher; but every one when he is perfected shall be as his teacher" (Lk. 6:40). Every once in a while it strikes me…I've been at Logos longer than any student and yet I never have and never will graduate from here! Also every once in a while, a student (usually in high school) will realize that lack in my life and bring it to my attention, with great glee. Then, should I reveal to this upstart my pathetic educational background, he or she tends to feel a whole lot better about a B- on the calculus test. How that knowledge affects the student's opinion of my qualifications to administrate Logos often (but not always) remains unspoken.

But this very issue of the lack of qualifications came up very often and with profound concern in the earliest days of the formation and annual conferences of the Association of Classical Christian Schools (ACCS). It was one of the top issues in our earliest conferences, when Logos provided most, if not all, of the workshops and plenary sessions. I heard from many folks who, after getting a vision for what classical, biblically based education could be, expressed real dismay at the seeming paradox of trying to provide what they never received.

I understood their quandary. Consider our own history: Out of the four founding board members of Logos School, only Doug Wilson had any background in classical studies; we did not all have bachelor's degrees; my own degree was a BFA (Fine Arts), with a minor in history and education; only one of us had a child older than eight; none of us had any experience serving on any kind of school board, or any classroom teaching experience, not to mention running a school; our first and only introduction to the idea of teaching the Trivium came from a short article by an English author (Dorothy Sayers) that I knew only from her mystery novels, and Doug happened to recall from reading the article while in the Navy. Such, and more, characterized the "qualifications" of the original, founding board of Logos School.

So, if a poorer readiness on the part of adults seeking to build an outstanding classical, Christian school can be found, I haven't met it. Really.

With all that incredible lack of preparation in knowledge and experience, how do we answer the original question: "How do you give what you haven't been given?" The simple answer is: by being obedient to your calling, not looking at your lack, but looking to your Lord to fill up that lack. G.K. Chesterton put it more bluntly: "Anything worth doing is worth doing badly."

The words of our Lord (above) used to give me considerable pause, especially in light of what we've attempted to do at Logos (i.e., teach students). I thought that He meant the student (or disciple) would never exceed the works, knowledge, and wisdom of his teacher. If that were really the case, then all instruction would be doomed to spiral downward in its quality and benefit to succeeding generations. But our Lord also told His disciples that *they* (fishermen, zealots, tax collectors, and other "uneducated" lowlifes) would do "greater" works than He did (John 14:12)! Greater than the works that Christ did? How can that be? Again, simply put, because that's how God likes to work—Scripture is loaded with God using the most worthless people and things (even donkeys and worms) to bring glory to Himself. And by being used by the Creator, those "worthless" people become the channels of very worthwhile works which God blesses.

Our job in starting or building classical, Christian schools is not to first gather the wise and experienced of this world, but rather to just obey His calling and study His Word. I wouldn't be doing this if I didn't believe, down to my bones, that this is what He's called me to do. I know *that*, even if I don't know *why* He chose to do so. But that's His concern, not mine. That is the same message I tell other folks in ACCS and other venues in this renaissance of effectively educating the next generation in the Word of God. A wonderful "side-effect," if you will, of this kind of obedience and faithful adherence to our calling is that we, along with the students, grow in our understanding of God's world and work. I date my best education beginning *after* I started working at Logos.

Does that mean, as we look to the future, that we only want inexperienced or clueless people to shape a school like Logos for the next generation? No. If our students truly 'become like their teacher,' a significant characteristic of their teachers, and founding board members, has been a trust in and a love of the Lord God and His Word. May that characterize all our students, all our children, as well. Thereby, they will do greater works than we have done.

And someday, I personally hope, Logos School will indeed be led and governed largely by people who have graduated from here!

THE MINEFIELD OF TEACHING MODERN U.S. HISTORY

> I wonder whether any other generation has seen such astounding revolutions of data and values as those through which we have lived. Scarcely anything material or established which I was brought up to believe was permanent and vital, has lasted. Everything I was sure or taught to be sure was impossible, has happened. (Winston Churchill)

For over thirty years, it was my privilege and challenge to teach our Logos sophomores about 'modern' United States history in their spring semester. More precisely, I had been teaching and adding to that course since Ronald Reagan was President of the United States. Then, not long ago we needed a history teacher to pick up the War Between the States (Civil War) class that the sophomores had in the fall semester. I took the plunge, so then I taught the entire year of 10th grade United States history, from about 1820 to the present time.

Consider this era from Winston Churchill's lifetime: When Churchill was born in 1874, rail was the newest and most innovative form of travel, medical practice and knowledge were virtually unchanged from the previous century, i.e., brutal and ineffective. Electricity was being treated as a clever trick and warfare was still conducted with cavalry, sabers, and glorious charges. Mechanical flight was science fiction and life spans averaged about forty-five years. Kings and other monarchs from ancient lines ruled most of Europe, the United States had recently torn itself apart in a states' war and it was at best a third rate upstart country full of immigrants, farmers, and cowboys.

When Churchill died in 1965, everything just noted had radically changed. Most people owned a car, vaccines and antibiotics were eliminating diseases, average life spans were about seventy-five years, every city and house had electric lights—some supplied by nuclear power; warfare was governed by a philosophy called M.A.D., because of the potential for the Mutually Assured Destruction of virtually all life as we know it, held in check by two "super-powers," the USSR and the U.S. Men were preparing to land on the moon, and almost every European royal dynasty had disappeared. Those that remained, including his own monarch, were essentially figure-heads. Oh yes, and the United States had won the two largest wars in the history of mankind and now was unparalleled in its standard of living in the world. All in the span of one man's lifetime!

Though we emphasized our classical, historical roots at Logos School, we wanted the students to also understand where we as Americans have come from and where we are now. All the technological and medical improvements we've enjoyed over the last century have been accompanied by radical shifts in our moral and spiritual foundations. To teach these high school students modern American history is to walk them through a veritable minefield of issues. Why are they "mines"? Because they are volatile issues that even Christians often part ways on when they come (blow?) up. Why is that? One possible reason is frequently these are issues that Americans, if they have been taught anything about them, have been taught only *one* side. To even discuss any other side can incite a reaction or even condemnation.

A short list of these 'mines' (in chronological order) would include:

1. Was the "Civil War" just about slavery or about states' rights or what? Did the South have any legitimate arguments or was it an "evil empire," lock, stock, and barrel?
2. What are we to make of Southern generals like Lee and Jackson whose Christian faith was evident even to their enemies?
3. Did the North treat former slaves with compassion and support, or was there widespread racism there, too?
4. Did the change in the federal system of government after the war, in assuming far more power and taking much from the states, bring greater or less liberty to Americans?
5. Both Prohibition and women's suffrage were put into law at about the same time. Why is the former considered a joke today, but the latter is seen as a great social step forward? For that matter, social Darwinism teaches that mankind is basically good and only needs the right 'push' or enlightenment to become even better. Is that a biblical view of man?
6. How might we compare the way Americans largely responded to the Great Depression to the way the recent "Occupy Wall Street" Americans were seeking their "due"?
7. Many question the morality of using the A bombs on Japan. What biblical principles of warfare should we consider in forming an opinion on Truman's acts?
8. How should we view the Civil Rights Movement? Does private property justify prejudice? Does the Federal Government have the power and responsibility to change moral behavior?

9. What went wrong in Vietnam, as judged from scriptural principles, versus popular cultural thinking?
10. Is there a good comparison between the thinking and results of *Roe v. Wade* and that of the Holocaust by the Nazis? Just because something is "lawful" does that make it right?
11. What biblical monetary principles has the United States ignored? Should the rich be taxed more than the poor? Is capitalism biblical or just an American tradition?
12. If enough states say it's legal for two people of the same sex to marry, does that change the nature of marriage and the family?

We could also toss in the environmental movement and population control theories, since they also have shaped how American Christians think these days.

All this brings us to the question "Does the class consist of telling these students what to think on each incendiary issue?" Of course not. Not only would that be unfair to them, it would go against one of our primary purposes as a classical, Christian school, i.e., encouraging the students to think biblically, not blindly. However, by having the unchanging standard of the Scriptures, we can let them know God is not silent on *any* area of life. They are encouraged to "examine all things, and hold fast to that which is good" (1 Thess. 5:21). Our culture, especially today, tells our children there is no fixed standard or measure by which their lives may be led. We seek to show them that not only is there a measure, God's Word, there is a Person, Jesus Christ, who is the same yesterday, today, and forever.

AN UNFORESEEN TIDAL WAVE

As I've chronicled the beginning of Logos School in this volume, I've attempted to make demarcations where, in looking back, I can see a directional change, sort of like the bends in streams. Some of those bends were pretty obvious, as when we moved from the church basement to the roller rink. Others were so quiet and slow that they can only be seen by looking back upstream, so to speak. The arrival of the children of alums might have been anticipated by others, but that particular "bend" caught me by surprise.

Don't get me wrong; I certainly wanted our alums to love Logos so much that they would enroll their children in it, too. But, sort of like the idea of having actual teens attending Logos in sizable numbers was largely theoretical to me back in the '80s, so was the idea of having alum children show up to any extent.

I also recall thinking, when Logos started to get real "teenagers" (such an absurd term, isn't it?), that the idea of any of our alums actually marrying *other* alums was highly improbable. I mean, they spent *all* day, *every* day going to the same classes, for *years*! I figured that they would be so heartily sick of seeing each other that the idea of *marrying* each other would be about as attractive as marrying their cousins. But, hardly for the first time, I was proved wrong over time. Perhaps, in some of their cases, it was like Lewis' explanation of why Cor and Aravis got married in *The Horse and His Boy*:

"Aravis also had many quarrels (and, I'm afraid even fights) with Cor, but they always made it up again: so that years later, when they were grown up they were so used to quarreling and making it up again that they got married so as to go on doing it more conveniently."

So our alums grew up and tended to get married, mostly to people they met after leaving Logos, but some ended up marrying other Logos alums. In any case, once married, they tended to have children like it was the most natural thing in the world or something.

One of those children, Bekah Wilson, you might recall as being the real impetus for the founding of Logos. She had been in our first kindergarten class in 1981, spent thirteen years being one of our guinea pigs (I know it sounds harsh—it's just the truth) enduring our first clunky attempts at this form of education, then graduated from Logos High School in 1994.

If you've been following the story to this point, it may not surprise you to hear that a new college in Moscow, New Saint Andrews, officially began in that same year—1994. Yup, Doug again: he and a number other key folks thought that having kids graduate from a classical, Christian education without having a substantive higher-ed program to go into was sort like being dressed up with no place to go.

So Bekah and a few other students began their college studies in New St. Andrews that year and in the spring of 1998 formed the first graduating class of the classical, Christian college. Bekah looked a bit different by the commencement ceremony; she had married a fellow named Ben Merkle the year before and was obviously pregnant with their first child. Those roomy graduation gowns came in mighty handy for her on that occasion. Not long afterward, Knox Merkle made his first official appearance.

Four years later, young Knox appeared in Logos Preschool. To use a fairly apt analogy he was the 'cloud the size of a man's fist.' Over the next few years he was followed, initially in ones and twos, then in tens, by fellow children of Logos alums. As with many visionary types of thinking, I hadn't foreseen this tide of incoming children. No matter; I was thrilled to see them come! Spending time at recess with these strangely familiar little people produced many deja-vu moments: I was sure I had pushed this same child on swing many years before. Or as I began to repeatedly say: "Same face, different name."

This new influx was of course noticed by many of us who had been connected with Logos for many years. At our annual fundraiser in the winter of 2007, John Sawyer, one of our earlier board members and the father of three K-12 alums, was asked to speak. He was also a grandfather of some little ones soon to enter his wife's kindergarten class. His comments struck a chord with me that evening. He easily remembered the early days of Logos, since his children were some of our first students. To paraphrase his comments, he was very grateful that Logos had been very good for his children, but it would have to be even better for his grandchildren!

John wasn't playing the grandfather card of "nothing's good enough for my grandkids"; he was making the very important point that Logos needed to keep improving in fulfilling its original vision. The children we helped train up during our first twenty-five years could truly be considered our first generation. What we did for them was wrought out of a lot of experimentation—trial and error. The vision was and continued to be worthy of implementing, but that didn't mean we, the board and teachers, had known what it would take initially to put feet on that vision. So we really did make some mistakes, errors in judgment, including not setting the "bar" high enough for ourselves, and by extension, for the students. That included the important cultural bar. At the same time, by God's grace, we did a lot of things pretty well and we were still here.

Now we were starting to see the next generation coming in, the children of our first grads. These young parents had their memories of what Logos was like for them and, apparently, they enjoyed and valued it enough to want something similar for their own prodigy. But they also wanted more for their children. They were rightly expecting that Logos had matured and would not repeat the same mistakes, but rather offer higher quality than they received. In other words, these families were very familiar with a classical, Christian education and they wanted it even more richly, wonderfully bestowed on their children.

Those great expectations did and should put a lot of real pressure on the staff and board of Logos. We took on a serious obligation with every child we enrolled at any time. However, the second generation came with an even greater obligation for us. These new parents were much more informed and convinced about this form of education than their own parents, our first families. They knew what they wanted and Logos needed to step-up to LOGOS 2.0!

MR. TRAIL GOES TO BOISE (AND LOGOS WINS!)

Almost as soon as we began to have real athletic students, we also learned that they could not go the distance, so to speak, and compete at any district or state level competition. This was not the athletes' fault, but rather the way the educational/political situation in Idaho was for many years.

We had been allowed to join the Idaho High School Athletics Association (IHSAA) rather easily, as soon as we were able to field a team in a sanctioned sport, such as volleyball or track. But, since we did not seek (or desire) state accreditation of our school's academic program, we could only be Associate, not Full, members of the IHSAA. Practically that meant that our teams could compete against similar sized local schools, but only in a non-league status. For instance, our boys' basketball team could play Deary, but win or lose, it didn't make any difference for either team since we were not in a league with Deary.

By not being in a league, no matter how good they were, our teams could not move on to district or state competitions. In other words, the IHSAA and the State Board of Education in Idaho worked hand-in-glove to put pressure on independent schools to become state accredited, if they wanted their students to be able to compete for a state-level championship.

Our biblically based educational philosophy held that only families have any authority in educating children. Hence, there was no way we would submit our school's program to the State for its approval (or disapproval).

This rock and a hard place was the way it was for over twenty years of our having sports teams. The really tough pill to swallow was in our track and cross country programs. With our other team sports, in any given season we could only conjecture how we would stack up against other local teams, wondering if we could compete well at state level play. With track and cross country, however, we had solid, empirical evidence of how our kids would do. Qualifying times and distances don't change according to the size or make-up of the teams competing. Any coach could determine what it would take for his athletes to win a state championship in the long-jump, for instance. But we were not allowed to compete and prove we could do it.

Then, in 2012, we had a political champion take up our cause. You might remember Tom Trail, the first special visitor we had in 1981. He had shown the entire (!) school slides from his and his wife JoAnn's visit to Israel. Well, after his career as a college professor, Tom became a State Representative for our region to the legislature located in Idaho's capital, Boise.

Tom heard of our dilemma and decided to challenge the status quo. He contacted the IHSAA and suggested that they consider changing their standards so that all qualified student athletes in any Idaho school could compete at every level. They responded with a polite but firm no.

So Tom took it up in the legislative branch. He prepared and submitted a bill that would not only allow our students to compete at every level, but allow all students in private schools in Idaho to do the same. In the meantime, we did some "politicking" ourselves. We knew that if Tom's bill passed, we would request to be part of the local public school league, the Whitepine. We wanted to be a blessing to them, not a curse; we'd rather knock on their door politely instead of kicking it in. So our intrepid and winsome Activities Director John Carnahan paid visits and made calls to the Whitepine coaches and ADs.

John asked each of them if they would be okay with our potentially joining their league. Overall, their responses were very positive and welcoming. They knew our students' reputation, as well as the fact that we had a very viable gym in which to compete.

Tom didn't have to filibuster or anything that dramatic. His bill met with a great degree of support and legally changed the landscape for our athletes. It was passed in time to allow our cross country teams to be the first teams we were able to send to league districts. The Knights did a superb job there so they advanced to state. And like the Cinderella ending to many stories, the Logos Cross Country team won the State Championship in our league for 2012!

(Over just the next two years, the Knights won five state-level championships in a number of sports.)

ALL CREATURES, GREAT AND SMALL

Children love animals. That is one of those givens, like saying children love ice cream. However, unlike ice cream, animals can and should be used quite regularly to further a child's love for God's creation. (Yes, while it could be argued that ice cream, both as a bribe and a reward, can influence a child's education, I will stick to legitimate, classical education techniques, if you don't mind.)

So Logos School has had its fair share of animal-related experiences and practices. Being located in northern Idaho, where moose sightings in neighborhoods are no more noteworthy than the latest movie release (possibly less if it's *Star Wars*), we have probably had more than our fair share. A few examples to make my point:

I walked casually out of my office door one day and literally ran into the back of an alpaca. For the uninitiated, these animals are sort like smaller versions of llamas. One of our staff families had a farm where they raised these creatures for their hair (fur, wool?). I have an alpaca scarf to prove it. This particular alpaca was visiting classrooms. Once I excused myself for invading his personal space, I checked to make sure he had a Visitor's Badge. He didn't, but he was with a staff member, so he was OK.

A former science teacher from years long past decided her students should have the real-life experience of raising chickens. I didn't see a problem. What could go wrong? The chicks arrived in a box, bundles of yellow fuzz, cheeping their little heads off, so cute! They were placed in a...what else... chicken-wire sided pen in a classroom. Then they grew. And stank. Oh man! In many ways, they were like human teenagers: as they grew they got ganglier, smellier, and ravenous. The breaking point came when I found out that some of the boys discovered that chickens are cannibalistic. They (the boys) had purchased some McNuggets from our nearby McDonalds and fed them (the nuggets) to the chickens. I could almost hear the chickens commenting on the meal:

"You know, these aren't so bad...they taste like *us*!"

"Hey, this one looks like Uncle Henry!"

April Fool's Day has got to be the dumbest holiday of them all. It even beats out the Brits' bizarre celebration of Guy Fawkes Day (you know, the creep that tried to blow up the King and Parliament in 1605?). I mention April Fools here because on one of those days some of our lads tried to use frogs in the hope that they would somewhat replicate the plague of the same creatures on Egypt, I suppose. Nothing went right for them (the lads, that is). The frogs would have none of it. About half-a-dozen of them were quietly placed at various spots in the hallways during class. Then, as the boys no doubt pictured it, the frogs would leap about randomly and send girls shrieking in all directions.

Instead, a very calm girl came to my office and quietly mentioned that frogs were sitting around the hallway. I went out with her and sure enough, there they sat, all with looks of complete boredom and weariness.

"Really?" they seemed to say with their round, half-lidded frog eyes.

We scooped them all up with no resistance on their part and placed them in a pail. The criminals were easily identified: one of the janitors had overheard them plotting up in the guys' locker room. That, and the fact that they left the frogs' original transportation, a glass terrarium, in the locker room. I guess a classical education doesn't make for clever lawbreakers.

While snakes making Great Escapes in classrooms or feral kittens living under storage sheds were very popular, personally my favorite animal visitors were the raptors. Almost every year our local Raptor Refuge & Repair (not their real name) organization would come and do a presentation for our elementary students. With two local universities, there usually wasn't a dearth of the creatures being found and turned in. If you live in Rhode Island you may not know that raptors are birds, such as owls, hawks, and falcons that, well, kill smallish animals and rip them to shreds for snacks. Julie and I, while on a walk in daylight, witnessed a falcon dive down, snag an unassuming robin off the street and swoop up to a rooftop where it gave Red Robin restaurant a run for its money, if you follow me.

The college-aged groups with the show-and-tell raptors were always very helpful and informative as they opened covered cages much like a magician performing a trick. The kids loved seeing a red-tailed hawk emerge, for instance, with its sharp talons grasping the leather glove of the handler. There were always stories of how the birds came to these young vets for help. Once they even had a damaged bald eagle to show. Whoa. Very noble looking. Probably the students' favorite type of owl was one that stood only about four inches, fully grown, I believe. It might have been called the Midget Owl, or something like that, which would fit. I always wondered, but never asked, what it ate. Full scale owls help keep the mouse population under control; I thought it would be anybody's guess who would win in a Midget Owl vs. mouse fight.

"ALL THE WORLD'S A STAGE"

The Logos drama productions changed rather radically in just about every way, from our first attempts at the Paradise Hills Church of God. I was a late comer to the stage, but when the acting bug bit, it never let go. I'd like to think that twenty years of being heavily involved in the Moscow Community Theater had the side benefit of preparing me to develop the Logos drama program.

After the move to the Baker Street campus, we built a little stage on one end of the auditorium. It was about ten feet deep and thirty feet wide. Later we built temporary extensions that pushed out the playing area another four feet along the entire front of the stage.

For twelve years, 1987–99, we did all our productions, junior high and varsity, as well as all the elementary skits, on that stage. Initially our 'curtains' were king-sized, dark blue bed sheets, ably sown together by Sandy Hoeft, a school mom. Finally, when I had enough money in the drama fund, we bought actual custom-made, navy blue, thick velour curtains!

That little stage saw us do many favorite American plays like *Harvey, Father Knows Best, Heaven Can Wait*, and *Arsenic and Old Lace*. We got into doing British shows, too, like *The Importance of Being Earnest*, Agatha Christie's *A Murder Is Announced*, and Shakespeare's *Much Ado About Nothing*. Our last varsity production on that stage was a non-singing version of *Les Miserables*.

Then in 1998 the gym started to become a reality and I was privileged to design a much larger stage for it. That one was thirty feet deep and forty feet wide. It had back entrances/exits that led to the guys' and girl's locker rooms, respectively, which doubled as dressing rooms during shows. It had a long catwalk along the back wall that not only allowed actors to cross unseen from one side of the stage to the other, but it also housed our pin rail. The pin rail is where the lines (ropes) for lowering and raising backdrops or curtains are tied off.

One end of the catwalk led to the drama/make-up room and the other led to the weight room. Eventually, we built three floors on each side of the stage, so drama had two rooms. The third floor room held our costume racks.

With the amazing ingenuity of Jody Jacobs, our custodian and so much more, we built an actual fly loft above the stage so we could raise and lower (fly) backdrops and set pieces. Lights and sound were added and improved over time, as well as a control booth built above a basketball stanchion on the other end of the gym. From that 'lofty' height, tech guys could run all the effects of a show.

On the "big" stage (as it was referred to by student actors), we began to present summer theater for our Teacher Training week, such as

Leave It to Psmith (Wodehouse) and *David Copperfield* (Dickens). Finally, Donna Grauke, a fellow thespian and a school mom with drama experience, went where I had always feared to go: she offered to direct a *musical*! Her choice was *Seven Brides for Seven Brothers* and it was a tremendous hit!

From then on we did musicals every other year: I took the plunge with *Oklahoma!*, which is essentially the same story as *Seven Brides*, but set in Oklahoma instead of Oregon. The bar had been raised, both in terms of production requirements, but more importantly, in terms of acting, singing and dancing. Costuming, set construction, special effects, and instrumental music also took a big tic upwards. All this enabled us to do dramas, comedies, and other musicals during the next years that pleased large audiences and brought in community members who came to Logos just for the drama productions. Among others, we presented *The Sound of Music, Annie,* and *Music Man* as musicals, and *Nicholas Nickleby, Ideal Husband, Leave It to Psmith, The 3 Musketeers,* and *Fiddler on the Roof* as dramas. We also continued our junior high productions each spring on the auditorium stage.

As I saw it, acting, whether in a kindergarten play or a varsity musical production, was a wonderful, God-given tool for telling great stories. It was a tool that every good teacher uses every day, and a skill that benefits every student receiving a classical, Christian education. No other practices give students the same level of confidence and boldness in public presentations. I am very confident that our Lord used those skills to tell His stories to thousands while He was with them. So am I saying that drama is biblical? Absolutely! Therefore, the shows must go on!

LOGOS 2.0: "THE END OF THE BEGINNING"

So, I'm writing this book at the close of Logos School's first thirty-five years. It is also the close of my career as its first head administrator. Being a history teacher for that same period of time, I think one of Sir Winston Churchill's statements is rather applicable at this juncture. After the Blitz was over for England in World War II and Germany was concentrating its efforts elsewhere, someone asked the Prime

Minister if the war might be ending. He replied: "This is not the end. It is not even the beginning of the end; but it is the end of the beginning."

I've had to skip a lot of details from recent years, as I fear they would be less interesting to the reader than to me (e.g., the powerline-damaging struggles of adding portable classrooms due to enrollment spiking, dealing with the global recession at the local level, etc.). But I did want to touch on a few important changes specifically, some of which I've alluded to already: In June of 2016, Dr. Larry Stephenson formally replaced me as Logos School Superintendent, and I began teaching more classes in our upper school, as well as doing some consulting with sister schools. But my last two updates are some of the most exciting: First, we are seeing the obvious and very delightful presence of second-generation Logos students. In 2015–16, out of 375 students there were sixty-eight children of alums. These alum families are forming the new nucleus of Logos 2.0. In combination with this, early in 2016 Logos School was able to purchase thirty acres on the east side of Moscow from the Trail family (the same folks that had been cheering on Logos since 1981), and Logos is, Lord willing, on the cusp of building a campus that will fully reflect the nature and beauty of a classical, Christian education.

As I reflect on what God has accomplished for His kingdom through Logos School, starting in a small, agrarian community in the sparsely populated region of north Idaho, I am rather overwhelmed. From eighteen students in a church basement, God has not only caused Logos to flourish as a strong Christian school with almost four hundred students, He built an organization, ACCS, that has over 240 member schools located throughout the world. Who would have ever seen that coming? But He likes to write stories like that, doesn't He?

In these closing comments, I need to draw attention to an aspect about which you, the reader, may have been wondering. Logos' history is not serendipitous; I have purposely not included some of the hardest, heart-breaking stories we've endured: staff firings, great sins, student expulsions, deaths of alums and others we loved, major "head bonks" between staff members or between the administration and board. I don't believe those stories would be edifying and could even cause hurt where God has brought healing. The fact that we have had those hardships and are still opening our doors is a testament to God's great grace and forgiveness, certainly not due to our wisdom or abilities. At the same time, I would be ungrateful to Him if I didn't acknowledge that He has taught us some worthwhile things along the way, many in fact. Here are just two of the significant elements of Logos that I believe have fostered the kind of school we became:

1. *From day one we advertised and held to our conviction that no family would ever be turned away for not being able to pay the total tuition cost.* Since I had a fair bit to do with the financial dealings we had with all our families for thirty-five years, I can say with a great degree of accuracy that we held true to that promise. Please don't misunderstand: we have turned away many families over the years. But the reasons were never due to the financial status of the families. Without going into details you might be able to guess anyway, there have been, and will be, families who don't have the same convictions we have regarding a classical, Christian education.
2. *Our staff members are strong, joy-filled Christians, who are happy to show up for work each day.* Of course they are real humans who struggle with sin at times, who get sick, who have heart-aches and sorrows. They get tired and even weary; stacks of papers to be graded or carpets needing to be vacuumed again can discourage the most stalwart of soul. I think it's been a very good thing that I have taught classes ever since we began. That has enabled me to empathize with the requirements we place on our teachers. And one of the most critical requirements that we place on them and all staff members is this: You have no right to a "bad day." Another way I've put it at every year's Orientation time is this: "Righteousness—don't leave home without it!"

To come and work at a Christian school, representing Christ before young ones, while being in sin is the height of hypocrisy. That means keeping short accounts with sin, whether at home or at Logos. Again, by God's grace, this has resulted in staff members who are not perfect, but they also don't indulge sin either. Gossip, for instance, is one of the most prevalent sins among Christian schools. I am extremely grateful that it has rarely gotten a toe-hold among our staff.

Another reason that our teachers are usually happy people is that we, the administration, have purposely treated them as they should be treated. That is, as professional, knowledgeable people who should be given a lot of respect and academic freedom. Within our adopted classical philosophy there is a lot of room for improvement and great ideas. Most of those improvements and great ideas over the years have come from our faculty members. By listening to and implementing those ideas, Logos' program has improved, our students have been blessed, making our families happier, which, coming full circle, makes our teachers happy.

As I close out my term as superintendent, I need to note that I've written this admittedly incomplete recollection in the comfort of my Theodore Roosevelt chair, a gift from my board for twenty years of work at Logos. While not actually belonging to that great man, it is a natural leather chair and ottoman, custom-made after a style TR used. I love it! It has become my go-to comfort spot in our home for fifteen years.

Normally, I believe, authors acknowledge and thank people at the beginning of their books. I hope you don't mind, but instead I will do that here. (Paul did that in his epistles, too. Just saying.) This is a shockingly short and no doubt incomplete list, so please forgive me if you should be noted here; it's been a long haul.

- Meredith G., Debbie W., Debbie Q., Candace B., Karen M., Molly M., Carol A., Carol S., Mary Sue O., Martha S.—You were some of our earliest staff members. I don't know all of your current last names, but you know who you are. Thank you for helping Logos get its first breath of life.
- Jay, Oba, Lee McCoy—Owners of McCoy Plumbing. You were the first Christian businessmen who were convinced that Logos was worth your investment of generous support!
- Vern Davidson—Pharmacist. You also invested in Logos, your support allowed us to get into the Baker Street campus.

- Chris LaMoreaux and Ann Casebolt—Our first bus route drivers. Your courage and patience deserves a Medal of Honor.
- John and Jan Sawyer—Early board member, teachers, and most of all faithful friends. Your children were among our first students and you never stopped loving Logos. It was a joy to see your grands follow suit.
- Stan and Trish Miller—Board member and one our early Development Officers. Your family came here many years ago for Logos. Our children grew up together and our friendship is one of our greatest blessings!
- Bill Twigg—Early board member and carriage wheelwright. You were our go-to guy for all things mechanical for years! Thanks for welding broken cafeteria tables without number!
- Chris and Brenda Schlect—Both teachers in Logos at different times. Chris, thank you for your commitment to and passion for seeing the Logos Mock Trial teams succeed, numerous times. We both know the benefit to the students far exceeded the victories earned.
- Charlene Polek—Our first Registrar. Not only caring and kind to all at Logos, you pushed us into the twenty-first century with your database wizardry.
- Carla Courtney—Our varsity drama "Costume Mom" for many faithful years. Without your expertise our shows would not have been the marvelous productions they were. Thank you very much!
- Joe and Paula Casebolt—Two of first alums to marry each other. Though I think Logos should get some kind of "finders fee" for these matches, I am gratified that you put your children in Logos, even after we treated you like guinea pigs. Thank you for your special friendship and support.
- Dr. John and Donna Grauke—Doctor and drama director. You moved from your successful practice in Seattle to invest in your

children's education in Logos. You have blessed us all more than you can know!

- Marc Rust—Our board president and my dear friend for many years. You did more than support me; you prayed for me and encouraged me more than even a brother could, particularly during my darkest hours.
- Jim Nance—Logic and Rhetoric teacher for over twenty years. Thank you for all your investment in hundreds of students at Logos. Your friendship was a boon to me many times.
- Matt and Tora Whitling—Principal, teachers. Matt, your value to Logos has been incalculable! You have also been a blessing to thousands of students through your wisdom expressed through ACCS. Thank you for your friendship and patient help to me for many years!
- Bill and Vicki Church—You were among the first in ACCS to get a school going, and in Michigan, my home state! Your great friendship and move to Moscow, not to mention our children marrying, has been a gift that keeps giving!
- John and Brenda Carnahan—John, you gave to Logos so much through your teaching and AD work; it wasn't our fault that others didn't appreciate our shared, keen sense of humor. Brenda, thank you for countless hours of reading to and loving our students.
- Don and Shirley Quist—founding board member family. You were instrumental in putting Logos on its feet, and you never stopped praying for its success. God bless you!
- Larry and Connie Lucas—founding board member family. You had a vision for a Christ-centered school that is now a reality. Your legacy continues to resonate in the halls!
- Doug and Nancy Wilson—founding board member family, teachers in Logos. Only God could write a story like this, right? Thank you so much for your friendship and leadership ever since Ann Arbor. It's been a long, strange trip, but it's worth every step, pain, tear shed, and drop of sweat. I thank God for you both!

- Carolyn, Seth, Kajsa, and Kathryn- You endured many of Logos School's first attempts at education. You were blessed in the long run, but it wasn't always easy or even fun, especially being the offspring of the principal. I cannot express how proud I am of each of you—my highest praise is that you are raising your dear children in the Lord with wisdom your mother and I only wish we'd had for you. I love you all!
- Julie—Thank you for not only being by my side through all the ways Logos affected our lives, but you have been a faithful teacher for many years, too. God has richly blessed me with you! I love being a hobbit in this shire with you!

And thank you, dear reader, for taking the time and effort to read this story that is dear to my heart. I hope it has blessed you to some degree, as well. If you know of a classical, Christian school, please pray regularly for its work—it is a light shining in a dark generation.

While I was in the Navy, these verses brought me through hard times—they still do: "Trust in the Lord with all your heart, and do not lean on your own understanding. In all your ways acknowledge Him and He will make your paths straight" (Prov. 3:5–6).

Amen and amen.

POSTSCRIPT: IT'S MY DAD'S FAULT

(*This is from a newsletter column I wrote in our early years. My father, the wisest, kindest man I've ever known, was and remains my inspiration. He and my mother were unwaveringly supportive of my work at Logos. They frequently came to see us and Dad even helped a bit with the remodeling of the roller rink. Hence I include this column in this volume.*)

At some point in almost every school year, some little person will ask me, "Do you like being a principal?" or "How did you get to be a principal?"

The answer to the first question is easy. I cannot imagine doing anything else that would bring me greater joy and satisfaction! True, it also brings real sorrow and frustrations at times. The answer to the second question is more complicated and the little person usually doesn't want to hear the real explanation. So I've given the explanation I saw in a cartoon several years ago: two little boys were standing outside the principal's office, and one asked the other how he thought someone becomes a principal. The other little boy replied, "I think you have to be bitten by one."

Actually, as late in life as ninth grade I was so intent on *not* being an administrator "like my father," that I distinctly stated so in a vocational research paper at the time. My career options, as I saw them from that height of maturity, were to be a veterinarian or an FBI agent. My father was an administrator of student finances at a nearby university. I couldn't imagine too many jobs more boring than "shuffling papers" at a desk all day. I wanted to do something exciting! (My wife, Julie, often says that my life reminds her of the classic movie, *It's A Wonderful Life*. George Bailey didn't want to be like his dad, either, at first.)

After that adamant denial of pursuing such a dismal future career, imagine the shock I had when halfway through my master's degree work, I discovered that not only was I doing a very similar job to my father's, he had exactly the *same* master's degree! I never knew what he had done in college, such was my lack of consideration of his past. What happened? How did I come to walk precisely in my father's footsteps, when I had had no such intention? He had never put his arm around my shoulders in his office and, while choking back a tear of joy, told me that someday all this would be mine—file cabinets and all!

The serious conclusion I have come to is that because my father is the kind of man he is, and because my heavenly Father is the kind of God He is, I didn't stand a chance. You see, my dad is the only man on earth I would love to be exactly like—as a father, as a husband, as a godly man, and yes, even as an effective administrator. My heavenly Father is the only One who really knows me and how I can best serve Him. I know it was the combination of my desire to emulate my dad (primarily because of his life, not because he in anyway pushed me), and the Lord's consistent love and guidance, that placed me in this position, and I love it. Now, Lord willing, I hope I can help foster future "surprises" for these children at Logos School. They, too, may "wake up" someday and find that, to their great surprise and joy, they are indeed like their parents, thank God!

APPENDIX A

LOST TOOLS ILLUSTRATED CHART

BEGINNING GRAMMAR (PRE-POLLY) *Grades K–2 (Approximately ages 4–8)*
Student Characteristics 1. *Obviously excited about learning* 2. *Enjoys games, stories, songs, projects* 3. *Short attention span* 4. *Wants to touch, taste, feel, smell, see* 5. *Imaginative, creative* 6. *Likes to copy, imitate*
Teaching Methods 1. *Guide discovering* 2. *Explore, find things* 3. *Use lots of tactile items to illustrate point* 4. *Sing, play games, chant, recite, color, draw, paint, build* 5. *Use body movements* 6. *Short, creative projects* 7. *Show and tell, drama, hear/read/tell stories* 8. *Field trips* 9. *Reinforce conceptual understanding of letters, numbers, associated meanings* 10. *Provide copying, imitating opportunities*

GRAMMAR (POLL-PARROT)

Grades 3–7.5 (Approximately ages 9–11)

Student Characteristics

1. *Excited about new, interesting facts*
2. *Likes to explain, figure out, talk*
3. *Wants to relate own experiences to topic, or just to tell a story*
4. *Likes collections, organizing items*
5. *Likes chants, clever, repetitious word sounds (e.g., Dr. Seuss)*
6. *Easily memorizes*
7. *Can assimilate another language well*

Teaching Methods

1. *Lots of sensory work, projects*
2. *Field trips*
3. *Make collections, displays, models*
4. *Plan integration of material through variety of means*
5. *Teach and assign simple research projects*
6. *Recitations, drama, memorization, chants, sound-offs*
7. *Drills, games, songs*
8. *Oral/written presentations*

LOGIC (PERT)

Grades 7.5–9 (Approximately ages 12–14)

Student Characteristics

1. *Still excitable, but needs challenges*
2. *Judges, critiques, debates, critical*
3. *Likes to organize items, others*
4. *Shows off knowledge*
5. *Wants to know "behind the scenes" facts*
6. *Curious about "Why?" for most things*
7. *Thinks, acts as though more knowledgeable than adults*

Teaching Methods

1. *Time lines, charts, maps (visual materials)*
2. *Debates, persuasive reports*
3. *Drama, reenactments, role-playing*
4. *Evaluate, critique (with guidelines)*
5. *Formal logic*
6. *Research projects*
7. *Oral/written presentations*
8. *Guest speakers, trips*
9. *Collaborative work in groups*

RHETORIC (POETIC) Grades 10–12 (Approximately ages 15–18)
Student Characteristics 1. *Concerned with present events, especially in own life* 2. *Interested in justice, fairness* 3. *Moving toward special interests, topics* 4. *Can take on responsibility, independent work* 5. *Can synthesize* 6. *Desires to express feelings, own ideas* 7. *Generally idealistic*
Teaching Methods 1. *Drama, oral presentations, poetry* 2. *Research, integration of disciplines, synthesis of ideas* 3. *Classic literature, history, speeches, debates* 4. *Give responsibilities, e.g., working with younger students, organize activities* 5. *In-depth field trips* 6. *Worldview discussion/written papers* 7. *Construction/public defense of theses*

APPENDIX B

LOGOS SCHOOL TIMELINE

1968

- Jim Wilson family moves from Annapolis, Maryland, to Ann Arbor, Michigan

1968–1971

- Doug and Evan Wilson attend Pioneer High School in Ann Arbor, along with Tom Garfield

SUMMER, 1971

- Jim Wilson family moves to Moscow, Idaho

DECEMBER, 1975–SEPT, 1976

- After four years in the U.S. Navy, Doug Wilson attends the University of Idaho, marries Nancy Greensides; their first child, Rebekah, is born

JANUARY, 1977

- After also four years in the U.S.N., Tom Garfield moves to Moscow to attend the University of Idaho, marries Julie Olsen in September

1979–80

- Doug meets informally with other interested parents in Faith Fellowship; an initial school board is formed: Shirley Quist, Larry Lucas, and Doug Wilson

1980

- October: Doug Wilson asks Tom Garfield to consider applying for the principal's job
- January—August, 1981
- January: Tom Garfield is interviewed by the school board, they offer and he accepts the post of principal and fourth board member
- March: A public presentation and Q and A session is held by the school board
- Three other teachers (all single females) are hired, a home is found for the school: half of the basement of the Paradise Hills Church of God, renovations begin
- Teacher Debbie Quist (daughter of Don and Shirley), suggests "Logos" as the name for the school
- During one of the summer board meetings, Doug Wilson hands out copies of an article by Dorothy Sayers: *The Lost Tools of Learning*; the board decides to adopt it as the school's educational philosophy

1981

- Tuesday, September 8, Logos School officially opens in the basement of the Paradise Hills Church of God, with 17 students: 7 kindergartners, 7 first/second graders (combo), 1 fifth grader, 1 sixth grader, and 1 ninth grader, to be taught by four full-time teachers (including the principal)

1982–1984

- Logos doubles in enrollment each year, requiring expansion and renovation of the rest of the church basement and use of the church library; more teachers are hired (mostly single females)
- The 'food pantry' is begun in a back room, parents regularly donate grocery items for the faculty members

- Playground equipment is built by school dads
- Logos buys its first used school buses and begins routes in Moscow and to Pullman
- The board expands to six "founding" members: Bill Twigg and John Sawyer are added
- The board adopts the motto—"A classical and Christ-centered education" and writes a six-fold mission for Logos School (three goals for "Christ-centered" and three for "classical")

1985–1986

- The enrollment and grades continue to expand; a short-lived plan to have two campuses is tried: K-4th grades stay at the Church of God, 5th-8th grades use the Church of the Nazarene
- In May of 1985, Jim Quist (completing four years of high school work) becomes the first graduate of Logos School
- With the school at about 130 students, the school board seriously begins research into another facility, either purchase or from ground-up—estimated costs are a serious hurdle

1987

- After much research by the board into possible sites, Larry Lucas promotes the idea of purchasing and renovating the Rollin' Derby roller skating rink on Baker Street (then owned by the Small Business Administration)
- Costs are researched and a fundraising event (to raise $47,000 for a down payment) is held at the rink and the Church of God fellowship hall—the money is raised that night
- Renovation begins at the rink in July; the school moves from the church in November; a dedication service is held that month

1988

- The school board meets with the parents of the five 8th grade students to determine the future viability of Logos High School; the families agree to stay, the first 8th Grade Promotion (to High School) is held that spring for the five students

1989–1992

- The secondary (7th-12th) program grows; more faculty members are hired for this level, extra-curricular programs; Tom Spencer is promoted to Vice-Principal, then Secondary Principal (Tom Garfield remains Elementary Principal as well as Superintendent)
- Logos adopts '*Non Nobis*' (from the 1989 movie *Henry V*) as the school song (from Ps. 115:1, sung in Latin), the mascot becomes the Knight, blue and white become the school colors
- Both 1990 and 1991 classes have two girls graduate
- 1990: a serious financial crisis is resolved by God's grace and generous donors; the board forms new by-laws and expands its membership to include three elected seats
- In 1991, Doug Wilson's book, *Recovering the Lost Tools of Learning* (Crossway) is written, published, and read by thousands

1993–1996

- In June, 1993—The first classical, Christian conference is held at Logos, about 70 people attend; Doug Wilson, Marlin Detweiler, Tom Spencer, and Tom Garfield form the first Association of Classical, Christian School (ACCS) board and write by-laws
- Logos starts informally publishing and selling its curriculum guides, policy manual, by-laws and other in-house materials to new ACCS schools
- May, 1994: some of the first kindergartners of Logos School, including Rebekah Wilson, and other classmates graduate from Logos High School
- Summer, 1994, Logos builds a two-room annex for the growing secondary program
- In June of 1994 and 1995, ACCS holds two more annual conferences at the local Best Western; attendees grow to about 140
- In July, 1995, in response to the growing demand for more 'practical training' in classical education, Logos conducts its first week-long Summer Teacher Training in Moscow
- Logos forms and sends its first Mock Trial team to compete at State in Boise; Logos wins its first Mock Trial State Championship title

- In June, 1996, Logos faculty and administration 'take it on the road' and conduct the fourth annual ACCS Conference in Raleigh, North Carolina; about 400 folks attend

1997–1999

- The school board considers building a gym
- 1998: Logos purchases adjoining land, holds a one-month, $250,000 capital campaign to build a 13,000 square foot gym costing $400,000; the money is raised and construction begins
- In February, 1999, the Logos gym opens officially and hosts a basketball tournament of the Mountain Christian League (formed through Logos School's initiative)
- 2000–2001
- Larry Stephenson becomes elementary (K-6) principal (Tom Spencer continues as secondary principal and Tom Garfield as superintendent)
- Logos celebrates its 20th year of ministry
- The exploding market for classical, Christian school materials compels Logos to hire staff members to make and sell such items

2002–2006

- A local controversy between Christ Church and some local liberals arises
- Logos School's non-profit status and ability to sell its curriculum materials is challenged, first at the local county level (opponents lose), then appealed to Idaho State Board of Tax Appeals
- The State Board rules in favor of Logos School

2006–11

- Logos purchases Short Street house
- oak tables, chairs, masterpieces in rooms
- Logos purchases carwash property
- 25th anniversary celebration
- 2008: U.S. economy collapses, Logos staff take voluntary pay cuts

2011–16

- Board decides Logos needs to actively seek new campus site

- Largest enrollment increase happens—100 new students!
- Purchase of two large, 2-room portables to help house new students
- Doubling of classes begins
- 30 acres of land east of Moscow is purchased for new campus
- Dr. Larry Stephenson hired to be Logos School's second superintendent
- Tom Garfield becomes president of LEAF, and this book's record ends

APPENDIX C

THE PARTICULAR PROSPECTS OF THE PRE-POLLY STAGE

by Tom Garfield, Superintendent, Logos School

THE NEED FOR IDENTIFYING THIS STAGE—EARLY GRAMMAR

I Cor. 13:11: "When I was a child, I used to speak as a child, think as a child, reason as a child; when I became a man, I did away with childish things."

Children are profoundly different than adults—not just smaller versions. They speak but it is a different speech we must understand before we can correct it. They think but along lines different than ours. For example, impressions are made more through all the senses, not just seeing or hearing. They reason but not in the kind of adult logic we must train them in. Again, we need to understand this in order to best correct and guide them to maturity.

1. Problems with ignoring or not studying the unique elements of this age group—I will state up front and clearly that I wanted to

address this topic out of a concern I have for what I perceive is a widespread misconception in ACCS schools. That misconception is that children entering school for the first time, five and six year olds, should be taught and trained in the very same way as students who are eight and nine. So the age group I am identifying as being in the Pre-Polly stage are students from about five to seven, or as we normally place them, students in kindergarten through the first part of the second grade.

Essentially the problems with not identifying and "cutting with the grain" of this age-group are the same problems we would have if we ignored the distinctions between the Pert and Poetic stages. That is:

2. We deny the built-in, natural differences between these students and older students thereby likely wasting our teaching efforts in large measure, at the very least, and possibly doing some harm in the process in dulling them to the joys of learning. Just as it is possible to teach the fundamentals of formal Logic to fourth graders by making a force-fit, through memorization we can force a lot of higher level math into the minds of five year olds. But then we shouldn't be surprised if they take little interest in the topic, nor use it well in years to come, since it was thrust upon them too soon, with little consideration for their innate interests. We stole our own thunder, but worse, we will be trying to build absent a foundation.

3. We will not take advantage of the unique characteristics of this stage. They are just beginning school, it's the "wet cement" time in their lives. All their experiences up to this point have been at home and with their families. Impressions are made easily, but can last for quite some time. Try to remember your earliest memories—they are probably around four or five. Think of the things that impressed you: probably bright colorful objects, various animals, events that affected your body (pain, illness, thrills), first independent acts (using a strange bathroom, your first favorite book), first friends, first group of classmates doing exciting things—playing with the parachute, going on field trips, having theme days. Gregory's Seven Laws of Teaching says "As children approach maturity, their interests tend to change from the concrete and more self-centered things to the abstract and

ultimate." We'll look at more ways to use these distinct characteristics for effective teaching.

4. We will disregard the essence of Gregory's Law of the Lesson—Connecting the new material to be learned to what is already familiar. This is the time to establish the first layer of Legos. These building blocks are the foundation or first principles that all further learning will be connected to in the coming Poll-Parrot. Another way of understanding this critical first step is establishing mental categories for further data. These categories will and must be, to some extent, conceptual in nature.

5. The latent but largest problem with not identifying the need for teaching to a Pre-Polly level is that we won't see the results of a poor foundation until years down the road. One of the greatest failures of the government school system is in this very regard—trying to force feed little ones with "higher critical thinking skills," as though "critical thinking" was an art these schools were versed in at any level. And like most of the disasters foisted on us by that establishment, the downstream effects of their experiments are having disastrous results long after there's any chance to correct them. Teaching by its very nature is a long-term proposition; classical education is certainly no different. Our learning curve can't be forced. We will overlook opportunities even with all our good intentions. Therefore, we must exercise even greater care with the foundations we lay.

Historical pedagogies begin at 7–8, even in the classical trivium *(The Lost Tools)*.

When we adopted the Lost Tools as our road map for our educational philosophy, one comment Sayers made always bothered me. In the article she states that in her hypothetical school, she would teach students the Trivium, but she would start with children who could "read, write, and cipher." That would be her "raw" material. But we get students in our earliest grades who often cannot do any of those three things very well at all. Why was Miss Sayers ignoring that fact? I always chalked it up to the fact that she just wanted to get to the meat of the education process she was proposing and didn't want to get too detailed. Then, in doing some further reading of the "old school" methods, Greek and Roman, as well as Jewish, I came to understand that in those cultures and times, children didn't start formal education until they were seven or eight. Well, what do you know, Miss Sayers wasn't just being lazy- she was reflecting the historical practice of when formal training began!

So for millennia, western cultures have assumed that at about eight years of age children came to some point of maturity that was significantly different than the preceding years. They were now, in some sense, *ready* for a specific pedagogy or curriculum of study, even if not the Trivium. (I haven't researched the American Baptist's reason for identifying eight as the age of accountability—maybe it would have strengthened my argument, but oh well.)

LOOKING AT THIS AGE GROUP, 5–7 YEARS

So let's look at this age group. A slight tangent may be necessary here, though. As I stated a moment ago, most historical systems of formal education began at about eight years old. In the United States, our systems of education have adopted five or six as the age to begin. The practice of teaching a "kindergarten" (German for child's garden) comes out of Prussia and Germany in the last century. German-Americans brought the practice to the United States. In the "old country" the students began this form of semi-formal training at about four or five years old. So here we are: as private schools we have many choices, one of them being when and how we start our program. Do we buck the adopted tradition and expect the parents to teach their children to read, write, and cipher at home, then begin the Trivium at about eight, or second grade? That is an option.

I don't believe the Scriptures give us an age, as much as an attitude and principle regarding teaching our children. Deut. 6 makes it clear that our educating our children is 24-hour-a day job, beginning at birth. So, if parents think their educational responsibility ends after five or eight years and then they can pass it off to a school, they're wrong either way. If schools think they can assume control of the child or his education when he's either five or eight, they are wrong. Conventional wisdom and long-term practice seem to indicate that a child can adapt well to formal training at five years old, whether that's at home or in a home-respecting school is not an issue for this time. We represent schools, so I will work from that standpoint.

1. Characteristics—how are Pre-Polly children different from their "full" grammar brethren—Obviously, the basic characteristics that will come to full-bloom around eight, are present in an undeveloped form in these little guys. That is, they are already imitators, able to recall and recite material without much difficulty. Our first daughter, Carolyn, was "reading" the story of Sleeping Beauty at two years old, after our reading it to her about a zillion times. So that grammatical ability is there to be used to some extent in kindergarten. But what are some other characteristics that are very evident in k-2, and then tend to diminish after 2nd grade?

The biggest difference is their reliance on their senses. Like very little children, which these students are just emerging from, touching, tasting, seeing, hearing all are like six-lane highways speeding loads of information to their minds. Later on, seeing and hearing will play the larger roles, but at this Pre-Polly stage, they need to move their hands, their bodies, they want to see while listening. All six lanes are moving so why not make use of them to get the material through from lots of connected roads?

Another big difference is the speed at which their little bodies are changing. I am always amazed at how little the kindergartners look at the beginning of the year, and how much more mature they appear by May. I am not a doctor, but from years of watching (and living with) these little guys, it seems that their physical changes slow down a bit after eight. They still grow, but not quite so obviously in every way. From getting lost in the bathroom in September to confident self-assurance in checking out of the room in April.

Not the last difference by any means, but one I personally like the best and has great potential for teaching practices is what I call the Amazement Factor. This is the window of opportunity, sort of framed by the ages of five to seven, in which you can wow these guys. Others may call it the sense of wonder- that sounds better, but it's still fun to go for the amazement level. The saucer-sized eyes, the sharp intake of breath, the slack-jawed mouth, it's a real challenge but worth the work at any staff meeting. But the Pre-Polly stage kids exhibit it regularly. They are excited to learn in a way that makes their teachers want to stick with that level for years. The excitement changes to a more reasoned, mature level by about third grade. Still good, but contained. The potential for good use of this sense of wonder, easy excitement, and sensory input is profound.

2. Matching teaching methods to the characteristics- So let's be consistent with the methods behind the Trivium, let's cut with the grain. We've studied the direction of the grain, now to cut.

A. *Senses are there for the using – guided discovery, exploration* — Some may react just to those last terms, especially if you've only seen them used in a humanistic, whole language situation. But just get over it, there's nothing wrong with using what works. Consider it plundering the Egyptians if it helps, but frankly I believe good teachers have been doing these things since the Ark. Pre-Polly children respond wonder-fully (get it?) to discovering patterns in math, exploring the different combinations of sounds with phonics, discovering what happens when vinegar and baking soda are mixed (things are never old to these guys!). And remember, Gregory of *The Seven Laws of Teaching* fame states that a child learns best what he learns on "his own" (guided discovery). For these guys, tangible makes it real.

B. *Integration with all involved* — Integration of knowledge is greatly aided by using those active senses at this stage. In math, for instance, sorting, counting objects by name (which happen to start with the phonic blend they're learning) and then writing the numbers derived illustrate the natural overlap or integration the students benefit from. Or science studies that correspond to the stories they are reading together, then using the animals, for example, for math practice. Then writing illustrated stories themselves to reinforce good handwriting as well as the material. This takes a lot of planning by the teacher, few programs have the total practical as well as philosophical aspects teachers in the Pre-Polly need. That sort of activity also involves every child being involved, vs. many watching while one or two answer or go up front. This is also good practice for the full-participation in chanting and reciting that the poll-parrot students enjoy.

C. *From simple to complex*—The law of teaching (Gregory again) regarding moving from the known to the unknown is very critical for teaching these little ones. Beginning with what they understand and can relate to, usually something that they did yesterday, is the frequent starting point. Here again, planning is key, but so what else is new? But the goal is to move from, for example, the simple sounds of letters to the complex concept of actually reading. Relying only on the recitation of facts, as is appropriate in the poll-parrot, is inappropriate here because they need to get the foundation laid for so many areas. Reciting alone will not move them from simple tasks to a more complex practice. Recognition and use of the letters of the alphabet is frankly just a necessary concept, not sheer memory. They need to develop (and they will) a "feel" for the connection between the written symbol and the sound associated with it.

This, by the way, is why Logos School designed its elementary history program the way we did. We start by acquainting the kindergarten students with the very basic grammar of history, i.e., history has to do with important places, people, and events (dates come later). We begin literally where the children live since that is what is best known to them. Then we "expand" from there as the students mature in their understanding of place and time from five to eight years old. (For a more complete explanation, see Logos School's *Apologetic for Teaching Elementary History*.)

D. *From physical to abstract*- An example of this would be the simple identification of a pattern in beads, to the concept of written numbers representing a similar pattern. Here they move again the appeal to their senses works—concrete objects having a relationship to written symbols, because they just do!

THREE CRITICAL PREPARATIONS FOR MAKING MOST OF THE FULL GRAMMAR STAGE

Everything they learn is a preparation for learning more.

1. *Conceptual/preparatory needs.* God designed these active little ones to learn from their imitation, from their being led to discover a truth, and just generally through their heightened senses. And they are

learning to make some order or sense out of the world. Even though they don't grasp the greater cause behind the concept, it is important that they do learn some concepts. That is, they do need to understand HOW certain things work the way do. The WHY isn't as important as HOW many beads make up 4, or HOW a paint brush is held, or HOW to form an H so it looks "right." It all leads to knowing HOW things are supposed to be done before you go on with the next step.

2. *Strong foundations of building on previous knowledge (Laws of Teaching).* As I have referred to before, the Seven Laws make it clear that all learning and teaching needs to be inter-connected to be the most productive. To make the most of the full-grammar stage, a teacher must rely on the foundations of learning that the students have gained, at home or at school, before entering her poll-parrot classroom. Again, this is historically marked at about eight or the third grade in most schools. We have seen the very real necessity of these students to read, write and cipher BEFORE they can do all we wish to do beginning at that level, not the least of which is learn Latin. Reading, writing, and math are foundational means to ends, not ends in themselves. The ends being the obtaining of further knowledge. History, science, even studying God's Word require a good grasp of the importance and skills of reading, writing and math.

3. *Setting patterns of learning, more to everything than is presented.* Finally, one of the best lessons to be learned in the Pre-Polly stage is that the world is a very big place and that there is far more to what they have heard, touched, tasted, and seen than the teacher showed then, or that they learned "themselves." This idea can be impressed, and understood in a limited way, even by second graders, without overwhelming them. Then they are prepared to read more and listen more in third grade. The patterns of learning have started well, and are now ready to mature into the full Poll-parrot practices.

CONCLUSION:

To repeat—Don't waste/misspend this "wet cement" time.

A. *Repeats more often, appropriately, in K-2.* There is no fire. Don't rush into teaching materials or methods the students as a whole are not ready for. Reading readiness, for instance, is affected by maturation, as well as instruction. Rushing boys into and through kindergarten or first grade, is often a sure-fire means to have them spend two years in second grade. On the other hand, repeats are necessary even when there was no conscious effort to rush. That's ok, better to take the time to set the foundations than to move on without them. Our record of repeats is very positive. There is no fire to get to in any case.

B. *Sets tone for view of school/learning.* The Pre-Polly stage should be an overall time of security, good memories of lots of wonderful experiences, steady growth in understanding things, and a love for school. This is a unique period of time, one of the significant stages children grow into and out of, and we must not overlook it or waste its potential for setting the joy of learning in the students' hearts.

APPENDIX D:

AN APOLOGETIC FOR LOGOS GRAMMAR SCHOOL'S APPROACH TO TEACHING HISTORY

by Tom Garfield, Superintendent

1. In keeping with Dorothy Sayer's treatise, *The Lost Tools of Learning*, we believe that there is a historical and educational precedent for what we call the "*Pre-Polly*" stage in addressing children*s learning characteristics. This stage manifests itself during the five to eight year-old period. It necessarily and appropriately precedes the "full" Poll-Parrot or Grammar stage, the first level of the ancient Trivium. Historically children were not considered ready for formal education until they reached the age of about eight years old. (Hence, Sayers' allusion to "starting" with students who could already "read, write, and cipher" in her hypothetical school. She was merely assuming that the children would have learned those skills prior to beginning the Poll-Parrot stage. It behooves us to examine how best to prepare the students for that stage.

2. This Pre-Polly stage is a time when students need to develop mental categories and concepts that are requisite for the full Grammar

instruction, beginning in about third grade. For example, before the students memorize addition facts (which they could probably do), they need to form the concept of numbers and their values in their minds. The written symbol—2—should be equated with two "somethings" in their thinking lest further math work lack a foundation in reality. The same foundational approach applies to reading; the students *could* memorize words (as in the Whole Language approach), but instead we ensure they equate the written symbol,—A—with an aural sound through training in phonics. In a sense, we are helping them develop mental "cubby holes" for subsequent related data. Future knowledge needs a place that fits with old knowledge, i.e., the cubby holes.

3. Students in the Pre-Polly stage are bundles of high energy, with all their senses and curiosity working overtime. They have little interest in or understanding of the concept of linear history through vast amounts of time or different cultures. To them, next week is about the same as next year, especially if they have to wait for an exciting event. They best relate to what they've known. They need to build a mental cubby hole for the concept of something as huge as history. What does "history" deal with? Well, it acquaints us with important people, places, events, and times.

4. So, in kindergarten through second grade (approximately the Pre-Polly stage for most students), we introduce them to the foundations of history through teaching them about specific and various famous people, places, events, and times, using beginning grammatical teaching techniques, e.g., singing, chanting, and especially activities that make use of their active little senses (touch, taste, hearing, etc.), as well as material that touches their lives. Wherever possible, we also try to integrate the history material with their beginning reading, writing, and math work. Remember, our emphasis is on equipping them with the means (tools), not the particular content, for future learning.

5. In kindergarten, these famous people include their families and the president; the places include spots in our town, e.g., their homes, the hospital, the fire station. Events include their birthdays, holidays, etc., and times include seasons. In other words, we begin with material they are already somewhat familiar with and build from there. In first grade they learn about famous (historical) and easily identifiable

places in the United States, including some of the monuments in Washington, DC. This instruction integrates nicely with their learning of money values in math, since many of the monuments are pictured on coins and bills. They know who the current president is, so memorizing all the presidents is an obvious activity. In second grade, we widen their exposure to history, since their understanding of time and places has expanded and matured. Think of their learning and our instruction as ever-widening circles, starting from where and when they live. By the end of second grade they will have learned about our region (the Northwest), Indian tribes, famous presidents and other people. All this grounds them in the concept that those kinds of things comprise the study of "history." (We don't worry too much about their understanding of "why" these are important people, etc., but rather just give them the "what," i.e., the grammar.)

6. Finally, in third grade, with the advent of the full Grammar stage and the students' matching of Poll-Parrot characteristics, the linear study of history begins. But even here, we begin with what is most familiar to the students, i.e., where they live—the United States and its geography. They memorize certain State Facts and then move on to the beginning of the history of the United States through European exploration and colonization.

7. From there, during fourth grade, we move linearly and by specific period (vs. a full survey) through key times and people critical to the history of the United States. Not only does this teaching from the familiar to the unfamiliar match the Seven Laws of Teaching, the material taught in the Pre-Polly stage is reintroduced in a fuller, chronological manner. The students, now more mature and experienced with time and travel, are better able to grasp the significance of the historical nature of the material presented.

8. Beginning in fifth grade the students commence the broad study of World History, starting with an introduction to geographical grammar (e.g., latitude, longitude) as it's used in studying the world. This again gives them a sense and understanding of place before they look at what happened there. Formal history begins with Creation and moves through the major civilizations of the world.

9. After two years of World History (fifth and sixth grades), the history studies in the last quarter of sixth grade are an entire review of World History, in keeping with the seventh Law of teaching. By the end of Grammar school and sixth grade, the students are very acquainted with the grammar, as well as the linear chronology, of history, and are now ready for the next stage, the Dialectic.

10. By using the unique characteristics of both the Pre-Polly and Poll-Parrot stages, we have made the best use of those fleeting years to prepare these students to learn later.

APPENDIX E

THE ARTS AND THE CHRISTIAN WORLDVIEW

By Tom Garfield

Affirming the reality of the trivium of Truth, Goodness and Beauty is easy for a school to put in their mission statement, putting feet on these necessary elements of a Christian education is another matter. That can get downright messy. Here are some short and admittedly incomplete definitions of terms with some examples from Scripture:

Truth: *That which is unchangeable over time and place: God's Word and work*

> Examples: Jesus Christ is God incarnate (John 1:1). God made the heavens and the earth (Gen. 1:1).

Goodness: *That which is always appropriate to express or do: Holy actions.*

> Examples: You shall love your neighbor as yourself (Lev.19:18). Speak so as to edify and build up others (Col. 3:16,17).

Beauty: *That which is always comely and adorning: Truth and goodness magnified creatively.*

> Examples: The beauty of holiness (Ps.29:2). The heavens declare the glory of God (Ps. 19:1).

Presenting Truth in a Christian school is a glorious and relatively straightforward activity. Actually, it's more of a commitment to faithfully present God's Word unflinchingly, in and out of the classroom. Whether Truth is being consistently presented or not can be seen and recognized by all, and virtually no Christian parents or teachers would object to Truth being presented in an unvarnished way.

Goodness also is a fairly popular aspect in Christian education. Kindness, love in the details of living together, boys holding doors for girls, and general pleasant speech and behavior are either the norm in daily life at school, or not. Here again, this is all recognizable, as well as universally admired and desired in a Christian education.

Beauty, on the other hand, while still a valued element of a Christian education, can cause some serious heartburn. With Beauty we seemingly and suddenly enter the realm of the 'subjective', illustrated often with remarks in the vain of, "Who's to say what is good or bad in art, or music, or theater, or...?" Is Beauty really relegated to the 'eye of the beholder'? Are there really no biblical standards by which we can determine what earns the title of "beautiful" and what doesn't? There have been many fine books written on this very issue; the focus of this essay is to address some biblical worldview elements to consider in constructing, presenting and encouraging the visual arts in a Christian school. We are including all formal presentations of the arts that we require from the students: paintings, drawings, songs, plays, etc.

Therefore, keeping in mind the necessary consideration of the ages and frames of our students, below are some basic biblical principles applied to the arts. First, some appropriate Scripture passages are referenced, then some applicable principles that may be drawn from those biblical foundations.

SCRIPTURE	PRINCIPLE/APPLICATION
1. Genesis 2:19,20	*Man was designed to be a small 'c' creator, imitating his Father and using the elements found in the Creation to 'name' things.*
2. Exodus 12:35–36	*Even the pagans (Egyptians in this case) can make beautiful objects that God's people not only may admire, but desire and use.*
3. Exodus 31:1–5	*The first "artist" God calls has the Spirit of God, is wise, knows a great deal that's worth knowing, and is very skilled in the technical aspects of many arts. He certainly doesn't do "art for art's sake."*
4. Exodus 20:4–7	*In our 'creating', no work of art is to receive the adoration or reverence due the Lord God and His Name. Thoughtless or meaningless use of His Name is forbidden.*
5. Christ's parables/ stories	*Jesus used many verbal illustrations to tell people about God and His kingdom. As the Master Story Teller, He must have used every acting device at hand to make His stories memorable and clear. For instance:*
6. Matt. 18:23–35	*Jesus tells a story with an evil servant in it and He delivers the servant's cruel lines. Evil is clearly evil in the story and it is dealt with appropriately.*
7. Matt. 6:28,29	*Beauty in the Creation, although transient, outshines the best that men can do. Even a Rembrandt is no match for a fleeting, but glorious sunset.*
8. Romans 14:14	*(Actually all of chapters 14 and 15.) There are varying levels of discernment and temptations among believers. What may be lawful for one to do, another may not do without sinning. Liberty may need to give up its 'rights' for the sake of the weak.*
9. I Cor. 5:9–13	*Blatantly immoral people (as we all were) exist; we should and must interact with them. (Hypocritical brothers are the greater problem.)*
10. Phil. 4:8	*Probably the best summation of a biblical worldview of the arts (and other areas). We need to recognize and honor all that is worthwhile. Lifting up what is noble often means concurrently dismantling and revealing what is dishonorable.*

PRACTICAL EXAMPLES OF ISSUES IN ART AND DRAMA:

1. Art Instruction—Creation is our best model for what God considers beautiful and fitting for imitation and meditation. This doesn't limit a student's scope—just the opposite. Creation, including man's shaping and use of it (historical events, architecture, landscapes, everyday life), provides us with an almost inexhaustible source of subjects. Art history and training should include the best of artists in the past (most of them non-Christians). We 'plunder the Egyptians' (e.g., the Impressionists) and recognize that, self-consciously or not, these artists gave glory to God through beautifully reflecting (emphasizing) His light, color, mood, and other true and accurate displays of His character in the work of the Creation.

What about studying and portraying the human body and the issue of nudity? The human body, like all things created, is not in itself a sinful object to view. People, individually or in groups, are the most popular subjects in art. Therefore, in studying the human body for artistic rendering, a great deal depends on the purpose, context, and the viewer. For instance, little children should not be shown or required to draw the full statue of David by Michelangelo. They are not mature enough. Older students, with a working knowledge of anatomy, should be able to maturely look at that statue, as well as the marvelous Greek statutes left to us. The students should be old enough and adequately prepared to understand that these works and paintings like the Sistine Chapel ceiling, were not composed to excite lasciviousness. Context matters: naked people in a battle scene or in a similar grim situation are objects of pity or admiration, not lust.

Great art can and should ennoble even harsh or ugly subjects, (e.g., Christ on the cross, beggars on a city street) in such a beautiful and skillful manner that they point to God's truths (mercy, justice, man's evil vs. God's kindness). By contrast, Creation should not be presented in a way that lies about it or degrades it, e.g., cubism or "motel" art.

Creatively using trained skills to portray a unique vision is the appropriate work of an artist. Glory to God, not oneself, is the primary goal of Christian artists. This conviction, combined with skill and the love of real beauty, will set Christian students and artists at odds with the relativistic, humanistic view of art today.

2. Drama productions—The primary purpose of a dramatic production is to tell a story using live actors to portray the characters. Therefore, much of the biblical worldview reasoning that applies to literature also applies to drama.*

The selection of what makes a "good" story—a story that is not only worth telling but worth seeing, requires careful consideration. Sadly there is a dearth of godly playwrights, so here again, as in painting, we frequently plunder the Egyptians. (Lord willing, this state of affairs will turn around as Christians retake the culture.)

Adapting some of the Logos Guidelines For Literature Selections, the following illustrates some of the thinking we have behind the selection of the stories (scripts) we will perform in drama:

1. What worldview does the selection communicate? Stories from a secular worldview will be analyzed according to Scripture. Directors will actively guide the students through the reading, analysis, and performing of secular materials. By "secular" we don't mean (or select) stories that ennoble lives and ideas that are contrary to God's Word. Rather we mean high quality stories that, most often unconsciously, present and support a biblical view of the world (e.g., good ultimately triumphing over evil, self-sacrifice for others, kindness and forgiveness trumping hate, etc.). We believe that this is also helpful in preparing the students to handle non-biblical ideas in the future.

2. Directors will consider the age, gender, and maturity levels of the students. Only scripts that are appropriate for the frames and understanding of the students will be used.

3. Age and maturity levels will also be considered when using stories that include allusions to illegal, sexual, or violent acts, due to the possible temptations to sin in the minds of the actors. Such references, if necessary to do justice to the story, will be minimized and blunted, as appropriate. At the same time, we agree with G.K. Chesterton: "A book with no evil characters is an evil book." Also C. S. Lewis: "Let there be

* See "Philosophy of English and Literature, and Guidelines for Literature Selections" in the Logos School Secondary Curriculum Guide, available from Logos Press.

wicked kings and beheadings, battles and dungeons, giants and dragons, and let the villains be soundly killed at the end of the book."

4. We recognize that the Bible condemns irreverent, coarse, vulgar and obscene language, and language that takes God's name in vain. The amount and context of this type of language in the script will be carefully considered, also keeping in mind the make-up of the audiences.

APPENDIX F

HOLIDAY GUIDELINES

1. We are a Christian school. That means we are not a church, but it also means we must consider Scripture in all that we teach, model, emphasize, and celebrate.

2. Because we are a non-denominational Christian school, we must not, through our teaching, practices, etc., encourage divisiveness among believers. This includes how we address holidays. Hence, we need to determine where our balance is, without following one church's practices over and against another's. In many ways, what we do should even "look" rather different than a church's methods.

3. Scripture is not silent about recognizing days of importance and teaching their importance to our children (Deut. 4:9, Ex. 13:14, for instance). Therefore, we may not be silent.

4. As a school with a classical, thinking emphasis, we must provide good instruction to our students about why and what we celebrate. This means we need to know our history and the purposes behind what and why we are celebrating, or even just remembering.

5. Celebration, in a Christian context, has its foundation in thankfulness to the Giver of memorable events. Christians have the most to be

thankful for and therefore should have the best understanding of the importance of celebrating with our whole hearts and minds.

6. At the same time, we recognize that, even though we are a private school, we live in community with thousands of people locally, as well as millions of others in the United States. Therefore our calendar will acknowledge, without particular teaching on our part, certain cultural, traditional holidays, e.g., Labor Day and Memorial Day. This acknowledgment is similar to our entire calendar, i.e., going to school for nine, mostly non-farming months, taking two weeks off at Christmas, and a week of spring vacation.

7. Therefore, in considering which days/events to celebrate, we consider their priority within one or more of the following categories:

A) *Days and/or events that are recognized as truly "holy days" or events, related as they are to Christ's work.* These would obviously include Christmas and Easter (Good Friday).

B) *Days and/or events that have a particularly Christian aspect and historical significance.* These would include Reformation and Thanksgiving.

C) *Days and/or events that are worth noting for their impact on our American country/culture.* Some of these are simply traditional in our culture, e.g., Labor Day, President's Day, and Memorial Day. Others we chose to note, so far as they fit within our curricular and/or philosophic scope as a Christian school, e.g., important people's birthdays, Veteran's Day, the anniversaries of Roe v. Wade and 9/11, etc.

APPENDIX G

A FEW ALUM STORIES

ANNIE (LAMOREAUX) MACINTOSH—1996

When I was in fourth grade, we raised tobacco moths and at the old building (Church of God) would take the caterpillars out and observe them. That year (1987) we moved to Baker Street, so the moths grew to adults there. Unfortunately, Miss Sebring couldn't let them go because they would eat the farmers' fields around, so they were frozen to death.

The Fall Retreats were choice: Josh drinking tons of Mountain Dew, then getting his appendix out. Chris and Brenda Schlect as chaperones when they were engaged; Jessica getting cut while carving pumpkins and freaking out; Natali capsizing in the pond at Camp Sanders and Mr. Spencer having to save her.

Once we set up the entire classroom of Mr. O outside before class to surprise him. He made us have class outside.

CAROLYN (GARFIELD) WILSON—1997

I could tell many stories of my time at Logos, particularly given the fact that I was one of the Superintendent's daughters! The good, the bad, and the ugly are all present as they are in any story. But the most pivotal memory I have, the one that shaped my decision to become a teacher, was in ninth grade. At that time, we Freshman were studying European history, and soaking in the enthusiasm of Chris Schlect as we gazed upon the glories of ancient Rome. In Latin, we were translating parts of the Aeneid with Mr. Wilson, while in literature we were also reading part of the *Aeneid* with our own Virgil in Mr. Callihan. I do not recall where in the school year we were, but I recall very distinctly sitting in Latin class and having a very bright light bulb switch on. These classes were overlapping!! We were seeing connections in our education—an integration of subjects if you will. Had our teachers planned this? Surely it was too much for coincidence! I believe I asked Mr. Wilson this question later on and I received a knowing chuckle and a confirmation regarding my suspicions. I was very impressed by this and oddly satisfied to have seen this overlap. I felt as though I had pulled aside a curtain and seen the inner workings of my education and it was this revelation. I wanted to see that light bulb go on for other students, perhaps help turn it on. And thus the seeds for my future career were laid.

AMANDA STOLL MOORER – 2005

As a 10th grader, we took Science from Mr. Struble. For those of you who never had Science from Mr. Struble, you need to know two things: 1) Mr. Struble reminded all of us girls of a young Sean Connery, so paying attention was never an issue and 2) no one could understand Science when he wasn't there. He was that good! My most memorable moment of him was the day he got sick, and his voice cracked...2 octaves. Seeing Sean Connery with a cracked voice caused me personally, large amounts of amusement. It was great!

If you ever had Mrs. Marston, you know what I'm about to say...everyone loved her. We loved making her laugh, we loved telling her stories, we loved learning from her...we loved everything that was/is Mrs. Marston. I still cannot smell Hazelnut coffee without thinking of her.

I finally have to talk about the School Superintendent. Not only was he an amazing artist – and still is...his artwork is on display at every county fair winning Grand Champion, but he was also a fantastic history teacher. I wish to God that I hadn't gotten sick and had to have open heart surgery that year because I missed so much of 20th Cent. History class. I do have one memory that I still cherish. We were discussing WWII and Mr. Garfield described Poland as being caught in between the Hells Angels and the Mafia (Germany and Russia respectively). The best part was his facial features...all of us kids were cracking up.

SCOTT GRESSARD – 2005

It was exciting to hear about all the expansion and plans for a new location, although I have to say the idea of losing the roller rink makes me a little sad. That place will be forever installed in my memory. I feel that I can remember every unique length of carpet lining the halls and each square of tile on the auditorium floor, even to this day. It is great you are writing this book, I will definitely be interested in reading it and am happy to make my small contribution.

I remember when I was much younger, there were "unofficial" before and after school activities that took place in that auditorium that everyone spent hours participating in and the competition was stiff. It actually was a stroke of genius for the staff to let that all develop so organically. I don't think there were nearly as many tardies during the time they were going on. I would actually try to rush my mom and brother out of the door earlier in the morning so that I could get a solid 30 min. of 4–square in before I had to go to class. I think I was in 3rd or 4th grade at the time. There would be 4 games of four square going at a time in each of the 4 blue "arenas" pre-painted into the tile flooring. I remember the feeling of pride when I made it to the 4th square the 1st time and the sharp sting of defeat when someone would slam the ball across my square, sending me "out" and to the back of the line. One particular day, an older student got so carried away with the competition that he spiked the ball into the floor and it bounced up and smashed the fluorescent light above sending bits of glass raining everywhere. The auditorium went silent before he was given the wave back to the office and I think that might have been around the time that after school 4 square ended. I believed the boys around my age moved our competition outside that winter to the massive pile of snow that had built up in the corner of the parking lot and had a number of colossal games of king of the hill before that got a little out of hand and we were forced (for the best) to move on to the next activity, but those remain some of my fondest memories of my younger years at Logos.

ABBY GRAY – 2008

What a grand old place. I spent a good portion of my life there at Logos and I tell anyone who asks me that they were the best years of my life up until that point. Truly. I loved it.

We may be remembered as the super loud and obnoxious class of 2008—the class who would sing "Happy Birthday" at the top of our lungs, off-key (unless of course we were in Mr. C's classroom). We would holler loud and clear, resounding our perfect out-of-pitchness through the halls. Everyone LOVED us. And if being amazingly good at singing off-key wasn't enough, we were also very intent on practicing our cleverness on our teachers. You see, we all were varying levels of clever, some more devious than others, but clever all the same. Mr. Nance could talk dream states all class period long, Mr. Garfield (yes, that's right) would follow any historical rabbit trail we could come up with, and we could get Mr. C to talk about heaters, thermostats and coffee breaks for a good solid 20 minutes. None of these achievements, however, will ever reach the sheer genius of our clock prank on Mrs. Mahaffy. 8th grade, 2003, English class, right before lunch. High School lunch bell was at 11:35 am, a whole half hour before ours. So one day, we decided that the High School lunch bell would be our salvation. We put the clock forward 25 minutes and held our breaths as we waited for Mrs. Mahaffy. She ended up being about 5 minutes late, by her watch, but when she looked at our clock, she stopped. We could tell she was already flustered and her squinting at the 25-minute-ahead clock on the wall made us cringe with anticipation. Will she buy it? Then with a shake of her head, she said "I am so, SO sorry I am so late. My watch must have stopped," and she matched her watch to the clock. Boom. Success. We all looked around incredulous and giddy: We get a WHOLE extra half hour for lunch. By this time, she only had 20 minutes left of class so after a quick lesson, the bell rang and we left without a word. Sadly, our escapade did not last much longer. One of our more conscientious classmates told Mrs. Mahaffy what had been done after we had all scurried out, and so, with not a small amount of controlled anger I am sure, she called us all back in. After a well-deserved scolding, we hung our heads as the clock was set back to the present. I suppose, looking back, if we weren't forced to eat lunch in the classroom that day, we should have been.

APPENDIX H

PHOTOS

September 1981: First all-school photo

PHOTO: MARK LAMOREAUX

Fall 1981: Paradise Hills Church of God—Logos School's first home
PHOTO: TOM GARFIELD

Fall 1981: First lunches together
PHOTO: TOM GARFIELD

Winter, 1982: Sledding during recess

PHOTO: TOM GARFIELD

Spring, 1982: Logos School food booth at Moscow's Renaissance Fair

PHOTO: TOM GARFIELD

1983: Logos gets its own outside entrance with sign painted by Tom Garfield
PHOTO: TOM GARFIELD

1983: 'New' playground equipment, made of stripped logs
PHOTO: TOM GARFIELD

1983: "Issachar," Logos School's first bus

PHOTO: TOM GARFIELD

c. 1984: Hard at work

PHOTO: TOM GARFIELD

1984: First sign for Logos School, painted by Tom Garfield

PHOTO: TOM GARFIELD

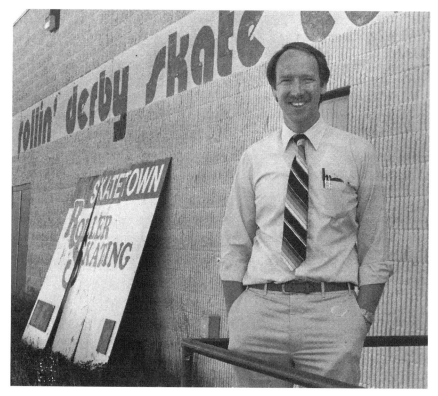

1987: Shortly after the purchase of 110 Baker Street

PHOTO: DAILY IDAHONIAN, ©1987.

REPRINTED BY PERMISSION OF THE MOSCOW-PULLMAN DAILY NEWS.

1987: The roller rink when Logos purchased the facility
PHOTO: TOM GARFIELD

1987: New location at 110 Baker ready for school
PHOTO: TOM GARFIELD

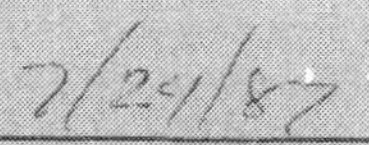

THE NEW LOGOS SCHOOL, in an artist's rendition.

Logos School gets rollin' to new spot

Logos School is on its way to the roller rink.

The private Christian school in Moscow, operated by Community Evangelical Fellowship, has cleared all the necessary financial and legal obstacles to take over the abandoned Rollin' Derby Skating Center on Baker Street.

Tom Garfield, principal at Logos, said he would like to have classes at the new facility on Sept. 1. Logos is moving from the Paradise Hills Church of God on Styner Street because of an expanded enrollment.

"There's been a real outpouring of support for the school," said Garfield. "This is a chance for Logos to become something more of a physical entity in the community and it will be an asset to the city as one more visible alternative for education in the area."

The school's enrollment has grown from 18 in 1981 to 140 today and has been seeking to move to a larger location since this spring. The students range in grades from preschool to ninth grade.

Garfield said First National Bank of North Idaho has granted the school a $350,000 loan to remodel the skating center. The school raised $100,000 itself through fundraising and donations. Associated Architects of Moscow have drawn up some plans for the new Logos School.

The plans for remodeling include putting in some windows and more doors, a sun-room style entrance and subdividing the interior into classrooms and offices. Garfield said they will be depending on volunteer labor for much of the work.

July 24, 1987: Original *Daily Idahonian* article with drawing by Tom Garfield

PHOTO: TOM GARFIELD

Spring, 1988: First 8th Grade Promotion ceremony

PHOTO: MARK LAMOREAUX

Summer, 1998: The new Logos gym takes shape

PHOTO: GWEN SPENCER

Fall, 1998: Seniors working on the retaining wall for the gym

PHOTO: GWEN SPENCER

Fall, 1998: Gym stage and pediment being built

PHOTO: TOM GARFIELD

1999: First practices in new gym

PHOTO: GWEN SPENCER